Evaluating Natureness

Measuring the Quality of Nature-Based Classrooms in Pre-K through 3rd Grade

Patti Ensel Bailie, PhD
Rachel A. Larimore, PhD
Arianna E. Pikus, MS

www.gryphonhouse.com

Copyright

© 2023 Patti Ensel Bailie, Rachel A. Larimore, and Arianna E. Pikus

Published by Gryphon House, Inc.
P. O. Box 10, Lewisville, NC 27023
800.638.0928; 877.638.7576 [fax]

Visit us on the web at www.gryphonhouse.com.

All rights reserved. No part of this publication may be reproduced or transmitted in any form or by any means, electronic or technical, including photocopy, recording, or any information storage or retrieval system, without prior written permission of the publisher. Printed in the United States. Every effort has been made to locate copyright and permission information.

Cover images used under license from Shutterstock.com. Interior images courtesy of the author.

Library of Congress Control Number: 2022947529

Bulk Purchase

Gryphon House books are available for special premiums and sales promotions as well as for fund-raising use. Special editions or book excerpts also can be created to specifications. For details, call 800.638.0928.

Disclaimer

Gryphon House, Inc., cannot be held responsible for damage, mishap, or injury incurred during the use of or because of activities in this book. Appropriate and reasonable caution and adult supervision of children involved in activities and corresponding to the age and capability of each child involved are recommended at all times. Do not leave children unattended at any time. Observe safety and caution at all times.

Suggested Citations for NABERS Tools

Bailie, Patti Ensel, Rachel A. Larimore, and Arianna E. Pikus. 2022. *NAture-Based Education Rating Scale for Pre-K Education: Comprehensive Assessment Rubric*. Lewisville, NC: Gryphon House.

Larimore, Rachel A., Arianna E. Pikus, and Patti Ensel Bailie. 2022. *NAture-Based Education Rating Scale for K-3 Education: Comprehensive Assessment Rubric*. Lewisville, NC: Gryphon House.

Praise for *Evaluating Natureness: Measuring the Quality of Nature-Based Classrooms in Pre-K through 3rd Grade*

"Evaluating Natureness is an important guide for early childhood education professionals, from teachers and staff to school and district administrators to policy makers. This book will support ongoing reflection and continual improvement in nature-based early childhood education practices. The ability to implement a common rating scale for our PreK–3rd-grade schools, classrooms, and programs helps us all work together to better support young children's healthy development and connection with the natural world."

—**Tara Williams**, Executive Director, Maine Association for the Education of Young Children (MaineAEYC)

"As nature-based education has expanded, so too has the need for tools that help evaluate programs in action. The NABERS tools are an invaluable resource for evaluation, research, and decision-making in nature-based early childhood education."

—**Christy Merrick**, Director of the Natural Start Alliance

"This book represents the maturation of the nature-based early childhood movement in the United States. Thanks to Patti, Rachel, and Arianna for making these assessment tools available to everyone. Patti created the first version of these assessments almost a decade ago for inclusion in the Nature Preschools and Forest Kindergartens book. The original tool has undergone mitosis, has developed into separate preschool and K-3 versions, and has become more specific and user friendly. With this book, early childhood educators now have a clear roadmap for how to make their programs more nature based and their students more rooted in the natural world."

—**David Sobel**, author of *The Sky Above and the Mud Below: Lessons from Nature Preschools and Forest Kindergartens*

"The positive significance of children being immersed in nature cannot be denied. Scientific research continues to uncover why being in and with nature is an important contributor to children's well-being, including their physical, cognitive, and social-emotional development. Understanding nature's magnitude, figuring out how to offer indoor, outdoor, and beyond spaces, and connecting children with the natural world is an essential responsibility for those who walk beside these young stewards of the Earth. Yet, sometimes we need a bit of help, some knowledgeable guidance, and perhaps a nugget of inspiration. If you're looking for innovative and creative ways to be intentional about nature-based pedagogy, offering natural experiences for young learners, and creating nature-infused places for children to inhabit, look no further. The NAture-Based Education Rating Scales (NABERS) are observation tools that invite educators to review and reflect on children's indoor and outdoor spaces from a nature-based perspective. This book is a practical guide to observing the "natureness" of your program and is an extraordinary resource for fostering important connections and confident relationships with nature."

—**Sandra Duncan**, EdD, coauthor of *Through a Child's Eyes: How Classroom Design Inspires Learning and Wonder*

"The authors, nature-based early learning pioneers and experts in the field, have created a tool that can both inspire educators and evaluate natural and built environments, programming, and leadership for NbECE programs serving children ages 3-8. Their intent to encourage reflexive thought is inherent in the tool, inviting professional conversations about nature pedagogies and the evidenced nuances that lead to high-level practices."

—**Victoria Carr**, EdD, Professor of early childhood education at the University of Cincinnati and Executive Director, Arlitt Center for Education, Research, and Sustainability

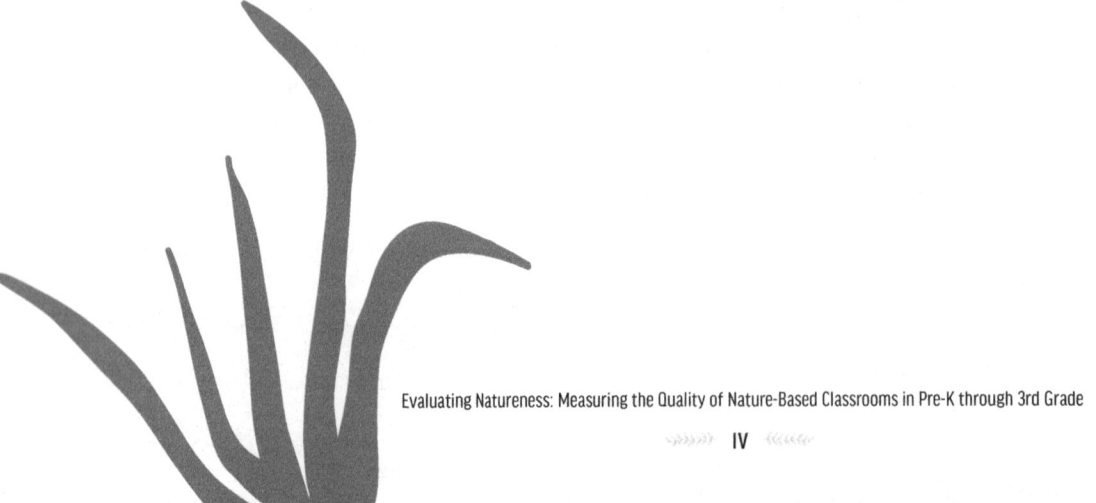

Dedication

To early childhood educators everywhere who strive each day to connect young children to the wonders and joys of our natural world. May you find support, encouragement, and inspiration within the pages of this book.

Table of Contents

Acknowledgments **VIII**

Introduction **1**

Using the NAture-Based Education Rating Scales **7**

NABERS Sections and Items:

SECTION I: Program Goals and Curriculum Practices **17**
    Category A: Program Goals **18**
    Pre-K Category B: Program Practices **35**
    K-3 Category B: Program Practices **48**
    Pre-K Category C: Curriculum **59**
    K-3 Category C: Curriculum **79**

SECTION II: Staffing **113**
    Category A: Administrator's Role **114**
    Category B: Teacher's Role **121**
    Pre-K Category C: Staff Qualifications **128**
    K-3 Category C: Teacher Qualifications **130**
    Category D: Professional Development **131**

SECTION III: Environment **135**
    Category A: Indoor Classroom (Inside) **136**
    Category B: Natural Play Area (Outside) **151**
    Category C: Natural Ecosystems (Beyond) **164**

SECTION IV: Community Partnerships **171**

Category A: Nature Educator **171**

Category B: Artifacts/Resources–On-Site **175**

Category C: Special Programs–Field Trips **178**

SECTION V: Family Engagement **181**

Category A: Family Communication and Education **181**

Category B: Family Nature Experiences **186**

Category C: Family Involvement **190**

NAture-Based Education Rating Scale for Pre-K Education: Comprehensive Assessment Rubric **194**

NAture-Based Education Rating Scale for K–3 Education: Comprehensive Assessment Rubric **212**

Appendices:

Appendix A: Annotated Bibliography with Stories Featuring Diverse Children in Outdoor Spaces **229**

Appendix B: Additional Resources Related to Nature-Based Education **232**

Appendix C: Recommended Questions to Ask During Teacher/Administrator Interviews **235**

References and Recommended Readings **240**

Index **244**

Acknowledgments

The nature-based early childhood education movement has seen incredible progress in the last decade or so. There has been a rise in the number of immersive nature-based programs and more discussion of nature-based and outdoor learning in mainstream early childhood circles. A professional association for nature-based early educators—Natural Start Alliance—was established in 2013. More and more research is being conducted in nature-based settings, and we've even seen the publication of a recommended research agenda for nature-based learning (Jordan and Chawla, 2019). Our hope is this NABERS tool will contribute to that research agenda and the growing nature-based education movement. Yet, we recognize this growth did not happen magically. There are many scholars and educators who have dedicated their careers to work related to nature-based education, which laid the foundation for the growth we're witnessing today, including the development of this natureness scale.

We want to take a moment to acknowledge the many people who have contributed to the nature-based movement and to this natureness scale, in particular. Researchers, educators, and thought leaders who have provided a foundation for this work include Dr. Ruth Wilson, Dr. Mary Rivkin, Prof. Robin Moore, Dr. Claire Warden, Rusty Keeler, Marcie Oltman, and Ken Finch.

Specific to the development of the two natureness scales, we want to first thank our teammate, Dr. Patti Bailie, for drafting an early version of this tool based on her dissertation research (2012). Thank you to David Sobel for including an early version of the tool in his book *Nature Preschools and Forest Kindergartens: The Handbook for Outdoor Learning* (2016). Additionally, thanks to David, Dr. Rachel Becker-Klein, and Dr. Lori Skibbe for use of the tool in their various research projects examining nature-based preschools and more conventional preschool models. We also want to thank Dr. Lori Skibbe for her support of the development of the K-3 version of this tool in examining child outcomes at kindergarten and first grade in nature-based and more conventional elementary settings.

All of these studies were made possible thanks to the financial support of the George B. Storer Foundation. We are incredibly grateful for all the foundation has done for the nature-based education movement over the past fifteen years.

We also want to extend a particularly heartfelt thank you to the many schools, administrators, teachers, children, and families who were part of the research projects that included the development of this tool at the pre-K and K-3 levels. Further, there were many early childhood programs that piloted early iterations of the tools, provided thoughtful feedback, and/or provided photos for the current book.

As former nature preschool directors, Patti would particularly like to thank Schlitz Audubon Nature Preschool teachers, staff, and families, and Rachel would like to thank Chippewa Nature Center Preschool for the years of experiences and influence on our nature-based knowledge and philosophies. Thank you to these teams for their dedication to the growth and development of the nature-based early childhood education profession.

These two tools would not exist without the work and support of all of these nature-based practitioners, researchers, and thought leaders. Thank you to all of them!

Finally, the book you're reading would not have been possible without the support of the entire Gryphon House team and our families and friends. This project has been a labor of love, and we hope it provides a meaningful contribution to the field so that, eventually, all children will have high-quality nature-based experiences as part of their formal education.

Evaluating Natureness: Measuring the Quality of Nature-Based Classrooms in Pre-K through 3rd Grade

Introduction

Why Nature-Based Early Childhood Education?

Nature-based early childhood education stems from a deep tradition in both early childhood education and environmental education. The earliest kindergarten, meaning "children's garden," began in the early 1800s. Developed by Friedrich Froebel, this approach assigned a small garden plot for each child to cultivate and a larger one for several children to work on together (Morrison, 2001). Later, the nature study movement of the late-nineteenth and early-twentieth centuries, which encompassed John Dewey's progressive education, provided models for experiential education that many early childhood programs incorporated (Armitage, 2009).

Maria Montessori, who connected nature education with the natural development of the child, insisted that children cultivate gardens (Montessori, 1912). Both Waldorf education and the Reggio Emilia approach have included natural materials as a foundation for scientific understanding and as a basis for inquiry and development of theories (Schwartz, 2009; Edwards, Gandini, and Forman, 1998). Nature has always been a key part of preschool and kindergarten curricula, providing engaging experiences for young children to learn through their senses (Bailie, 2016).

Common threads run through the histories of both early childhood and environmental education. Both have an approach to education that addresses the whole child, includes authentic experiences, integrates subjects in the curriculum, and provides opportunities for sensory-based learning. However, the role of nature in early childhood education is primarily focused on child development, and the role of early childhood in nature study is the development of environmental stewardship.

Why Is It Important for Children?

Because young children learn through their senses, the natural world provides many opportunities for learning, such as listening to bird calls (a precursor to phonetic awareness), searching for animal tracks (patterns and spacing provide a foundation for math), and collecting tadpoles and catching frogs (a life-cycle concept in science). In addition to the foundation for academics that learning outside offers, a growing body of research suggests that nature's role in the developing child is significant and should be fostered. For example, studies have shown a decrease in symptoms of attention-deficit hyperactivity disorder (ADHD; see Faber Taylor and Kuo, 2009), higher development of motor skills (Fjørtoft, 2001), and increased resilience (Ernst, Juckett, and Sobel, 2021) in children who attend nature-based programs. Nature-based play has also been shown to instill a sense of place and stewardship (Chawla, 2015).

What Is NbECE and Nature-Based Pedagogy?

Nature-based early childhood education (NbECE) is a broad term describing the integration of two disciplines—early childhood and environmental education (Bailie, 2010; Larimore, 2011a, b). This pedagogical approach is sometimes also called *nature pedagogy* (Warden, 2015) or *nature-based pedagogy* (Larimore, 2019). Given the integration of early childhood and environmental education, NbECE has dual goals of whole-child development and environmental literacy (Bailie, 2012). Nature-based programs value not only cognitive but also social-emotional and physical development (Bishop-Josef and Zigler, 2011), along with children's connection to the natural world (Larimore, 2019). This approach includes any program model for children ages birth to eight years that does the following:

- Provides extensive daily outdoor time
- Operates with nature as the curriculum's organizing concept
- Follows a curriculum that emerges from children's interest in seasonal events
- Emphasizes learning *with* nature rather than learning *in* or *about* nature
- Supports learning across the boundaries of physical spaces indoors, outdoors, and in more wild spaces beyond the outdoor play space (Bailie, 2012; Finch and Bailie, 2015; Larimore, 2016; Sobel, 2014a; Andrachuk et al., 2014; Kenny, 2013; Larimore, 2011a; Moore and Cosco, 2014; Sobel, 2015; Warden, 2012, 2015)

In addition, teachers in nature-based programs are colearners with the children and partners in play as they discover and explore the natural world. The daily outdoor experiences and teacher-child interactions provide the foundation for learning that connects nature-based experiences through physical spaces and activities over time. The nuances of these characteristics of NbECE are the crux of the NAture-Based Education Rating Scales (NABERS; pronounced "neighbors") tools. The NABERS tools focus specifically on measurable features to determine how rooted a program is in nature-based pedagogy.

Today, under the broad umbrella of NbECE, there are a variety of program models throughout the world, such as nature-based preschools, forest preschools, forest kindergartens, nature kindergartens, and bush kindergartens. Some of these variations are based on cultural context, such as the term *preschool* versus *kindergarten* in different countries for children ages four to five years. Other variations include the emphasis on time outdoors and the use of an indoor facility (Larimore, 2016; Merrick, 2019). Whereas NbECE includes programs serving children from birth to eight years old, the NABERS tools measure a "natureness" focus in pre-K and K-3 settings specifically. Additionally, although the tools were originally developed in the United States with U.S.-based schools in mind, the basic principles are applicable no matter the sociocultural context. The most problematic part of NABERS may be the Staff (pre-K) and Teacher (K-3) Qualifications sections. The intent is that teachers meet the requirements of the governing body to which they report and also have nature-related formal education.

Why Assess Nature-Based Education in an Early Childhood Program?

Nature-based education is a growing educational practice in the United States, with the number of nature-based preschool programs doubling in recent years (Natural Start Alliance and NAAEE, 2020). Although organizations such as North American Association for Environmental Education (NAAEE) and Natural Start Alliance have created guidelines for how programs can include more nature, the NABERS Pre-K and K-3 tools are the first assessments created to determine the quality of the integration of nature into an early childhood education program.

NABERS was developed based on best practices in both early childhood education and environmental education, such as those outlined in the National Association for the Education of Young Children's (NAEYC's) *Developmentally Appropriate Practice in Early Childhood Programs Serving Children from Birth through Age 8* (Copple and Bredekamp, 2009), the NAAEE *Guidelines for Excellence* (n.d.), and the National Association for Interpretation (NAI) principles of interpretation (2019). In addition, *The Nature-Based Preschool Professional Practice Guidebook* (Merrick, 2019), developed by the Natural Start Alliance and NAAEE and released after the NABERS tools were created, greatly influenced our revisions. Although the NABERS Pre-K and K-3 tools incorporate the NAEYC developmentally appropriate practices, these tools focus more on the program characteristics that enhance and integrate nature-based pedagogy into a program.

This book is a guide to NABERS Pre-K and NABERS K-3. The goal of this guide is twofold: to bring clarity to the scoring of items within the NABERS tool and to describe tangible examples to support educators in shifting administrative and teaching practices to be more nature based.

Best Practices in Early Childhood Education and Environmental Education

The NAEYC book *Developmentally Appropriate Practice in Early Childhood Programs Serving Children from Birth through Age 8* is about meeting children where they are according to what is known about child development, the individual child, and the social and cultural contexts in which a child lives (Copple and Bredekamp, 2009). Best practices in early childhood education are based on research in child development. Central to developmentally appropriate practice (DAP) are the integrated curriculum, attention to the whole child, child-centered and play-based curriculum, and intentional teaching practices.

The National Project for Excellence in Environmental Education initiated several different but interrelated efforts from 1996 to 2010. The NAAEE *Guidelines for Excellence: Early Childhood Environmental Education Programs* (n.d.) focuses on six key characteristics of ECEE: program philosophy, DAP, curriculum framework for environmental learning, play and exploration, places and spaces, and educator preparation. The *Early Childhood Environmental Education Rating Scale* (2011), a formative evaluation tool developed by Dr. Yash Bhagwanji to help programs improve nature education for young children, was based on these guidelines.

Freeman Tilden, the preeminent voice of the field of interpretation, developed a set of guiding principles in the mid-1950s. Tilden's six principles (1957) incorporated the philosophy of nature guiding in the national parks developed by Enos Mills, a ranger at Rocky Mountain National Park. The NAI *Interpretation Standards* (2019) suggest that quality interpretation requires honing skills and knowledge as well as a commitment to professional development. Interpretation should be more inspirational than informational, address the whole person, and be provocative rather than just instructing. Finally, one must have a passion for the work, inspiring conservation and being intentional and thoughtful in developing programs.

Whom Is NABERS For?

The NABERS tools are designed to capture, in a relatively short amount of time, a snapshot of the current NbECE practices and glimpses into potential areas for improvement in a single classroom. As such, NABERS provides a way for practitioners, researchers, and policy makers to collect standardized information on the quality of nature-based classrooms from pre-K through third grade.

Practitioners

Our hope is that NABERS will encourage and support practitioners' ongoing reflection of their nature-based teaching. Through this reflection, we hope teachers and administrators will make continual improvement in their NbECE practices to better support young children's development and connection with the natural world.

NABERS is also intended to capture a relatively broad view of classrooms. This is not to say that tools exploring teaching and administrative practices at a more granular level are unnecessary. We value more focused, nuanced examination of nature-based programs, such as exploring the questions teachers use in teacher-child interactions. The NABERS tools, however, were designed to be an initial step and perhaps to point to areas for further explanation. Our hope is that the explanations and examples in this book will inspire tangible opportunities for growth in nature-based practice.

Researchers

Given that the field of NbECE in its current form is relatively new, we hope researchers will use the NABERS tools when conducting studies that report on the practices or outcomes of nature-based programs. Using NABERS as a way of defining the extent to which nature is used in the class curriculum will help scholars and practitioners make sense of comparable or differing results. For example, if a study is comparing two different nature-based kindergarten classrooms, the NABERS K-3 tool can be used to highlight similarities and differences in teaching practices in those two classes. If the study also compares child outcomes within those classrooms, the K-3 tool may provide additional insights as to why those outcomes were observed.

Although NABERS was designed to provide a picture of a nature-based classroom, we caution researchers to complete their own reliability among raters on the research team. This may involve multiple iterations of rating and clarification of items and terms. The tools themselves and the information in this book should be referenced heavily to clarify and establish agreement on interpretations. We also encourage that any significant areas of discrepancies using the tool be reported in study reports and manuscripts for the benefit of readers as well as for future research.

Policy Makers

The NbECE movement is growing rapidly. This is great news for young children, but it can be challenging for policy makers. For example, most states now have a quality rating and improvement system (QRIS) for preschool programs, which often includes an observation tool of some sort. However, the observation tools rarely focus on nature-based practices specifically. This is problematic for programs that define themselves as "nature-based." The NABERS tools will provide a common framework for determining the quality of these nature-based programs. In other words, it will serve as an accountability measure with clear, common language and standards. We can envision states using this tool, in conjunction with their other QRIS measures, to rate and support nature-based programs.

We also hope this tool will help move the emphasis for accountability away from individual child assessment (outcomes) to the inputs in a child's learning environment and a focus primarily on the behaviors of the adults who directly and indirectly influence young children's learning.

Using the NAture-Based Education Rating Scales

Overview of NABERS

The purpose of the NABERS tools is to distinguish high-quality nature-based early childhood (NbECE) practices. It is not intended to measure general high-quality early-childhood practices that are not related to the nature-based approach. NABERS is intended to encourage ongoing reflection to make continual improvement in NbECE teaching and administrative practices. Thus, the tools are designed to be completed during a three-hour observation. The NABERS tools assume someone other than the classroom teacher–such as a curriculum coordinator or outside assessor–will be completing the rating scale. We do, however, encourage using the tool as a self-assessment measure to identify strengths and areas of possible improvement.

NABERS for Pre-K

NABERS for Pre-K is organized into five sections. Within each section are multiple categories. Each category has multiple items with descriptors for each item. The items are scored across the row. Each row lists the Level 1 through Level 7 descriptors for a particular item. There are anywhere from one to nine items for each category, and these differences in the number of items are accounted for in the scoring process.

SECTION I: Program Goals and Curriculum Practices
A. Program Goals
B. Program Practices
C. Curriculum

SECTION II: Staffing
A. Administrator's Role
B. Teacher's Role
C. Staff Qualifications
D. Professional Development

SECTION III: Environment
A. Indoor Classroom (Inside)
B. Natural Play Area (Outside)
C. Natural Ecosystems (Beyond)

SECTION IV: Community Partnerships
A. Nature Educator
B. Artifacts/Resources–On-Site
C. Special Programs–Field Trips

SECTION V: Family Engagement
A. Family Communication and Education
B. Family Nature Experiences
C. Family Involvement

NABERS for K–3

NABERS for K-3 education is also organized into five sections. Within each section are multiple categories. In the K-3 tool there are additional subcategories within the category of Curriculum. Each category has multiple items, with descriptors for each item. The items are scored across the row. Each row lists the Level 1 through Level 7 descriptors for a particular item. There are anywhere from one to six items for each category, and these differences are accounted for in the scoring process.

SECTION I: Program Goals and Curriculum Practices
A. Program Goals
B. Program Practices
C. Curriculum:
  a. Environmental Literacy and Connection
  b. Literacy
  c. Math
  d. Science
  e. Social Studies
  f. Arts

SECTION II: Staffing
A. Administrator's Role
B. Teacher's Role
C. Teacher Qualifications
D. Professional Development

SECTION III: Environment
A. Indoor Classroom (Inside)
B. Natural Play Area (Outside)
C. Natural Ecosystems (Beyond)

SECTION IV: Community Partnerships
A. Nature Educator
B. Artifacts/Resources–On-Site
C. Special Programs–Field Trips

SECTION V: Family Engagement
A. Family Communication and Education
B. Family Nature Experiences
C. Family Involvement

Guidance for Observations and Scoring

The NABERS tools are designed to rate individual classrooms. Some items may apply to all classrooms in a building or program, but the majority will be specific to a particular classroom setting. The observations should last at least 3 hours on a typical day and include time when the class is outdoors. With this in mind, try to avoid using the tool within the first or last four weeks of the school year. "Typical" days should avoid special events, guest teachers, and extreme weather events. Observers should minimize their effect on the classroom as much as possible. This means not interfering with or participating in classroom activities–including talking with teachers or children during the class session. If observers are not able to observe all of the items on NABERS, they should conduct a teacher interview at a time when this will not affect the learning environment.

Step 1: Observe the classroom and conduct teacher interviews as appropriate to document supporting evidence.

- The NABERS for K-3 rating should include observation of *at least* three different curricular areas (environmental literacy and connection, literacy, science, math, social studies, art) taught by the primary classroom teacher.

- Supporting evidence for both tools (Pre-K and K-3) includes observation, teacher reports to the assessor, children's work products, and documents such as lesson plans and strategic plans. Supporting evidence may be relevant in multiple sections or subsections of the tool. This should be noted in writing next to the relevant items. If there is a question of whether a particular practice is present, the assessor should ask the teacher about this after the observation.

- If there are multiple teachers in a classroom as coteachers, the scores should reflect the practices of all teachers. Many preschool classrooms will involve a coteaching situation, but this will be less common at the K-3 level.

Step 2: Read each item and check one box per item row.

- Once you have observed and collected supporting evidence, score each item row by placing a check mark in one of the boxes in the columns labeled 1, 3, 5, and 7. Complete every row of items. If a category—such as one of the curriculum categories in K-3—does not apply, make a note to that effect. This will be relevant in Step 3.

- When scoring, keep in mind these clarifications of the terms *almost always/all, often/most, sometimes/some,* and *rarely/no/does not*. Almost always is every day children are present at school. Generally speaking *often* would be more than 60 percent of the time, *sometimes* would be 30-60 percent of the time, *rarely* would be less than 30 percent of the time, and *no/does not* would be never.

Step 3: Determine the score for each category.

Circle the corresponding level (1, 2, 3, 4, 5, 6, or 7) at the top of the category. The score for each category is determined using the following criteria:

- For categories with *three or more rows* of items:

  Level 1: Half or more of the Level 1 boxes are checked (regardless of the Level 3, 5, or 7 boxes that may be checked).

  Level 2: Fewer than half of the Level 1 boxes are checked, some of the Level 3 boxes are checked, and no Level 5 or 7 boxes are checked.

  Level 3: All Level 3 boxes are checked *or* one Level 1 box is checked, and the remaining boxes are checked at Level 5 or 7.

  Level 4: No Level 1 boxes are checked, half or fewer of the Level 3 boxes are checked, and the remaining boxes are checked at Level 5 or 7.

Level 5: All Level 5 boxes are checked *or* one Level 3 box is checked, and the remaining boxes are checked at Level 7.

Level 6: No Level 1 or 3 boxes are checked, half or fewer of the Level 5 boxes are checked, and the remaining boxes are checked at Level 7.

Level 7: All Level 7 boxes are checked.

* For categories with *two rows* of items:

Level 1: Both Level 1 boxes are checked.

Level 2: One Level 1 box and one Level 3 box are checked.

Level 3: Both Level 3 boxes are checked *or* one Level 1 box is checked, and the remaining box is checked at Level 5 or 7.

Level 4: One Level 1 or 3 box is checked and one Level 5 box is checked.

Level 5: Both Level 5 boxes are checked *or* one Level 3 box is checked, and the remaining box is checked at Level 7.

Level 6: One Level 5 box is checked, and the remaining box is checked at Level 7.

Level 7: Both Level 7 boxes are checked.

If a category, such as one of the curriculum categories in the K–3 tool, does not apply or cannot be observed, compute the quality level based on the number of subcategories completed for that category. For example, if all subcategories except Art in the category of Curriculum are scored, the number of subcategories scored would be six.

Making Meaning of Scores

Early childhood programs, whether pre-K or K-3, are influenced by many factors, including specific contextual factors such as culture, geography, pedagogical beliefs, and so forth. The specific context of a school will greatly influence the scores on NABERS. That is, every school has a different emphasis on nature-based education, different access to natural ecosystems, and so on. Further, most early childhood programs are shifting their practice to be more nature-based rather than starting their program with that clear intention. As such, it is unlikely that programs will score a Level 7 on all of the items in the NABERS tool. Instead, the scores will help identify both strengths in a nature-based practice and opportunities for improvement.

An "ideal" score is also dependent on the particular program. Scores are not intended to be interpreted as "good" or "bad" but, rather, to offer a broad glimpse of where a program is on a continuum of nature-based practice. Lower-scored items are potential areas for improvement, but whether or not to shift practice is always the choice of teachers and administrators. It may be that it is not physically possible to achieve a higher score on some items. Or it may be that a program chooses to invest time and energy on other areas of the program. For example, a school might have access to only one ecosystem within walking distance and also may choose not to invest funds on transporting children to access an additional two ecosystems. Thus, they would not score a Level 7 on access to natural ecosystems. The NABERS tools are designed to support these as being intentional and well-informed decisions.

> **NABERS scores will help programs identify both strengths and opportunities for improvement in their nature-based practice.**

Tips for the Observer and Tips for Growing

This book focuses on clarifying the components of the NABERS tools. We've tried to clarify each item in more detail. In some places, we offer more extensive examples of evidence for a particular item; we've titled these boxes Tips for the Observer. Throughout this book you'll also see boxes called Tips for Growing. We've included these for times when it may be less obvious what changes could be made in order to improve the nature-based teaching practice. We hope these features will be resources for both observers and practitioners as a way to reflect and build on their practice to be even more nature-based.

Additional Explanation of Terms

The individual NABERS tools and information in this book include many terms, some of which may have different meanings for different audiences and contexts. For example, in the tools we use *school* and *program* interchangeably. We recognize K–3 programs tend to use *school*; whereas, pre-K programs will use a mix of *school* or *program*. Whenever we use one of these terms, we mean the organization that is housing the teachers and children. Below is a list of terms that are helpful in making sense of the information and the NABERS Pre-K and K–3 tools.

Administrators are those in a decision-making capacity for running a school or program. In a public K–3 setting, they might include the superintendent, assistant superintendent, principal, outdoor-learning coordinator, and possibly school board members. In a private school, they might be the head of school or trustees. In a pre-K setting, they could be the owner, director, or board members. The degree to which their involvement will vary is based on the size of the school and their particular role.

Authentic nature refers to images, objects, and other items that accurately represent what is found in the natural world rather than anthropomorphized or caricature versions of nature. This also includes intentionally disrupting stereotypes of nature such as, "Wolves have red eyes," or "All pigs are pink."

Beyond (natural ecosystems) is the area beyond the boundaries of the designated outside play area, which may or may not be fenced. This is one of the three spaces commonly discussed in nature-based education: inside, outside, and beyond.

Child-led activities are those in which children make the majority of the decisions regarding what activities to engage in and how they will engage.

Classroom is a group of children and adults who interact and function as a group within a school or program. The term is used interchangeably with *class*.

Environmental education is a process that helps individuals, communities, and organizations learn more about the environment and develop skills and understanding about how to address global challenges.

Environmental literacy encompasses environmental knowledge, attitudes, and skills by which individuals understand their relationship with the natural world so they can make responsible decisions for future generations. This is often thought of as the outcome of environmental education.

Environmental stewardship refers to the responsible use and protection of the natural environment through active participation in conservation efforts and sustainable practices by individuals or groups.

Healthy ecosystems is a concept widely debated among ecologists. In this context, we generally mean an ecosystem with rich biodiversity and minimal exotic or invasive species.

Inside refers to the space inside a four-walled structure. This is typically a permanent, built structure but could also include a semipermanent structure such as a yurt or platform tent. This is one of the three spaces commonly discussed in nature-based education: inside, outside, and beyond.

Learning *about* nature means learning content focuses on the natural world; it does not necessarily include the physical presence of nature. Learning can occur indoors or outdoors.

Learning *in* nature is learning that occurs outdoors but does not depend on nature for learning to occur.

Learning *with* nature is learning that relates to or emerges from outdoor experiences with the natural world and relies on the natural world as another teacher.

Leave No Trace© Seven Principles (1999) are guidelines for responsibly behaving in the outdoors to minimize our impact on the natural world. These principles were developed by the nonprofit Leave No Trace Center for Outdoor Ethics.

Licensing, for the purposes of these tools, refers to any regulatory guidelines governing legal program operations. For example, in U.S. contexts at the preschool level, *licensing* means state approval to legally operate a child-care program.

Local nature refers to climate, plants, and animals found geographically close to the classroom—the nature found right outside the classroom door or within the region. For example, a black-capped chickadee is local to Vermont, but a flamingo is not. However, the reverse is true for Florida—the flamingo is a local natural feature.

Managed outdoor spaces are the natural outdoor play spaces found in nature-based programs. These spaces are managed in that, although they are natural, they are not as wild as natural ecosystems (for example, plants are kept trimmed, grass mowed) but are more natural than a typical playground.

Natural ecosystems (beyond) are natural communities rich with living (plants, animals) and nonliving (water, soil) elements. Natural ecosystems include ponds, rivers, wetlands, marshes, meadows, fields, prairies, lakes/beaches, vernal pools, and woodlands. They can also include spaces that have been cultivated by humans, such as arboretums, gardens, and ponds.

Natural history knowledge refers to an understanding of animals and plants in their natural environment gained through observation and interacting with the natural world.

Natural materials are objects found in nature and not created by humans, such as leaves, rocks, sticks, pine cones, shells, flowers, and animal bones.

Natural play area (outside) is a designated outdoor play space with a general appearance of nature and emphasis on natural materials, loose parts, and some built elements to support learning with nature (rather than more conventional playground climbing structures).

Nature educator is an expert in natural history, ecology, outdoor education, interpretation, or a related field; examples include a naturalist from a nature center, a park interpreter, or a child's family member with natural history or environmental science expertise.

Nature-based early childhood education (NbECE) is a pedagogical approach to teaching that blends the two disciplines of early childhood and environmental education to support children from birth to eight years old through extensive daily outdoor time and nature as the curriculum's organizing concept. It is also referred to as *nature based pedagogy*.

Outdoors, in this tool, is a collective term for any space independent of the indoor space within a building or shelter. Outdoors could include either outside or beyond spaces or both.

Outside, in this tool, refers specifically to the designated outdoor play area. This is one of the three spaces commonly discussed in nature-based education: inside, outside, and beyond (see also *Natural play area*).

Play is an activity that is (1) self-chosen and self-directed; (2) intrinsically motivated; (3) guided by mental rules; (4) imaginative; and (5) conducted in an active, alert, but relatively nonstressed frame of mind (Gray, 2013).

Program is used interchangeably with *school*. We recognize K–3 programs tend to use *school*; whereas, pre-K programs will use a mix of *school* or *program*. Whenever we use one of these terms, we mean the organization that is housing the teachers and children.

School is used interchangeably with *program*. We recognize K–3 programs tend to use *school*; whereas, pre-K programs will use a mix of *school* or *program*. Whenever we use one of these terms, we mean the organization that is housing the teachers and children.

Seasonal experiences are those rooted in what is occurring outdoors at the present time. Conversation about these experiences might compare the present moment with other times of the year, but the experience is primarily rooted in what is currently happening outdoors.

Teachers are those directly implementing the curriculum in a classroom. They might include lead teachers, assistant teachers, or coteachers, depending on the setting (public/private) and age (K–3/pre-K).

Teacher-led activities are those organized and directed by the teacher and involving the whole class or a subset of children.

Unstructured nature play is play that occurs outdoors while using nature as props or tools in the play. *Play*, by definition, is an activity that is (1) self-chosen and self-directed; (2) intrinsically motivated; (3) guided by mental rules; (4) imaginative; and (5) conducted in an active, alert, but relatively nonstressed frame of mind (Gray, 2013). Thus, we realize it is somewhat redundant to say *unstructured* nature play. We use that term to emphasize the importance of children's time in nature during which they—the players rather than the teacher—determine the activity and rules.

Section I:
Program Goals and Curriculum Practices

NbECE is a term that describes the integration of early childhood and environmental education (Bailie, 2010; Larimore, 2011a; Finch and Bailie, 2015). Each of these disciplines has different goals, but when the two come together in NbECE there are dual goals: developmentally appropriate early child education and environmental education. NbECE implements best practices of both disciplines.

As such, when determining the natureness of a nature-based program, it's important to examine the value a program demonstrates for ongoing experiences in nature during which children have agency in deciding the focus and direction of their learning. Additionally, through daily practice, a nature-based program demonstrates values of environmental stewardship and minimal impact on the land by following the Leave No Trace Seven Principles. In addition to these goals, nature-based programs value ongoing experiences outdoors and structure their operations and procedures, such as how the day is structured and safety-related policies and procedures, to support positive outdoor experiences.

Another way nature-based program goals are brought to life is through the curriculum. In these programs, nature is the central organization concept, and the curriculum is based on local, seasonal, and authentic experiences. These experiences are then integrated into all developmental domains and disciplines. Children's ongoing experiences in nature are connected to and build on their learning throughout the class day and the school year. Further, through this process children are leaders in the learning process as much as possible, making them agents in their own learning.

The categories and items are generally the same for pre-K and K-3 settings. However, when it comes to curriculum, we recognize the pre-K and K-3 worlds function somewhat differently based on the systems they operate within (such as funding, policies, and governance). Thus, Category B: Program Practices and Category C: Curriculum are divided into two parts: Pre-K and K-3.

Category A: Program Goals

About This Category

The items in this category evaluate to what extent a program is structured to include the goals of both early childhood (child development) and environmental education (environmental stewardship). A program scoring at the highest level implements best practices for both early childhood and environmental education consistently. A program scoring in the mid-range implements best practices of one discipline or the other, or perhaps a bit of each, but not both at the same time. Furthermore, mid-range programs do not consistently implement practices of both disciplines over time. A low-scoring program implements neither high-quality early childhood nor environmental education practices.

Item 1: The program has a mission or purpose statement that indicates dual goals of both child development and environmental stewardship.

The dual goals of a high-quality program—both child development and environmental stewardship—can be observed explicitly (shared in a mission statement, posted on a wall, declared in a family manual, or provided in other written documentation) and implicitly (observed in actions by the teacher, in lesson objectives, or in the environment of the classroom). The NABERS tool measures implicit indications of mission and purpose throughout the tool; Category A focuses on how the goals are *explicitly* expressed. The documentation (for example, mission statement, website, family handbook) that illustrates these goals is shared widely with families and the community.

Environmental stewardship goals include a coherent environmental philosophy or set of practices that support children's positive connection to the natural world. This enhances their environmental literacy—their knowledge, skills, and emotional connection with the natural world. Nature is mentioned as a vehicle for accomplishing the child development goals. For example, evidence may include statements in written school or program documents that indicate that physical development is promoted through hiking on trails, balancing on logs, or climbing trees.

Depending on the age of the children, environmental stewardship goals can include a range of children's environmental awareness, from developing appreciation and respect for nature to nature study and sustainability practices. For example, evidence statements may include that environmental stewardship is supported when children express an increasing appreciation and affinity for nature, demonstrate actions that reflect a sense of respect for nature and the environment, understand that plants and animals need many of the same things from the environment that humans do, and engage in activities such as recycling and composting that promote sustainability.

Child development goals include the areas of social, emotional, physical, and cognitive development at a minimum and could include development in other areas, such as creative/aesthetic, spiritual, and approaches to learning. Many of these goals may stem from local, state, and national early learning standards. Nature-based programs make explicit the ways activities in nature support development; for example, social development is supported by children working cooperatively to plant a garden or build a fort, emotional development is encouraged by children taking care of classroom animals, and cognitive development is supported through problem solving in natural environments.

Level 7: The program has a mission or purpose statement that indicates dual goals of both child development *and* environmental stewardship.

The highest-rated programs explicitly mention their dual goals of both child development and environmental stewardship; that is, nature is not only a tool for supporting child development but also serves to develop children's environmental literacy. Level 7 programs share their goals widely within and outside the school community.

Level 5: The program has a mission or purpose statement that indicates a goal of child development with mention of nature as a tool to accomplish that goal.

Programs at this level explicitly express goals of child development but do not explicitly express goals of environmental stewardship. Level 5 programs may mention nature as a vehicle or tool for achieving child development rather than also being a way to support children's environmental stewardship.

Level 3: The program has a mission or purpose statement that indicates a goal of child development with no mention of nature.

Programs at this level explicitly state child development goals in a mission or purpose statement (or other written documentation). Environmental stewardship is not mentioned, and there is no mention of nature as a vehicle or tool to accomplish child development goals.

Level 1: The program has no mission or purpose statement.

Although goals may be implicit in a Level 1 program, they are not explicitly stated in a mission or purpose statement, posted on a wall, or included in a family manual (or other written documentation). They are not shared widely with families and the community.

Tips for the Observer: Program Goals

It is not always easy to find evidence of program goals. Here are some ideas that might provide evidence of what the program goals are. We also provide questions an observer might ask to collect more information about program goals.

Examples of evidence:

Goals of the program may be explicitly specified in a

- mission statement,
- family handbook,
- family newsletter,
- display on the wall in the school or classroom,
- strategic plan,
- marketing brochure, or
- website.

Questions to ask if evidence isn't apparent:

- What are the goals of the program?
- Where are these goals documented (for example, in a mission statement, family handbook, poster, or other forms of written documentation)?
- How are the goals of the program communicated to families and the community?

Item 2: The program models that all children, no matter their background or ability, deserve and can participate in positive outdoor experiences.

Implicit in nature-based education is the idea that all children, no matter their background or ability, are not only able to but also have a right to experience positive outdoor experiences. It is important to recognize the two key components of this item.

The first is *all children, no matter their background or ability.* The idea is that outdoor experiences should be inclusive of every child and that programs are intentional about supporting all children who want to participate in outdoor experiences. In addition, program materials, conversations, and the like should reflect children and families representing diverse communities enjoying outdoor experiences.

The key second component of this item is *positive outdoor experiences.* This implies that experiences will vary from child to child and that the adults will adapt activities and support children emotionally and physically to ensure they have a positive experience. In other words, nature-based programs are not intended to create a survivalist, tough-it-out-no-matter-what mentality. On the contrary, they recognize that children's prior experience, personality, and skills—along with the context of the school and activities—will influence their experience.

This belief can be demonstrated in myriad ways. In their written documents, such as philosophy statements, family handbooks, and staff manuals, programs may explicitly mention that all children can participate in positive outdoor experiences. Programs may also convey this belief in more implicit ways, such as representing diverse audiences in their marketing materials, limits (or lack thereof) on who may or may not enroll, and conversations within the program. The program may offer resources to support all children experiencing the outdoors in different weather, terrain, and so on. For example, a program serving lower-income families will provide enough extra appropriate clothing to ensure every child can be safe outdoors in all weather—no matter the family's financial situation.

Level 7: The program *almost always* models that all children, no matter their background and ability, deserve and can participate in positive outdoor experiences.

Highest-rated nature-based programs live, day in and day out, the belief that all children, no matter their background or ability, deserve and can participate in positive outdoor experiences. At this level, there will be evidence of outdoor inclusivity in multiple ways, such as the enrollment materials, family handbook, materials or equipment to support children's unique needs for outdoor experiences, and even additional staff.

Level 5: The program *often* models that all children, no matter their background or ability, deserve and can participate in positive outdoor experiences.

Although Level 5 programs are intentional about expressing that all children deserve and can participate in positive outdoor experiences, there may be limits to how this belief is implemented. For example, a program may demonstrate extensive support for children with social-emotional disabilities but state it is unable to support the needs of a child who uses a wheelchair because the facilities and terrain are not wheelchair accessible.

Level 3: The program *sometimes* models that all children, no matter their background or ability, deserve and can participate in positive outdoor experiences.

Programs at this level sometimes model that all children deserve and can participate in positive outdoor experiences, but there are many times when they do not. For example, they may have written policies limiting who may attend the program, such as requiring a certain language proficiency or stating an inability to support a child with limited physical mobility. They may also use deficit language when referring to groups of children and their ability to participate in outdoor activities. This might include phrases such as, "They just need too much help" or, "Folks from that culture don't like to be outside anyway."

Level 1: The program *rarely* or *does not* model that all children, no matter their background or ability, deserve and can participate in positive outdoor experiences.

A Level 1 program does not model an inclusive approach to participation in outdoor experiences. Programs at this level will likely be reinforcing notions of ableism, racism, sexism, and other prejudices about who can and deserves to participate in outdoor experiences. For example, a program might respond to questions about inclusion with, "We just can't support children with special needs."

Materials in a nature-based classroom, whether indoors or outdoors, will include mix of human-made and natural materials.

Tips for Growing: Modeling Positive Outdoor Experiences for All Children

If a program has a score on this item that is less than desired, here are considerations for being more intentional, inclusive, and asset based.

Examples of outdoor experiences:

Many different activities can create positive outdoor experiences. Some will lean toward adventure/physical movement, and others will lean more toward deep nature study. Still others will fall somewhere in the middle along that continuum. When considering the positive outdoor experiences represented consider these questions:

- How are the outdoor interests of the children in the classroom reflected and represented?
- How are the popular outdoor activities in our community represented in the classroom? (These are usually deeply connected to place.)
- Who is represented as participating in these activities? Are children from a variety of backgrounds and abilities portrayed as being able to participate in outdoor activities?

Outdoor experiences come in many different forms. Here are a few different types of outdoor activities to consider:

Hiking	Birding
Camping (tent, RV, and the like)	Geocaching
Hunting	Swinging in a hammock
Fishing	Painting the scenery
Canoeing, kayaking, rafting	Picnicking/cookouts
Sailing	Gardening
Biking	Swimming
Rock climbing	Foraging
Horseback riding	Collecting shells
Skiing	Playing games
Photography	Singing and dancing

Item 3: Emphasis is placed on learning *with* nature.

Nature-based education involves child-led emergent curriculum emphasizing learning *with* nature. Given that children spend so much time outdoors, their interests will almost always be aligned with the seasons. They will be curious about what they are observing and experiencing in nature at that point in time. A child-led curriculum allows those curiosities to drive the learning and for nature to serve as another teacher. This is the core of learning with nature, which is different from learning in or about nature. However, if we are truly addressing the whole child, it's impossible to ignore learning in and about nature.

Learning *in* nature means any learning that physically occurs outdoors but doesn't depend on nature for learning to occur. The learning activity would be the same if it occurred indoors. These activities may be teacher- or child-led and don't typically connect to other experiences in time.

Learning *about* nature means the content of the activity focuses on the natural world and, as with learning in nature, does not necessarily need the physical presence of nature to occur—the learning can occur indoors or outdoors. Learning-about-nature activities are mostly teacher led during large- or small-group time or when teachers are providing information in a moment during play. These activities may build over time and connect with prior experiences.

Learning *with* nature requires an outdoor experience with the natural world for children to relate to and connect with. The learning emerges from those experiences, which means they're almost always child led. This learning is typically outside of the teacher's original plans, but not necessarily, and relies on the natural world as another teacher. The result is learning that has personal meaning to the child, whether through a cognitive or emotional connection. Learning with nature typically builds over time because children are immersed in the natural world and noticing patterns or disruptions to patterns. Evidence of learning in, about, or with nature may be observed in curricular scope-and-sequence documents, lesson plans, and/or observed lessons.

Level 7: Emphasis is placed on learning *with* nature versus learning in or about nature (i.e., integration of nature in learning).

Learning *with* nature positions experiences first, followed by sharing information after children have had a meaningful experience. Teachers allow the children's interests to drive the learning and emphasize open-ended exploration. There will be moments of learning *about* nature even with emphasis on learning *with* nature. These moments, however, will emerge from children's experiences learning with nature. For example, while out exploring a child might find an interesting insect and ask, "What is it?" The teacher's answer is a form of learning about nature, but the question is sparked by the child's interest and thus should be considered learning with nature. However, if the teacher started the lesson telling the students names of insects in the area and then asked them to go look for them, this would be considered learning *about* nature.

With the lack of specific standards related to content outcomes, pre-K will have more freedom for exploration so each day can truly be child led. K-3, on the other hand, will likely have more specific outcomes in mind. A teacher, for example, may need to teach about the life cycle of plants. With that broad goal in mind, the teacher can still emphasize an open-ended opportunity for learning with nature by, for example, having the children wear tall athletic socks over their shoes and walk through a meadow to see what seeds stick.

Level 5: Learning primarily emphasizes learning *about* nature.

Learning emphasizing learning *about* nature will involve a more didactic approach in which teachers convey information to children either indoors or outdoors. In learning about nature, there is little engagement or experience with the natural world. In some cases, the children will have a chance to explore, but the teacher shares information about the topic at hand before exploration. For example, a teacher might tell the group about the life stages of a frog and then have children explore a pond for each stage. This activity could be shifted to learning *with* nature by exploring the pond first and then discussing the stages of a frog's life after the experience. (Note: A whole-group time before exploration to discuss safety measures and tool use is not considered a learning *about* moment.)

Level 3: Learning primarily emphasizes learning *in* nature.

Programs at this level regularly conduct learning activities outdoors, but the activities do not rely on or connect to nature in any way. Pre-K programs at this level might, for example, move the art easel, sand and water table, or dramatic play materials outside for children's use during play. In K-3 settings, a class might conduct a shared reading lesson or complete math worksheets outside. These activities do not rely on nature to occur and are not inspired or influenced by nature in any way. Thus, the activities are considered learning *in* nature.

Level 1: No integration of nature in learning.

Programs at this level do not integrate nature into the learning. This means there are no learning activities with nature as the topic or focus and no learning activities occurring outdoors.

Tips for the Observer: Identifying Emphasis on Learning *with* Nature

Identifying how much a class is emphasizing learning with nature can be a challenge, so we've included some examples of evidence to look for during observations. We have also provided questions an observer might ask to determine whether an activity is learning in, about, or with nature. (By the way, these questions may also be helpful to teachers when planning class activities.)

Examples of evidence:

- Lesson plans
- Documentation of learning experiences prior to the day of observation:
    - Journals
    - Bulletin-board displays
    - Social-media posts
    - Website/blog posts
    - Newsletters to families
    - Media coverage such as newspaper clippings
- Anecdotes shared during a teacher interview

Questions for an observer to ask themselves when observing a lesson:

- How would this same activity be similar or different if it occurred inside? outside?
- If a lesson is focused on learning about nature, was there an experience with this nature topic before the current activity? Which came first—a nature-based experience or learning about nature?

Question to ask if evidence isn't apparent:

How do you identify the activities for upcoming class sessions?

Item 4: Learning topics and scope are developmentally appropriate (for example, are concrete, locally focused).

Author David Sobel (2013) in *Beyond Ecophobia: Reclaiming the Heart in Nature Education* says, "What's important is that children have an opportunity to bond with the natural world, to learn to love it and feel comfortable in it, before being asked to heal its wounds." Item 4 of the rating scale is intended to address this issue. Ideally, learning topics in nature-based programs are *developmentally appropriate*—that is, appropriate to the child's age, developmental status, and the social and cultural context in which they live (Copple and Bredekamp, 2009). For nature-based programs, this means emphasizing concrete, locally focused learning rather than abstract concepts such as global climate change and faraway places. This isn't to say that young children can't begin to see a connection between their behavior and the planet. Rather, those connections should be rooted in a child's particular place in their world, in things they can observe and experience firsthand for their own sense-making. Evidence of learning topics may be found in classrooms scope and sequences, lesson plans, and/ or observed lessons.

Level 7: Learning topics and scope are *almost always* developmentally appropriate (for example, are concrete, locally focused).

Classrooms at this level demonstrate developmentally appropriate practices by focusing on phenomena (natural events, plants, animals, and culture) in their particular place in the world, all of which they can observe or experience directly. Although the primary focus of learning at this level will not be large, abstract ideas, Level 7 programs will engage in developmentally appropriate learning that is foundational to later understanding of those large concepts. A teacher might, for example, facilitate a phenology study in which children observe the cycles of the natural world and compare those to previous years. Although this activity isn't explicitly connected to climate change, it builds conceptual understanding of cycles and patterns over time. Developmentally appropriate environmental stewardship might focus on service learning projects in the program's particular setting. For example, students might decide they want to start a campaign to clean their schoolyard of garbage and debris, a tangible, personally meaningful activity and, thus, developmentally appropriate.

Level 5: Learning topics and scope are *often* developmentally appropriate (for example, are concrete, locally focused).

A Level 5 score should be awarded when a program mostly provides learning topics and scope that are developmentally appropriate but may occasionally provide lessons that are abstract or focused on distant locations. Note that a program discussing far-off places in comparison with local ones is considered developmentally appropriate. If, for example, children in the United States have been studying Virginia opossums, they might also conduct a study of kangaroos as a comparison to a marsupial in another part of the world. Only focusing on the kangaroo, however, would not be developmentally appropriate because kangaroos are not fauna naturally found in U.S. habitats. Thus, if the kangaroo-focused lesson was the only learning topic that was not developmentally appropriate, the classroom would receive a Level 5 score. It should be noted here that if the class had gone on a field trip to a local zoo, observed a kangaroo in person, and then wanted to learn more about it, that would be developmentally appropriate.

Level 3: Learning topics and scope are *rarely* developmentally appropriate (for example, are concrete, locally focused).

A classroom should receive a Level 3 score if learning topics and scope are sometimes developmentally appropriate but primarily are above children's understanding (i.e., abstract and distant). For example, focusing on the life cycle of an animal that does not live in their place in the world would not be developmentally appropriate.

Level 1: Learning topics and scope are above children's understanding (for example, are abstract aspects of climate change, faraway places).

Level 1 programs will consistently provide learning activities that are above the children's developmental understanding and thus not developmentally appropriate. For example, discussing climate change in terms of average global temperatures and carbon levels would not be developmentally appropriate for most of early childhood. However, keeping a journal of daily temperatures from year to year to see long-term trends would be developmentally appropriate.

> ### Tips for the Observer: Learning Topics and Scope Are Developmentally Appropriate
>
> We recommend observations be 3 hours long, so it is difficult to know what happens in the classroom on other days or at other times—particularly when it comes to developmentally appropriate topics. The following are some observation considerations for developmental appropriateness.
>
> **Examples of evidence:**
>
> - Lesson plans
> - Scope-and-sequence documents
> - Curriculum materials
>
> **Questions to ask if evidence isn't apparent:**
>
> - How do you decide what curriculum to teach in your classroom?
> - How do you decide what nature-based content to focus on?

Item 5: Sustainable practices are evident.

One of the goals of NbECE is environmental stewardship. Teachers can facilitate this outcome by supporting learning around the concepts and also by modeling sustainability-related behaviors. This item focuses on the sustainable practices the adults in a classroom are modeling for children.

Sustainability is based on the idea that development should meet the needs of the present without compromising the ability of future generations to meet their own needs (National Research Council, 2011). Using sustainable practices in a school and classrooms demonstrates the ways humans can live in conjunction with the natural environment and helps to foster environmental stewardship in children. Although this tool primarily focuses on the processes within a school (i.e., human behavior), it's important to note that the building itself can be designed, built, and maintained using sustainable practices. Although the frequency of some of these practices may be due to school policies or other external factors, incorporating sustainable practices in the school and classroom environment demonstrates the overall program goals and environmental stewardship. (See the following textbox for examples of sustainable practices.) Evidence of sustainable practices will primarily be observed but may be noted through interviews with teachers and administrators if they occur at times not observed, such as during different seasons or different parts of the day.

Sustainable Practices in Schools and Classrooms

- Providing cloth napkins or hand towels
- Using reusable utensils, plates, and cups
- Using reusable water bottles
- Eating locally grown food for meals and/or snacks (for example, from a school garden or local farm)
- Recycling
- Composting
- Using rain barrels
- Using natural light

Level 7: At least *3* sustainable practices are evident in the program.

Programs at this level show evidence of incorporating many sustainable practices into the indoor and outdoor classroom environments. Throughout the day, this may look like intentionally limiting electrical light use and using natural light instead. At mealtimes, it may look like creating a chart of mealtime trash to reduce the amount of waste. It could also include composting, washable plates, silverware, and cloth napkins. Special projects could include having rain barrels or a garden to grow fruits and vegetables for meals or snacks.

Level 5: At least *2* sustainable practices are evident in the program.

Programs at this level show evidence of incorporating at least two sustainable practices, such as intentionally limiting electrical light use and using reusable materials at mealtimes, into the indoor and outdoor classroom environments.

Level 3: At least *1* sustainable practice is evident in the program.

Programs at this level show evidence of incorporating at least one sustainable practice into their indoor and outdoor classroom environments. A program at this level might, for example, use fabric towels rather than paper towels for cleaning up spills and messes, but demonstrate no other practices.

Level 1: *No* sustainable practices are evident in the program.

Programs at this level demonstrate no sustainable practices as part of their program. They may include single-use materials for meals and not provide any opportunities for recycling and so forth.

Tips for the Observer: Sustainable Practices

There are many ways a program or classroom can support environmental sustainability efforts. The following are some concrete examples of evidence that might be observed in a classroom as well as questions to ask if evidence isn't apparent.

Examples of evidence:

- Recycling and compost bins are available for children to use.
- Reusable materials are located throughout the classroom.
- Building certification for sustainable practices is displayed.

Questions to ask if evidence isn't apparent:

- What do you do in your classroom to promote environmental sustainability?
- How do you model sustainable practices to children in your class?
- Was your building designed using sustainable practices?
- In what ways are sustainable practices used to maintain the building?

Item 6: Program implements the Leave No Trace Seven Principles in natural ecosystems.

Leave No Trace is a movement led by the nonprofit group Leave No Trace Center for Outdoor Ethics to ensure people enjoy the outdoors responsibly, in a way that minimizes our impacts on the natural world. Leave No Trace principles not only benefit the natural environment but also ensure that other people can also enjoy the wonders nature has to offer.

The Leave No Trace© Seven Principles

❀ Plan Ahead and Prepare

❀ Travel and Camp on Durable Surfaces

❀ Dispose of Waste Properly

❀ Leave What You Find

❀ Minimize Campfire Impacts

❀ Respect Wildlife

❀ Be Considerate of Other Visitors

© 2021 Leave No Trace. For more on the Leave No Trace Seven Principles and how to implement them in your program's environment, visit www.LNT.org. The Leave No Trace Center for Outdoor Ethics provides resources, lesson plans, courses, and more for learning more about the seven principles.

These principles are most relevant to NbECE when exploring natural ecosystems beyond the designated outside play area and are important to reduce the impact programs have on the natural ecosystems they visit. As the number of nature-based programs continues to grow, so does the impact on the natural world. Because one of the goals of nature-based education is environmental stewardship, it seems logical for educators to model stewardship behaviors in our programs. Further, implementing the Leave No Trace Seven Principles in nature-based programs teaches young children to be environmental stewards through practices they can implement now as well as carry with them into the future.

How these principles are enacted will vary depending on the particular context—most notably, the ecosystem in which you find yourself. For example, in more resilient ecosystems, it may be best to spread out when traveling off-trail to minimize impact. In other ecosystems, it may be best to follow one another in a straight line if you must venture off the trail.

The scoring for this item is based on the extent to which a program implements all seven principles. Assessors will primarily observe evidence for this item, but they can also procure evidence through interviews with teachers and administrators. At this highest level, an assessor will see evidence of all seven principles appropriate to the program setting's particular ecosystem, which may include:

❀ a clear plan and preparations, such as appropriate equipment and gear, for trips beyond the outside play area;

❀ durable surfaces, such as constructed trails, sand, or gravel, for group travel, play, and group meetings; and

* observations of children leaving the area as it was found, including actions such as rolling logs back over after looking under them for insects, only using dead and downed sticks for play, and dismantling stick forts they have created.

The highest-rated nature-based programs will also minimize their campfire impacts, dispose of all waste properly, respect wildlife, and be considerate of other visitors.

In implementing these ideas, teachers and children will inherently talk about how to reduce their impact outdoors and why they do that. By living these principles, we are developing children's skills and knowledge related to stewardship.

Level 7: The program *almost always* practices the Leave No Trace Seven Principles in natural ecosystems.

To score the highest level on this item, a program must almost always practice the Leave No Trace Seven Principles in natural ecosystems. Although the observer will be seeing only one point in time, the extent to which this item is met will be in evidence through the physical wear and tear of the spaces the group uses.

Level 5: The program *often* practices the Leave No Trace Seven Principles in natural ecosystems.

Programs that often, but not always, adhere to the Leave No Trace Seven Principles are rated a Level 5. For example, there may be some minimal evidence of a class's human impact on a natural space, such as a few pieces of litter, after the group has left the area.

Level 3: The program *sometimes* practices the Leave No Trace Seven Principles in natural ecosystems.

Level 3 programs sometimes adhere to the Leave No Trace Seven Principles. These programs make some efforts to reduce their impact but do not make a comprehensive, intentional effort. For example, they may pick up trash when they leave a space but may have trampled vegetation in the area and created a high-impact campfire. As a result, even once the group has left a natural space, there will be some evidence of their presence and impact on that space.

Level 1: The program *does not* practice the Leave No Trace Seven Principles in natural ecosystems.

Programs at this level do not adhere to the Leave No Trace Seven Principles; there is no indication of any of the seven principles in action. As a result, once the group has left a natural space, there will be extensive evidence of their presence and impact on that space.

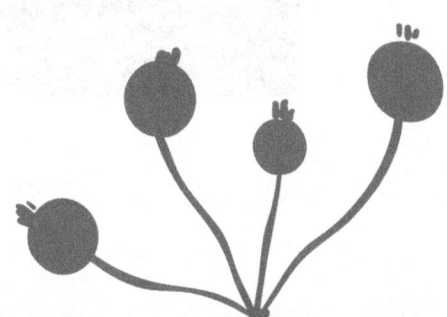

Tips for the Observer: Program Implements the Leave No Trace Seven Principles

We realize observing a class at one point in time may make it difficult to confidently say whether that class is always adhering to the Leave No Trace Seven Principles. However, observers should be looking for behaviors in the moment as well as for evidence of prior impact.

Examples of evidence:

- Collecting and packing out garbage
- Teachers talking about minimizing impact
- Well-worn paths
- Campfire ashes that have built up over time
- Trampled or broken vegetation

Questions to ask if evidence isn't apparent:

- How do you reduce the impact your class has on the natural environment?
- How are these procedures communicated to staff? through a policies and procedures manual? through activity protocols?
- Are there other groups that use this same space?

Evaluating Natureness: Measuring the Quality of Nature-Based Classrooms in Pre-K through 3rd Grade

Pre-K Category B: Program Practices

About This Category

The items in this category evaluate to what extent a class demonstrates a value for ongoing experiences in nature through the daily class structure. A class demonstrates this by prioritizing children's outdoor time during the day, having children spend extensive time outdoors, and ensuring unstructured nature play is a large part of that outdoor time. Teachers facilitate children's ongoing reflection on their outdoor experiences and plan activities that build on children's knowledge of and experiences with nature. In doing so, teachers take advantage of outdoor experiences as teaching and learning opportunities rather than seeing them as a "break" from the indoor classroom. Teachers implement all of these experiences while following safety-related policy and procedures that are written to ensure children's positive experiences outdoors.

A pre-K program scoring in the upper range of this category starts class outside and spends at least half of the day outside, including time to explore beyond the outdoor play area. A program scoring in the mid-range might not start the day outside but still spends about a third of the class time outdoors, including occasionally visiting natural ecosystems beyond the fence. A mid-range program might not have daily opportunities for children to reflect on those experiences outdoors; however, the teachers regularly plan teacher-led activities that draw on children's outdoor experiences. A low-scoring program, on the other hand, will spend little time outdoors and will not incorporate those experiences into children's learning through reflection and teacher-led activities. For example, a low-scoring program might go outside for 20 minutes at the end of every class day and not reflect on or connect the outdoor activities to other learning in which the children are engaged. Thus, the outdoors serves more as a recess space than as a learning environment.

We recognize that pre-K and K–3 settings have different daily structures, particularly because K–3 settings have a greater emphasis on academic skills. Thus, the measures of quality are slightly different between the two settings and are listed separately. Although we recognize the systemic pressures of K–3 to focus on academic skills, we do not believe academic skills and outdoor learning are mutually exclusive. In fact, there are many ways the natural world can serve as another teacher at all grade levels.

Item 1: The class day starts outdoors.

Starting the class day outdoors conveys a message about the value of outdoor experiences in children's learning and the many social-emotional benefits of being outdoors. Outdoor experiences may provide a more successful class day when children are back indoors through their increased ability to attend to more sedentary, focused tasks. With this in mind, this item examines the frequency with which classes start their day outdoors.

Level 7: The class *almost always** starts the day outdoors.

To score the highest level on this item, a program must always start the class day outdoors. This could mean beginning the day either in the natural play area or in areas beyond. By starting outdoors, teachers prioritize outdoor learning and ensure there is enough time for children to become immersed in their play. Further, when children start the day outdoors, they will arrive dressed appropriately for outdoor play, thus reducing the time spent on transitions throughout the day.

Level 5: The class *often* starts the day outdoors.

Level 5 pre-K programs often start their day outside. A program might, for example, start outdoors every Monday, Wednesday, and Friday but not on Tuesday and Thursday. At this level, teachers and children will talk about starting the day outdoors as more of the norm, but with regular exceptions.

Level 3: The class *sometimes* starts the day outdoors.

Pre-K programs that rarely start their day outdoors, for example, once a week, are rated a Level 3. In conversation with teachers and children, they should be able to recall several times they've started outdoors, but this will likely not be described as the norm.

Level 1: The class *does not* start the day outdoors.

Level 1 pre-K programs do not typically start their day outdoors. It will likely be hard for teachers and children to name a time they started outdoors.

---

* Note: A rare exception would be days when the weather is dangerous and, as a result, the program adjusts the schedule for that day. For example, on an extremely cold morning, teachers might shift the schedule so outdoor time occurs an hour later than normal to allow the sun and temperatures to rise. It will be evident that this is an unusual event when children and families comment or appear visibly surprised that the class is not starting outdoors.

Tips for the Observer: The Class Day Starts Outdoors

Although it will be clear on the day of observation whether the class begins the day outdoors, it's hard to know about days when you are not observing. Look at the following items to help find evidence.

Examples of evidence:

- Daily schedule board: Where in the schedule does outdoor time appear?
- Comments and behaviors by adults and children in the program, such as the following:
  - "Oh, we're not starting outside today?" suggests being indoors is out of the ordinary. A score of Level 7 or 5 is appropriate in this case.
  - A parent says, "Look, you're starting the day outside again!" suggests starting outdoors is not every day but has been done before. Thus, a score of Level 5 or 3 would be logical. Clarify with a follow-up question to the parent or with another adult in the program such as, "How often does the class start the day outside?"
  - "Why are we going outside now? We usually do that later," suggests starting outdoors is a novel or unusual event. This might suggest a Level 3 or 1 and would need more evidence to make a final determination.

Questions to ask if evidence isn't apparent:

- If the class starts outdoors during the observation, clarify the frequency by asking, "Are there times you start the day indoors?"
- If the class starts the day indoors during the observation, consider questions such as, "When in the day do you usually go outdoors?"
- In either case, ask questions such as, "Are there times in the year when you shift the schedule? If so, when? Why?"

Item 2: A majority of the class time is spent outdoors.

In addition to starting the day outdoors, high-quality nature-based programs spend a large portion of their day outdoors either in the natural play area or in natural ecosystems beyond. Ideally, the class will spend at least 50 percent of its time outdoors. Generally, this section is scored based entirely on what is observed on a given day. If there is reason to believe the observed length of time is out of the ordinary, for example, on an extremely cold day*, then the observer might want to ask about this during the post-observation interview.

---

* Note: A rare exception to this would be days when the weather is dangerous and, as a result, the class adjust their schedule for that day. As a reminder, observations ideally would be scheduled on typical days and not on extreme weather days.

Level 7: At least 50 percent of total daily class time is spent outdoors (in a natural play area and/or beyond).

To score at this highest level, a pre-K program must spend at least half of their classroom time outdoors. If the class day is 3 hours long, the children must spend 1.5 hours or more outdoors to score a Level 7. Similarly, if the class is 6 hours long, the children must spend at least 3 hours outdoors. This outdoor time can be any combination of time in the natural play area or beyond. For example, a program might spend 25 percent of their time outside in the natural play area and 25 percent in the beyond. Or a program might spend all of their outdoor time in the beyond. Either scenario would score a Level 7 so long as the total time outdoors was at least 50 percent of the class day.

Level 5: Thirty to fifty percent (30-50 percent) of total daily class time is spent outdoors in the natural play area and/or beyond.

Children in a pre-K program at this level will spend more than 30 percent but less than half of the day outdoors. If the class day is 3 hours long, they will score a Level 5 if they spend 1-1.5 hours outdoors. If the class is 6 hours long, they must spend 2-3 hours outdoors to score at this level.

Level 3: Daily outdoor time in the natural play area and/or beyond of up to 30 percent of class time is equivalent to or greater than that required by regulations.

Level 3-rated programs spend up to 30 percent of the class time outdoors, and this amount is greater than or equal to the time required by regulations such as state licensing. For example, a state might stipulate children must be outside for 30 minutes if they are in care for 3 or more hours. If the program spends 30-60 minutes or more outside, the score would be a Level 3. (If the class spends more than an hour outdoors, they would move to a Level 5.) However, if the program only spends 25 minutes outside, that would be scored a Level 1.

Level 1: Daily outdoor time is less than that required by regulations.

Most regulatory agencies specify in their pre-K regulations or licensing requirements the amount of time children must spend outdoors each day. If a program does not meet this requirement, it should be rated a Level 1.

Example Time Scoring

Let's say there are three programs in a state that require children to be outside at least 45 minutes a day if they are in continuous care for 3 or more hours.

Program 1:

On the observation day, children in Program 1 spent 45 minutes in the outdoor play area and 20 minutes beyond during their 3-hour class. This totaled 65 minutes and is greater than the licensing requirements of 45 minutes, thus being equal to or higher than a Level 3. However, the time is also greater than 30 percent of the class day but not more than 50 percent, so this program scored a Level 5.

Program 2:

During the observation, children in Program 2 went outside in the outdoor play area for 30 minutes during their 3-hour class. Although this is approximately 17 percent of the class day spent outdoors, the percentage is irrelevant because the class did not meet the licensing requirements of 45 minutes. Thus, this program scored a Level 1.

Program 3:

Program 3 was a 6-hour class that spent 2 hours in the outdoor play area and 2 hours in the beyond. The children went inside only for lunch, rest time, and brief free-choice time. Thus, they were outdoors 4 out of the 6 hours. Because they spent more than half of their day (>3 hours) outdoors, this program is scored a Level 7.

Tips for the Observer: Time Outdoors

Observations will almost always include outdoor time. However, this may not always be possible. Consider different sources of evidence that may indicate the time a class spends outdoors.

Examples of evidence:

- If observing when a class is outdoors, record the time spent there.
- Review the daily schedule and calculate the total time, outside play area time, and time in the beyond.
- Listen for language by adults and children indicating frequency and length of outdoor time.

Question to ask if evidence isn't apparent:

On the rare occasion that severe weather limits a program's ability to go outdoors during the observation, ask the teacher to describe the daily schedule if a printed version is not available.

Item 3: The class regularly visits natural ecosystems.

Previous items in this section focus on the time and timing of outdoor time, whatever areas that outdoor space might include. This item focuses on the quality of the nature children experience when they are outdoors. Although being outdoors is important, a core component of nature-based education is connecting with the natural world in meaningful ways. The more natural the ecosystems, the more opportunities children will have to learn *with* nature.

Natural ecosystems are communities rich with living and nonliving components. Ponds, rivers, wetlands, marshes, meadows, fields, prairies, lakes/beaches, vernal pools, and woodlands are all examples of natural ecosystems. However, natural ecosystems can also include human-cultivated spaces such as arboretums, gardens, and ponds. Wherever the location, the more biodiversity in these spaces, the better for learning with nature.

These natural ecosystems do not have to be separate from the natural play area. However, given the frequency of permanent or semipermanent human-built features in natural play areas, visits to natural ecosystems will most often occur beyond. For a natural play area to meet the requirement of a natural ecosystem, it must be primarily dominated by natural living and nonliving organisms (not human built). Forest preschools, for example, often include a base camp within a natural space. The base camp typically includes a meeting space and other human-built features. In this case, the forest preschool would need to go beyond the boundaries of base camp into more natural spaces to score high on this item.

How much time the program spends in these natural ecosystems is captured in other items within the NABERS tool. For the current item, the level is based solely on whether children and staff went there.

Level 7: The class visits natural ecosystems daily.

Pre-K programs at Level 7 visit natural ecosystems every day they are in session. So, if a pre-K session operates five days per week, the children must visit the natural ecosystem each of the five days to achieve this highest score. Similarly, if the program operates two days per week, the children must visit the natural ecosystem both days to score a Level 7.

Level 5: The class visits natural ecosystems at least once a week.

Level 5 pre-K programs visit natural ecosystems at least once a week out of their normal class sessions. A five-day-per-week pre-K session that visits a natural ecosystem anywhere from one to four days per week would be rated a Level 5 for this item. A three-day-per-week session that visited a natural ecosystem one or two days would also score a Level 5. However, if this three-day-per-week program visited this natural ecosystem all three days, they would move up to a Level 7 rating.

Level 3: The class visits natural ecosystems at least once a month.

Pre-K programs that visit natural ecosystems at least once but fewer than four times a month (in other words, weekly) are rated a Level 3 on this item.

Level 1: The class visits natural ecosystems less than once a month.

Level 1 pre-K programs visit natural ecosystems less than once a month.

> ### Tips for the Observer: Visiting Natural Ecosystems
>
> An observation will most likely include a visit to one natural ecosystem at most. Yet, Item 3 is examining how often the class visits different ecosystems. Following are some suggestions for determining where and how often a class visits natural ecosystems.
>
> **Examples of evidence:**
>
> - A teacher leads a vote on where to hike to today, saying something like, "So far this week you have chosen to go to the pond and the meadow. I wonder where you'll choose today."
>
> - While hiking to the forest, a child says something like, "Why aren't we going to the pond like we did yesterday?"
>
> **Questions to ask if evidence isn't apparent:**
>
> Today we went to the ____. Are there other places you sometimes visit during the class day? If so, how often do you visit those places?

Item 4: Extensive daily class time is unstructured nature play.

Play is an activity that is (1) self-chosen and self-directed; (2) intrinsically motivated; (3) guided by mental rules; (4) imaginative; and (5) conducted in an active, alert, but relatively nonstressed frame of mind (Gray, 2013). *Nature play* occurs outdoors while using nature as part of the play; nature becomes a prop or tool in the play and sometimes even the focus of the play.

We realize it is somewhat redundant to say *unstructured* nature play. We use that term to emphasize the importance of children's time in nature where they (rather than the teacher) determine the activity and rules. Unstructured nature play is time for children to determine who they will play with, the rules of the play, and how they will use the natural world in their play. For true unstructured nature play to occur, a class will be present in a natural space with no direction from the adults other than a timeframe and safety parameters. For example, a teacher might say, "We'll be in this space for 30 minutes. Please remember to stay within the marked boundaries and follow our rules for outdoor play." This is comparable to free choice, free play, or choice time in an indoor classroom.

When scoring this item, base the assessment on days the class is outdoors. Consider, when a class is outdoors, how much of their time is spent in unstructured nature play. We don't want to additionally penalize a program for this item simply because it wasn't outdoors in the first place. If, for example, the class has outdoor time three days per week, then the frequency of unstructured nature play should be based on those three days and not five.

Level 7: At least 50 percent of the outdoor class time is unstructured nature play.

To score at this highest level, children in the pre-K program must spend at least half of their outdoor classroom time in unstructured nature play. If the class day is outdoors for 3 hours, they must spend 1.5 hours or more in unstructured nature play to score a Level 7. Similarly, if the class is outdoors for 2 hours, they must spend at least 1 hour engaged in unstructured nature play. This nature play time can be any combination of time in the outside play area or in natural areas beyond.

Level 5: Thirty to fifty (30-50) percent of the outdoor class time is unstructured nature play.

A pre-K program at this level will spend more than 30 percent but less than half of their outdoor class time in unstructured nature play. For example, if the time outdoors is 3 hours, the program will score a Level 5 if the children spend 1-1.5 hours of that time in unstructured nature play. If the class spends 6 hours outside, the children must spend 2-3 hours in unstructured nature play to score at this level.

Level 3: Up to 30 percent of the outdoor class time is spent in unstructured nature play.

Level 3-rated programs spend up to 30 percent of their outdoor class time in unstructured nature play.

Level 1: No outdoor class time is spent in unstructured nature play.

If a program does not spend any of the day in unstructured nature play, it should be rated a Level 1.

Sometimes evidence for items within NABERS may come from unusual places. A row of well-used boot scrapers indicates a need for this equipment.

> ### Tips for the Observer: Unstructured Nature Play
>
> Item 4 examines how much time classes spend in unstructured nature play when outdoors. The following are suggestions for evidence to look for when scoring this item.
>
> **Examples of evidence:**
>
> ❋ Observe and record the time spent in unstructured nature play.
>
> ❋ Review the posted daily schedule, and calculate the total time in the class day and the portion in unstructured nature play.
>
> ❋ Notice the language children use in expecting unstructured nature play or reacting to the absence for the day. For example, "Can we have a longer play time today?" or, "Why aren't we getting play time today?"

Item 5: Safety-related policies and procedures based on ongoing site and benefit-risk assessments are in place.

Nature-based programs should have policies and procedures in place to ensure the ongoing safety of children and adults in the program. These policies and procedures should be based on the program's context, which is determined through ongoing site and benefit-risk assessments.

A *site assessment* is an evaluation of the physical environment for hazards in both nonliving and living forms. Nonliving hazards include landscape, weather, and other natural events such as earthquakes or wildfires. Living forms include plants and animals—including humans. The site assessment should be revisited regularly, particularly as seasons change or after major weather events.

A site assessment is about the physical environment, but *benefit-risk assessments* identify how adults and children are to behave in that space to stay safe. The benefit-risk assessment was originally developed by David Ball and colleagues (Ball, Gill, and Spiegal, 2013). Although it has been modified through the years for different contexts, the assessment comes down to three questions:

1. What are the benefits of doing this activity?

2. How might we (or nature) get hurt doing this activity?

3. How can we keep ourselves, each other, and nature safe doing this activity?

The answers to these questions become the foundation for written policies and procedures and also for ongoing conversations between adults and children.

This item is intended to capture whether a program has safety-related policies and procedures in place and to what extent those policies and procedures are based on ongoing site and benefit-risk assessments. (See Common Risk-Related Terms Defined on page 46.)

Level 7: Safety-related policies and procedures based on ongoing site and benefit-risk assessments are written for *almost all* activities.

Pre-K programs at Level 7 have extensive policies and procedures related to safety. These policies account for the hazards, risks, and appropriate behaviors for all activities within the program.

Level 5: Safety-related policies and procedures based on ongoing site and benefit-risk assessments are written for *most* activities.

Level 5 pre-K programs have clear policies and procedures related to safety for most activities in which the class engages. If, for example, a program has policies related to excursions to the beyond, fire making, tool use, and tree climbing but does not have a policy for stick play, then the program would be scored at Level 5.

Level 3: Safety-related policies and procedures based on ongoing site and benefit-risk assessments are in place for *some* activities.

Pre-K programs that have benefit-risk assessments, policies, and procedures in place for some, but not all, activities, are rated a Level 3 on this item.

Level 1: *No* safety-related policies and procedures based on ongoing site and benefit-risk assessments are in place for activities.

A Level 1 pre-K program does not have safety-related policies and procedures in place.

Policies and procedures should be based on the living and nonliving hazards identified during a site assessment and benefit-risk assessment related to the activities that will occur on the site.

Common Risk-Related Terms Defined

Beneficial risk is a situation in which hazards are easy to identify and children have some element of control and engagement with the activity that will lead to growth not harm.

Benefit-risk assessment means identifying potential risks of an activity and ways to mitigate that risk.

Fear is an unpleasant emotion caused by the belief that someone or something is dangerous.

Hazard is a source of potential damage, harm, or adverse health effects. (Note: These are things children can't see or control.)

Policy is a rule designed to reach certain objectives of the organization.

Procedure defines a set of steps to be followed during a given task; it is often used interchangeably with *protocol*.

Protocol defines a set of steps to be followed during a given task; it is often used interchangeably with *procedure*.

Risk is the probability that someone will be hurt if exposed to a hazard. (Note: These are things children can decide whether or not to engage in or with.)

Site assessment means identifying potential nonhuman and human hazards in a particular place.

Item 6: Safety-related policies and procedures are followed.

Although written policies and procedures are important, they are of little value if they are not followed in practice. This item addresses the extent to which a program follows the written guidelines they have established, which can include everything from appropriate clothing for the weather conditions to implementing protocols for higher-risk activities such as the use of fire. Programs can score high on this section by following clear safety-related procedures even if they do not have these procedures written down as reviewed in Item 5.

Level 7: Safety-related policies and procedures are *almost always* followed.

To score at this highest level, children in the pre-K program must almost always follow in practice the written policies and procedures related to safety.

Level 5: Safety-related policies and procedures are *often* followed.

A pre-K program at this level will follow the written safety policies and procedures most of the time. There may be minor exceptions during which adults and children veer from the written guidelines; for example, the written procedures indicate teachers should carry two-way radios and first-aid kits, but the teachers have cell phones with them and no first-aid kit.

Level 3: Safety-related policies and procedures are *sometimes* followed.

Level 3-rated programs occasionally adhere to the written policies and procedures, but the majority of time the lived behavior does not align with the written guidelines.

Level 1: Safety-related policies and procedures are *not* followed.

If a program is unsafe and/or not following their own safety-related policies and procedures, it should be rated a Level 1.

Programs may have protocols describing the way to set up a tool station. Item 6 asks the observer to identify whether those protocols are being implemented.

Tips for the Observer: Safety-Related Policies and Procedures

Safety-related policies and procedures are critical for providing children with positive outdoor experiences. The NABERS tool includes two different items related to these policies and procedures: the presence of written guidelines and the extent to which a program adheres to those guidelines. Following are examples of potential evidence and questions to ask if there is no apparent evidence.

Examples of evidence:

- Policies and procedures manual
- Printed procedures by an activity site, such as a campfire; by activity equipment, such as with a box of hammers and nails in a shed; or elsewhere
- Language adults and children use that refers to the policies and procedures. For example, "Remember, the rule is you can only climb the tree if you can get up there yourself."

Questions to ask if evidence isn't apparent:

- "Tell me about your policies and procedures. How are these developed? How often do you review them?"
- "Do you have written procedures/protocols for any of the activities you do with children? If so, which activities? How were those procedures developed?"

K-3 Category B: Program Practices

About This Category

The items in this category evaluate to what extent a class demonstrates a value for ongoing experiences in nature through the daily class structure. Value is demonstrated by prioritizing outdoor time in the day and spending extensive time outdoors. In doing so, teachers take advantage of outdoor experiences as teaching and learning opportunities rather than as a break from the indoor classroom. All of these experiences are implemented with an eye to safety-related policy and procedures that are written and followed to ensure children's positive experiences outdoors.

A K-3 program scoring in the upper range of this category starts class outside and spends at least half of the class time outside, including time to explore natural ecosystems beyond the outside play area. An upper-range program will also be intentional about providing children opportunities for reflection about those outdoor experiences. Further, teacher-led activities will connect to and build on the children's outdoor experiences.

A program scoring in the mid-range might not start the day outside but still spends about half of the class time outdoors, including occasionally visiting natural ecosystems. A mid-range program might not have daily opportunities for children to reflect on those experiences outdoors, but teachers regularly plan and lead activities that draw on children's outdoor experiences.

A low-scoring program, on the other hand, will spend little time outdoors and will not incorporate those experiences into children's learning through reflection and teacher-led activities. For example, a low-scoring program might go outside for 20 minutes at the end of every class day and not reflect on or connect the outdoor activities to other learning in which the children are engaged. Thus, the outdoors serves as more recess space than learning environment.

Item 1: The class day starts outdoors.

Starting the class day outdoors conveys a message of the value of outdoor experiences in children's learning and the many social-emotional benefits to being outdoors. Time spent outdoors may provide a more successful class day when the children are back indoors, for example, by increasing their ability to attend to more sedentary, focused tasks. With this in mind, this item examines the frequency with which classes start their day outdoors.

Level 7: The class *almost always** starts the day outdoors.

To score at the highest level on this item, a program must almost always start the class day outdoors. This could mean beginning the day either in the natural play area or in areas beyond. By starting outdoors, teachers are prioritizing outdoor learning and ensuring there is enough time for children to become immersed in their play. Also, when they start the day outdoors, children arrive dressed appropriately for outdoor play, reducing the time spent on transitions throughout the day.

Level 5: The class *often* starts the day outdoors.

Level 5 K-3 programs often start their day outside. For example, a program might start outdoors every Monday, Wednesday, and Friday but not on Tuesday and Thursday. At this level, teachers and children will talk about starting the day outdoors as more of the norm but with regular exceptions.

---

* Note: A rare exception to this would be days when the weather is dangerous, and as a result, programs must adjust their schedules for that day. For example, on an extremely cold morning, teachers might shift the schedule so outdoor time occurs an hour later than usual to allow the sun and temperatures to rise. It will be evident that this is an unusual event when children and families comment or appear visibly surprised that the class is not starting outdoors.

Section I: Program Goals and Curriculum Practices

Level 3: The class *sometimes* starts the day outdoors.

K-3 programs that rarely start their day outdoors (for example, once a week) are rated a Level 3. In your conversation with teachers and children, they should be able to recall several times they've started outdoors, but this will likely not be discussed as the norm.

Level 1: The class *does not* start the day outdoors.

Level 1 K-3 programs rarely start their day outdoors. It will likely be hard for teachers and children to name a time they started outdoors.

Extra clothing that is easily accessible shows the program's emphasis on ensuring positive outdoor experiences in all weather.

Evaluating Natureness: Measuring the Quality of Nature-Based Classrooms in Pre-K through 3rd Grade

Tips for the Observer: The Class Day Starts Outdoors

Although it will be clear on the day of observation whether the class begins the day outdoors, it's hard to know about days when you are not observing. Look at the following items to help find evidence.

Examples of evidence:

- Daily schedule board: Where in the schedule does outdoor time appear?
- Comments and behaviors by adults and children in the program, such as the following:
    - "Oh, we're not starting outside today?" suggests being indoors is out of the ordinary. A score of Level 7 or 5 is appropriate in this case.
    - A parent says, "Look, you're starting the day outside again!" suggests starting outdoors is not every day but has been done before. Thus, a score of Level 5 or 3 would be logical. Clarify with a follow-up question to the parent or with another adult in the program such as, "How often does the class start the day outside?"
    - "Why are we going outside now? We usually do that later," suggests starting outdoors is a novel or unusual event. This might suggest a Level 3 or 1 and would need more evidence to make a final determination.

Questions to ask if evidence isn't apparent:

- If the class starts outdoors during the observation, clarify the frequency by asking, "Are there times you start the day indoors?"
- If the class starts the day indoors during the observation, consider questions such as, "When in the day do you usually go outdoors?"
- In either case, ask questions such as, "Are there times in the year you shift the schedule? If so, when? Why?"

Section I: Program Goals and Curriculum Practices

Item 2: The class spends extensive time outdoors.

There are many demands for time in the K-3 classroom, and daily time outdoors may not be possible. There is also value in longer, more immersive chunks of outdoor time. Thus, for K-3, time outdoors is calculated weekly rather than daily. (Note: We recognize, based on the current culture of elementary schools, that a Level 3 will likely be the most common score. Our goal with this portion of the tool is not to be punitive but to push thinking about what is possible.)

Level 7: At least 50 percent of total weekly class time is spent outdoors in a natural play area and/or beyond.

To score at this highest level, a K-3 program must spend at least half of their weekly classroom time outdoors. *Classroom time* means outdoor time that is part of the formal learning time above and beyond recess times–outdoor time in addition to recess or physical education times. For example, to score a Level 7, if the class day is 7 hours long, 5 days per week, children must spend 17.5 hours or more outdoors. Similarly, if the class is 6 hours long, they must spend at least 15 hours outdoors throughout the week. This outdoor time can be any combination of time in the outside play area or beyond the fence. For example, a program might spend 25 percent of their time outside and 25 percent in the beyond. Or a program might spend all of their outdoor time in the beyond. Either scenario would score a Level 7, so long as the total time outdoors was at least 50 percent of the class week.

Level 5: Thirty to fifty (30-50) percent of total weekly class time is spent outdoors in an outside play area and/or beyond.

A K-3 program at this level spends more than 30 percent but less than half of the week outdoors. If the class is in session 30 hours each week and children spend 10 hours outdoors each week, the program would score a Level 5. These 10 hours might be divided so they spend 2 hours each day outdoors on each of the five days in the week. Or the class might spend 5 hours outdoors on both Tuesdays and Thursdays.

Level 3: Less than 30 percent of total weekly class time is spent outdoors in a natural play area and/or beyond.

Level 3-rated programs spend less than 30 percent of class time outdoors throughout the week. For example, if the class day is 7 hours long, five days per week, and children spend less than 10.5 hours per week outdoors, the program would be a Level 3. A program that spends 1.5 hours each day outdoors would score a Level 3 because that adds up to 7.5 hours per week, which is less than 30 percent of the weekly total.

Level 1: The program has no outdoor learning time (i.e., no time separate from recess).

If the only outdoor time children have during the week is recess, a program is scored Level 1.

> ### Tips for the Observer: Time Outdoors
>
> Observations will almost always include outdoor time. However, this may not always be possible. Consider different sources of evidence that may indicate the time a class spends outdoors.
>
> **Examples of evidence:**
>
> - If observing when a class is outdoors, record the time spent there.
> - Review the daily schedule and calculate the total time, outside play area time, and time in the beyond.
> - Listen for language by adults and children indicating frequency and length of outdoor time.
>
> **Question to ask if evidence isn't apparent:**
>
> On the rare occasion that severe weather limits a program's ability to go outdoors during the observation, ask the teacher to describe the daily schedule if a printed version is not available.

Item 3: The class spends outdoor time in natural ecosystems.

Previous items in this category focus on the time and timing of outdoor time, whatever areas that outdoor space might include. This item focuses on the quality of the nature children experience outdoors. Although being outdoors is important, a core component of nature-based education is connecting with the natural world in meaningful ways. The more natural the ecosystems children are visiting, the more opportunities they will have to learn *with* nature. Given that K-3 schools may divide their outdoor time across the week, this item looks at what percentage of that time is spent in natural ecosystems.

Natural ecosystems are communities rich with living and nonliving components that may or may not be naturally occurring. Ponds, rivers, wetlands, marshes, meadows, fields, prairies, lakes/beaches, vernal pools, and woodlands are all examples of natural ecosystems. However, natural ecosystems can also include human-cultivated spaces such as arboretums, gardens, and ponds. Wherever the location, the more biodiversity in these spaces, the better for learning with nature.

These natural ecosystems do not have to be separate from the natural play area. However, given the frequency of permanent or semipermanent human-built features in natural play areas, visits to natural ecosystems will most often occur in the beyond. For a natural play area to meet the requirements of a natural ecosystem, it must be primarily dominated by living and nonliving organisms that are natural (not human-built).

How much time the program spends in these natural ecosystems is captured in other items within the NABERS tool. For the current item, the level is based solely on whether children went there.

Level 7: At least 50 percent of outdoor class time is spent in natural ecosystems.

The highest scoring K-3 programs for this item will spend at least half of outdoor class time (no matter the length of time outdoors) in natural ecosystems. For example, if children spend 3 hours outdoors each week, at least 1.5 hours must be spent in natural ecosystems to score a Level 7.

Level 5: Thirty to fifty (30-50) percent of outdoor class time is spent in natural ecosystems.

To score a Level 5, K-3 programs must spend 30-50 percent of their time in natural ecosystems. If, for example, a program spends 4 hours per week outdoors for class time, children must spend 72-120 minutes in natural ecosystems. If they spend more, they would score a Level 7; if they spend less, a Level 3.

Level 3: Less than 30 percent of outdoor class time is spent in natural ecosystems.

If a K-3 program spends less than 30 percent of outdoor class time in natural ecosystems, it would score a Level 3.

Level 1: The program spends no time in natural ecosystems.

Level 1 K-3 programs do not spend time in natural ecosystems at any point in their outdoor class time.

Tips for the Observer: Visiting Natural Ecosystems

An observation will most likely include a visit to one natural ecosystem at most. Yet, Item 3 is examining how often the class visits different ecosystems. Following are some suggestions for determining where and how often a class visits natural ecosystems.

Examples of evidence:

- A teacher leads a vote on where to hike to today, saying something like, "So far this week you have chosen to go to the pond and the meadow. I wonder where you'll choose today."

- While hiking to the forest, a child says something like, "Why aren't we going to the pond like we did yesterday?"

Questions to ask if evidence isn't apparent:

Today we went to the _____. Are there other places you sometimes visit during the class day? If so, how often do you visit those places?

Item 4: The class has unstructured nature play as part of daily outdoor time.

Unstructured nature play is play that occurs outdoors while using nature as part of the play. That is, nature becomes a prop or tool in the play. *Play*, by definition, is an activity that is (1) self-chosen and self-directed; (2) intrinsically motivated; (3) guided by mental rules; (4) imaginative; and (5) conducted in an active, alert, but relatively nonstressed, frame of mind (Gray, 2013).

We realize that it is somewhat redundant to say *unstructured* nature play. We use that term to emphasize the importance of children's time in nature where they (rather than the teacher) determine the activity and rules. In other words, unstructured nature play is time for children to determine who they will play with, the rules of the play, and how they will use the natural world in their play. For true unstructured nature play to occur, a class will be present in a natural space with no direction from the adults beyond a timeframe and safety parameters.

For this item, we are examining the presence of unstructured nature play as part of the outdoor class time separate from daily recess time. We realize time is a precious resource in any classroom, and particularly in K-3 settings. Sometimes this results in little time for children to experience free play during their outdoor class time. Thus, there is no timeframe for this item but, rather, a measure of the consistency of unstructured nature play in the outdoor routine. This means that even if a class only spends 5 minutes each day in unstructured nature play, it would still score a Level 7 if that 5 minutes occurred during *every* outdoor time period.

When scoring this item, base the assessment on days the class is outdoors. We don't want to additionally penalize a program for this item simply because they weren't outdoors in the first place. If the class has outdoor time three days per week, then the frequency of unstructured nature play should be based on those three days, not five.

Level 7: The class *almost always* provides unstructured nature play as part of daily outdoor time.

To score at this highest level, children in the K-3 program must have some portion of their outdoor classroom time in unstructured nature play. Every time the class is outdoors, separate from recess, the children must have opportunities for unstructured nature play.

Level 5: The class *often* provides unstructured nature play as part of daily outdoor time.

A K-3 program at this level often provides unstructured nature play but may have an occasional day during which free play is not included in the schedule. Generally, *often* is measured as more than 60 percent of days outdoors including unstructured free play. For example, a class that has outdoor time 5 days per week and provides free play 3-4 days each week would score a Level 5.

Level 3: The class *sometimes* has unstructured nature play as part of daily outdoor time.

Level 3-rated programs sometimes provide unstructured nature play as part of the outdoor time, but it's not a highly predictable experience. For example, at this level the class may have unstructured nature play less than 30 percent of the days they have outdoor time.

Level 1: The class *does not* have unstructured nature play as part of daily outdoor time.

Unstructured nature play is not an activity that is part of the daily outdoor time.

Tips for the Observer: Unstructured Nature Play

Item 4 examines how much time classes spend in unstructured nature play when outdoors. The following are suggestions for evidence to look for when scoring this item.

Examples of evidence:

- Observe and record the time spent in unstructured nature play.
- Review the posted daily schedule, and calculate the total time in the class day and the portion in unstructured nature play.
- Notice the language children use in expecting unstructured nature play or reacting to the absence for the day. For example, "Can we have a longer play time today?" or, "Why aren't we getting play time today?"

Item 5: Safety-related policies and procedures based on ongoing site and benefit-risk assessments are in place.

Nature-based programs should have policies and procedures in place to ensure the ongoing safety of children and adults in the program. These policies and procedures should be based on the program's context, which is determined through ongoing site and benefit-risk assessments.

A *site assessment* is an evaluation of the physical environment for hazards in both nonliving and living forms. Nonliving hazards include landscape, weather, and other natural events such as earthquakes or wildfires. Living forms include plants and animals–including humans. The site assessment should be revisited regularly, particularly as seasons change or after major weather events.

Whereas a site assessment is about the physical environment, *benefit-risk assessments* identify how adults and children are to behave in that space to stay safe. The benefit-risk assessment was originally developed by David Ball and colleagues (Ball, Gill, and Spiegal, 2013). Although the assessment has since been modified for different contexts, it comes down to these three questions:

1. What are the benefits of doing this activity?

2. How might we (or nature) get hurt doing this activity?

3. How can we keep ourselves, each other, and nature safe doing this activity?

The answers to these questions become the foundation for written policies and protocols and also for ongoing conversations between adults and children.

This item is intended to capture whether a program has safety-related policies and procedures in place and to what extent those policies and procedures are based on ongoing site and benefit-risk assessments. (See Common Risk-Related Terms Defined on page 46.)

Level 7: Safety-related policies and procedures based on ongoing site and benefit-risk assessments are written for *almost all* activities.

K-3 programs at Level 7 have extensive policies and procedures related to safety. These policies account for the hazards, risks, and appropriate behaviors for all activities within the program.

Level 5: Safety-related policies and procedures based on ongoing site and benefit-risk assessments are written for *most* activities.

Level 5 K-3 programs have clear policies and procedures related to safety for most activities in which the class engages. For example, if a program has policies related to excursions to the beyond, fire making, tool use, and tree climbing but does not have a policy for stick play, then the program would be scored at Level 5.

Level 3: Safety-related policies and procedures based on ongoing site and benefit-risk assessments are written for *some* activities.

K-3 programs that have benefit-risk assessments, policies, and procedures in place for some but not all activities are rated a Level 3 on this item.

Level 1: *No* safety-related policies and procedures based on ongoing site and benefit-risk assessments are written for activities.

A Level 1 K-3 program does not have safety-related policies and procedures in place.

Item 6: Safety-related policies and procedures are followed.

Although written policies and procedures are important, they are of little value if they are not followed in practice. This item addresses the extent to which a program follows the written guidelines they have established, which can include everything from appropriate clothing for the weather conditions to implementing protocols for higher-risk activities such as the use of fire. Furthermore, programs can score high on this section by following clear safety-related procedures even if they do not have these procedures written down, as reviewed in Item 5.

Level 7: Safety-related policies and procedures are *almost always* followed.

To score at this highest level, children in the K-3 program must always follow the written policies and procedures related to safety.

Level 5: Safety-related policies and procedures are *often* followed.

A K-3 program at this level follows the written safety policies and procedures most of the time. There may also be minor exceptions in which adults and children veer from the written guidelines. For example, the written guidelines might say teachers should put a sign up when tools are being used, and they haven't done that during the observation but followed the other guidelines in the tool-use procedures.

Level 3: Safety-related policies and procedures are *sometimes* followed.

Level 3-rated programs occasionally adhere to the written policies and procedures, but the majority of time the way teachers and children behave does not align with the written safety guidelines.

Level 1: Safety-related policies and procedures are *not* followed.

If a program is unsafe or not following their own safety-related policies and procedures, it should be rated a Level 1.

Tips for the Observer: Safety-Related Policies and Procedures

Safety-related policies and procedures are critical for providing children with positive outdoor experiences. The NABERS tool includes two different items related to these policies and procedures: the presence of written guidelines and the extent to which a program adheres to those guidelines. Following are examples of potential evidence and questions to ask if there is no apparent evidence.

Examples of evidence:

- Policies and procedures manual
- Printed procedures by an activity site, such as a campfire; by activity equipment, such as with a box of hammers and nails in a shed; or elsewhere
- Language adults and children use that refers to the policies and procedures. For example, "Remember, the rule is you can only climb the tree if you can get up there yourself."

Questions to ask if evidence isn't apparent:

- "Tell me about your policies and procedures. How are these developed? How often do you review them?"
- "Do you have written procedures/protocols for any of the activities you do with children? If so, which activities? How were those procedures developed?"

Pre-K Category C: Curriculum

About This Category

The items in this category evaluate the extent to which the central organizing concept of the curriculum is nature. This category also evaluates to what extent the experiences supporting these concepts are based on children's interests that emerge from local, seasonal, and authentic experiences in nature.

Local nature refers to the climate, plants, and animals found geographically close to the classroom—nature found right outside the classroom door or within the geographic region. *Seasonal experiences* are rooted in what is occurring outdoors at the given time. Conversation about these experiences might compare the present moment with other times of the year, but the experience is primarily rooted in what is currently happening outdoors. *Authentic nature* means the images, objects, and other materials in the classroom accurately represent what is found in the natural world, rather than anthropomorphized or caricature versions of nature, and do not perpetuate stereotypes of nature such as, "Wolves have red eyes," and, "All pigs are pink." For example, a game might ask children to match a picture of a beaver with a number and picture of that

Providing authentic nature means providing objects that highlight the diversity of the natural world and do not reinforce stereotypes of nature.

number of logs. This relates to an authentic event in nature. However, if the beavers are wearing overalls and hats, the game perpetuates an unnecessary and inauthentic representation of the beavers.

The curriculum category also measures to what extent teachers support and extend children's interests by facilitating play-based learning rooted in authentic experiences and the reality of their place in the world, by using natural materials for teaching, and by integrating activities with all developmental domains. An underlying assumption in this section is that nature-based programs emphasize play-based learning; didactic, direct instruction will be minimal in a quality nature-based program. Another assumption is that play inherently supports all developmental domains. Similarly, when teacher-led activities do occur, those nature-based activities should also address all developmental domains. In other words, nature should be used not just to support science development but to support all domains, including literacy and social-emotional development.

Although the majority of class time in a pre-K classroom is spent in free play, teachers sometimes lead activities. Teacher-led activities are organized and directed by the teacher and involve the whole class or a subset of children (referred to as *small group*, *large group*, *whole group*, or similar terms). When teacher-led activities occur, they should emerge from children's interests. Materials in the physical learning environment should also reflect children's interests. This emergent approach requires intentionally planning activities and materials based on children's interests. With extensive time outdoors, these interests will almost always be connected to seasonal events. These connections will, of course, be through the unique lens of each child, their prior experiences, observations, and curiosity.

Item 1: Teachers intentionally develop children's outdoor skills.*

Outdoor skills are those that allow children to have safe, positive outdoor experiences, including a range of self-care, from dressing appropriately for the weather to building a fire to whittling. The types of skills taught will vary depending on the age of the children, the amount of time spent outside, the climate, and the types of activities allowed in the class. At the very least, high-quality nature-based programs will make explicit connections between the weather and self-care, such as clothing to wear, such as rain boots for puddle jumping; places to play, such as shaded areas in extreme midday heat; and other techniques, such as sitting on a fabric cushion instead of a cold rock in cooler times.

Other skills might include children picking up their feet when walking through dewy grass, walking quietly through leaves, and identifying hazardous elements such as poison ivy and venomous snakes. The skills taught should be appropriate for children's development and the local place and should minimize impact on the environment. (See other portions of NABERS, such as Section I, Category A, Items 4-6, for these caveats.)

Teachers can explicitly teach outdoor skills, such as having a whole-class discussion before visiting a pond to assess the benefits and the risks. Teachers can also support skill development by interacting with individual children throughout the day—for example, helping children in conducting benefit-risk assessments or discussing appropriate clothing during free play. Ultimately, whatever specific skills are taught and whether the skills are taught individually or as a whole group, they should allow children to be safe and comfortable while maximizing connections with nature.

Level 7: Teacher-led activities *almost always* develop children's outdoor skills.

Pre-K programs at Level 7 are intentional about developing children's outdoor skills, a practice seen in explicit discussion and connections to children's behavior and to their safety and comfort outdoors. For example, as a teacher helps a child find a dry pair of mittens, they might discuss why it's important to keep hands dry while playing outside in cold weather. Or, when gathering a group for an outdoor circle time, a teacher might say, "Put a cushion under your bottom before you sit down to provide insulation from the ground and help keep you warm."

---

* There are a variety of terms for outdoor skills, including *woodcraft*, *bushcraft*, and even *survival skills*. Whatever term is used, the activities themselves should align with the other quality measures in the NABERS tool, such as *developmentally appropriate* and *environmental impact*.

Level 5: Teacher-led activities *often* develop children's outdoor skills.

Teacher-led activities within Level 5 pre-K programs often develop children's outdoor skills. There may not be daily discussion with children connecting their behavior with their safety and comfort, but this practice is a regular part of the children's classroom experience. For example, teachers may connect the weather to how children are dressed, narrate the safety procedures before going on a hike, explain the importance of changing into dry clothes, and conduct a benefit-risk assessment aloud with children before starting a new activity.

Level 3: Teacher-led activities *sometimes* develop children's outdoor skills.

Pre-K programs that sometimes develop children's outdoor skills are rated a Level 3 on this item. For example, during an observation there might be a couple of moments during which teachers are developing children's outdoor skills but perhaps very few moments or moments that only occur with a handful of children. If there are several moments, the program would likely score a Level 5.

Level 1: Teacher-led activities *rarely* develop children's outdoor skills.

Level 1 pre-K programs rarely develop children's outdoor skills. For example, the activities at this level will not provide any language related to why something is being done in relation to outdoor skills.

Tips for the Observer: Outdoor Skills

Outdoor skills generally refer to any skills needed to have safe, positive experiences in the outdoors. This includes ways of behaving outdoors that support our basic human needs for food, water, and shelter but also that keep people safe from injury or illness. Among the many different outdoor skills are practices such as these:

- Dressing for the weather
- Staying warm and dry in cold temperatures
- Staying cool and out of the sun in hot temperatures
- Building a fire
- Navigation (with and without a map)
- Knots for different applications
- Pitching a tent or tarp for shelter
- Creating a shelter out of natural materials
- Using the restroom outdoors
- Basic first aid
- Leave No Trace skills (See Section I, Category A for more on this topic.)
- What to do when encountering wildlife
- Whittling

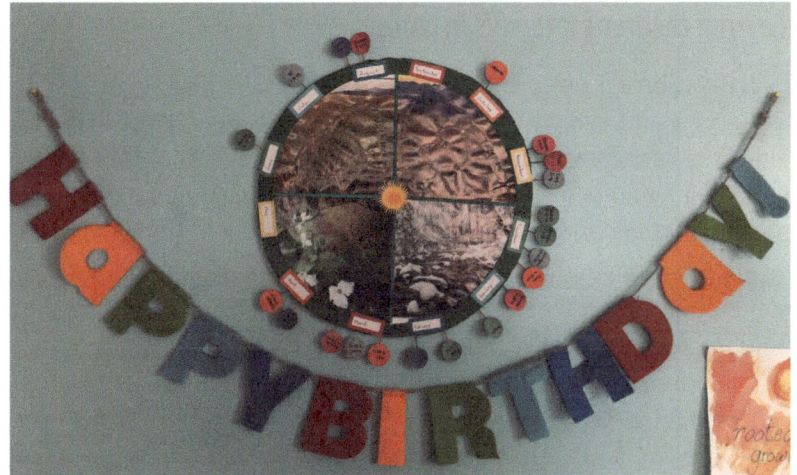

In this classroom, the teachers connected children's birthdays to the outdoors seasons, making connections between children's lives and the natural world.

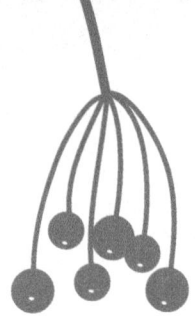

Item 2: Activities emerge from children's interests in nature.

Teachers in high-quality nature-based programs are intentional in leading activities that build on children's interests and avoid predetermined themes, topics, or activities. To be responsive to children's interests, teachers will generally plan no more than a week in advance. This does not mean teachers can't consider natural or social events that will occur in the future and think about activity ideas; rather, it means they will not set specifics of the day's plans beyond a week in advance. For example, a teacher might have a list of climate, plant, and animal events likely to occur in spring, such as wildflowers emerging and migrant songbirds returning. However, when spring arrives, the children discover salamanders under logs and are really curious to learn more about these creatures. The teacher then adjusts their plans to align with the children's interest in salamanders.

Level 7: Activities *almost always* emerge from children's interests in nature.

Pre-K programs at Level 7 are intentional about building on children's interests. The majority of activities in a Level 7 program connect to children's observations, questions, and play narratives.

Level 5: Activities are *often* connected to children's interests in nature.

Teacher-led activities in Level 5 pre-K programs often connect to children's interests in nature. There may not be connections to every child's interests each day, but this approach is a regular part of the children's classroom experience.

Level 3: Activities are *sometimes* connected to children's interests in nature.

Pre-K programs that sometimes connect to children's interests in nature are rated a Level 3 on this item. For example, a teacher might share an example of a time they adapted a lesson or study to build on children's interest, but they do not have extensive examples to provide.

Level 1: Activities are *rarely* connected to children's interests in nature.

Level 1 pre-K programs rarely connect to children's interests in nature. The activities focus only on predetermined topics or activities and do not account for children's interests in nature at all.

Item 3: Activities and experiences align with authentic, local, and current seasonal happenings.

Experiences in nature-based programs will primarily focus on authentic, local, and current seasonal events. When there is discussion of nature found elsewhere in the world or at different times of the year, it is usually as a means of comparison. Even if children don't spend time outdoors, activities and experiences indoors can relate to authentic nature that is found locally and is happening outside at the time. For example, in the spring a class might read a storybook about birds caring for their young, or a program located in a landlocked jack pine forest in mid-Michigan might focus on the Kirtland's warbler rather than on flamingos.

Level 7: Activities and experiences *almost always* align with authentic, local, and current seasonal happenings.

Pre-K programs at Level 7 work to ensure classroom activities and experiences always align with authentic, local, and current seasonal happenings.

Level 5: Activities and experiences *often* align with authentic, local, and current seasonal happenings.

Teacher-led activities within Level 5 pre-K programs often align with authentic, local, and current seasonal happenings. There may not be inclusion of authentic, local, or current seasonal events in every activity, but they are a regular part of the children's classroom experience.

Level 3: Activities and experiences *sometimes* align with authentic, local, and current seasonal happenings.

Pre-K programs that sometimes align with authentic, local, and current seasonal happenings are rated a Level 3 on this item. The activities primarily focus on nature found elsewhere in the world or from a season different from the current one.

Level 1: Activities and experiences *rarely* align with authentic, local, and current seasonal happenings.

Level 1 pre-K programs rarely align with authentic, local, and current seasonal happenings. At this level, if activities and experiences relate to nature at all, they will primarily be related to different locations and/or seasons.

Item 4: Children reflect on their nature experiences through conversation and documentation.

Ongoing experiences outdoors are vital to nature-based education. Although simply having outdoor experiences is valuable, even greater value for children's learning lies in reflecting on those experiences. This item of the NABERS tool is intended to measure teachers' intentionality in reflecting on and connecting nature-based experiences to children's prior experiences and learning while also setting the stage for future connections. This is done through oral, written, and pictorial documentation of children's experiences. Generally, these reflections relate to time spent in more natural ecosystems, particularly those beyond, but any outdoor experience is relevant to this item.

These reflections can happen in a variety of ways and at different times throughout the class day. For example, a teacher might ask children during mealtimes what their favorite part of the hike was that day. Or a teacher might say to a child, "Tell me what it was like when you caught that frog earlier today." Written documentation and reflection might involve recording children's observations from the day in a group journal, including photos of the experience if available. Teacher-led activities such as small or large groups might also encourage reflection on nature experiences. For example, a small-group activity might prompt children to draw the beach they visited the day before, opening the door for conversation around the experience as they draw. Children's reflections can happen individually, in a small group, with the entire class, with peers, or with the teacher. For scoring purposes, it's important to capture the extent to which *all* children in the classroom reflect: *rarely*, *sometimes*, *often*, or *almost always*. (Note: It is possible to reflect daily even if the class has not visited more natural ecosystems during the observation. For example, the class might discuss the time last week the children watched a butterfly emerge from its chrysalis.)

Level 7: Children *almost always* reflect on their nature experiences through conversation and documentation.

Level 7 pre-K programs provide opportunities every day for children to reflect on their experiences outdoors. These reflections may vary in format from day to day, but there are opportunities every day. For example, one day teachers might prompt children during snack with, "What was your favorite part of the hike today?" The next day a teacher might gather the children together around a large journal to document the "noticings" and wonderings they have about the forest they're playing in. The key for a Level 7 is that reflection about outdoor experiences happens every class day.

Level 5: Children *often* reflect on their nature experiences through conversation and documentation.

Pre-K programs at a Level 5 often provide children opportunities to reflect on their experiences outdoors. They don't reflect every day, but this approach is a regular part of the children's classroom experience. The days in which reflections occur outnumber the days they do not.

Level 3: Children *sometimes* reflect on their nature experiences through conversation and documentation.

A Level 3 pre-K program sometimes encourages children to reflect on their experiences with nature. The days they do not reflect on their experiences with nature are more frequent than the days they do reflect.

Level 1: Children *rarely* reflect on their nature experiences through conversation and documentation.

Pre-K programs at a Level 1 rarely provide opportunities for children to reflect on their experiences with nature.

Tips for the Observer: Reflecting on Nature Experiences

Reflecting on experiences with nature can come in many forms, such as in small or large groups, in discussions, or as written documentation. Consider the following examples of evidence to gather and questions to ask as you observe to determine how frequently reflections occur.

Examples of evidence:

- Teacher prompting reflection in conversation with statements such as, "Tell me what it was like seeing that hawk fly over."
- Group gathering around a journal
- Individual journaling prompts

How children react to reflection prompts can indicate consistency or the frequency with which the group reflects. For example, a child might say, "What do you mean we should journal?" or, "I want to write the question of the day at the top of the page!" The former suggests journaling is rare—a Level 1 or 3, depending on other evidence—whereas, the latter suggests the children are used to a journaling routine, which indicates a Level 5 or 7.

Question to ask if evidence isn't apparent:

How do you reflect on and document outdoor experiences with the children?

Item 5: Teacher-led activities build on nature knowledge and experiences.

Teachers in high-quality nature-based programs are intentional in leading activities that build on children's nature knowledge, outdoor experiences, and interests. Additionally, teachers are intentional about connecting ideas over time; the activities not only reflect the current week's experiences but also connect to previous weeks and months. For example, a teacher-led activity might involve reading a story about the pond in wintertime. During the read-aloud, the teacher stops and asks the children to recall what the pond looked like before there was snow on the ground. In another example, a teacher-led activity might involve taking daily photos of a tree in the outdoor play area over the course of two weeks to notice subtle changes as the leaves change from green to orange in autumn. The teacher is not only building this activity over time but also is connecting the conversations each day to previous experiences.

Level 7: Teacher-led activities *almost always* build on nature knowledge and experiences *over time*.

Pre-K programs at Level 7 are intentional about building on ideas over time. The majority of activities in a Level 7 program connect to children's previous knowledge of and experiences with nature.

Level 5: Teacher-led activities *often* build on nature knowledge and experiences *over time*.

Teacher-led activities in Level 5 pre-K programs often build on ideas over time. There may not be connections to experiences from previous days or weeks in every teacher-led activity, but this is a regular part of the children's classroom experience. For example, it is common to hear a teacher say something like, "How is this different from when we visited last week?" or, "Wow! The leaves weren't this colorful when we were here a few weeks ago."

Level 3: Teacher-led activities *sometimes* build on nature knowledge and experiences *over time*.

Pre-K classes that sometimes build on nature knowledge and experiences over time are rated a Level 3 on this item. These classes may occasionally relate the present learning to previous experiences or knowledge, but these connections are absent more than they are present. For example, a teacher might occasionally ask, "What else in nature does this remind you of?" but not frequently ask questions, make statements, or create activities to build on concepts or experiences over time.

Level 1: Teacher-led activities *rarely* build on nature knowledge and experiences *over time*.

Level 1 pre-K programs rarely build on nature knowledge and experiences over time. The activities focus only on that day's outdoor experiences or do not connect to outdoor experiences at all.

Item 6: Natural materials are used as tools for teaching curricular domains.

Natural materials are objects found in nature and not created by humans, such as leaves, rocks, sticks, pine cones, shells, and animal bones. Natural materials not only provide opportunities for connecting with the natural world but are also diverse—even when technically the same type of object. For example, a group of plastic objects made to appear like acorns will typically be uniform in shape, size, texture, and weight. Acorns collected from nature, even those from the same species of tree, will be diverse, with some being smaller or larger, some having insect holes, some being lighter or darker in color, some missing the cap, and so on.

These nuances in the materials provide opportunities for teacher-child and child-child conversations that would not be afforded by manufactured materials. The conversations, in turn, provide opportunities for learning that is connected across curricular domains throughout the class day. It should be noted that the presence of natural materials in this item does not have to be at the exclusion of manufactured materials. A program will score high on this item if they always use natural materials but never manufactured ones or if they always have a mix of natural and manufactured.

Teachers can use natural materials in teaching and for learning in a variety of ways. Natural materials could be objects for applying concepts or something children are making sense of. For example, children might use sticks and snow to practice writing. They might sort natural materials into groups of three or organize them into A-B-A patterns in math learning. Children might investigate sinking and floating with a variety of natural and manufactured materials. Natural materials can also be used to create a miniature replica of the school or perhaps to create art sculptures. The materials can also serve as an inspiration or model for activities. For example, a flower could be used as a model for drawing a still life image. The possibilities for using natural materials in different curricular domains are endless.

Level 7: Natural materials are *almost always* used as tools for teaching curricular domains (literacy, math, science, social studies, and art).

Level 7 pre-K programs always provide natural materials for children to use when learning in all curricular domains. For example, for painting (art domain), the teacher provides the students with paint, paintbrushes, and leaves to paint with. Related to literacy, children might create letters using sticks. In a small group, they might make patterns out of different leaves, which is an activity related to math and science.

Level 5: Natural materials are *often* used as tools for teaching curricular domains (literacy, math, science, social studies, and art).

Pre-K programs at a Level 5 often provide natural materials for children to use when learning in all curricular domains. There may be occasions on which an activity does not include natural materials, but those occasions are rare. Activities will likely include sticks, leaves, pine cones, soil, and other natural materials.

Level 3: Natural materials are *sometimes* used as tools for teaching curricular domains (literacy, math, science, social studies, and art).

A Level 3 pre-K program sometimes provides natural materials to support learning across curricular domains. For example, programs at this level might include natural materials in art activities but not in literacy activities. Or programs might include natural materials in a variety of learning domains, but natural materials are more likely to not be included at all.

Level 1: Natural materials are *rarely* used as tools for teaching curricular domains (literacy, math, science, social studies, and art).

Pre-K programs at Level 1 rarely provide natural materials for children to use in learning.

Section I: Program Goals and Curriculum Practices

Tips for the Observer: Use of Natural Materials

Not all classroom materials will be displayed in the classroom during an observation. Thus, it may be necessary to gather other evidence to score this item.

Examples of evidence:

- Children's language can be a clue to the regularity of natural materials in the classroom. For example:
    - "Why don't we have pine cones today?" suggests pine cones are typically present, suggesting Level 5 for this classroom.
    - "Oh, yay! We get to use the natural materials box today!" might imply a novel but not entirely new event and thus a Level 3.
    - A child holding a natural object and asking, "What are we supposed to do with this?" might indicate a Level 1.

Of course, children's language alone will not determine the score on this item. How objects are organized and stored, along with wear and tear, are all indications of which materials are being used most frequently in the classroom.

Tips for Growing:
Natural Materials to Add to the Classroom

Natural materials are powerful for learning in all domains, and there are many different options to include. Although any natural material is helpful, keep in mind the ideal materials will be local to your place. Children can help collect materials when outside or in the beyond.*

- Pine cones
- Seed pods, such as milkweed pods
- Acorns
- Dry corn kernels
- Rocks
- Seashells
- Tree "cookies" (a thin cross-section of a log)
- Stumps
- Leaves
- Logs
- Sticks
- Soil
- Sand
- Snow

*When collecting natural materials, be aware of other parts of the NABERS tool, such as Section I, Category A, Item 6, by selecting items that are "dead and down."

Natural materials can be used as teaching tools in all curricular domains, including art.

Item 7: Fictional texts represent authentic, local nature and align with seasonal happenings.

Fictional texts, such as picture books, are common in pre-K classrooms. This item focuses on the extent to which fictional texts represent authentic, local nature aligned with seasonal events. Many storybooks present anthropomorphized or caricature versions of nature. This item isn't suggesting eliminating those texts from the classroom but, rather, being intentional about the balance of messages within the library as a whole. This means emphasizing texts that provide accurate scientific facts about nature found in children's geographic place in the world. If a class is located in a desert, the storybooks should primarily emphasize desert ecosystems and species rather than stories about the ocean, for example. In regard to accuracy, a book might refer to a butterfly pupa as a *cocoon* rather than a *chrysalis*. Although teachers don't necessarily need to eliminate this book from the classroom, they should be aware of the error and, in most cases, use this as an opportunity to teach. A text with a factual error should also make a teacher question the accuracy of the rest of the book and analyze what percentage of errors like this occur in all texts in the library. At the very least, texts should not reinforce stereotypes of nature such as, "Wolves have red eyes," and, "All pigs are pink." Ideally, texts should disrupt these stereotypes.

Level 7: Fictional texts provided *almost always* represent authentic, local nature and align with current seasonal happenings.

Pre-K programs at Level 7 are intentional about providing fictional texts that accurately represent nature found locally and occurring at a given point in time. An observer looking at the bookshelf will see a collection of fictional texts that are almost entirely focused on natural topics. The nature represented is authentic and local to where the school is located, and aligns with the current season.

Level 5: Fictional texts provided *often* represent authentic, local nature and align with current seasonal happenings.

Fictional texts within Level 5 pre-K programs often connect to authentic, local, and seasonal nature. There may be inauthentic nature presented in some texts, but generally fictional texts represent authentic, local, and seasonal happenings.

Level 3: Fictional texts provided *sometimes* represent authentic, local nature and align with current seasonal happenings.

Pre-K programs that sometimes represent authentic, local, and seasonal happenings in fictional texts are rated a Level 3 on this item. When looking at books in a classroom at this level, there will be more that do not relate to authentic, local, and seasonal nature than those that do.

Level 1: Fictional texts provided *rarely* represent authentic, local nature and align with current seasonal happenings.

Fictional texts in Level 1 pre-K programs rarely represent authentic, local, and seasonal happenings or do not connect to nature at all.

Tips for Growing: Nature-Based Pre-K Fictional Texts

There are so many fictional texts available for young children related to nature that the choices can be overwhelming. Here are a few examples to consider:

- *999 Frogs Wake Up* by Ken Kimura
- *Around the Pond: Who's Been Here?* by Lindsey Barrett George
- *Bones, Bones, Dinosaur Bones* by Byron Barton
- *Carmela Full of Wishes* by Matt de la Peña
- *Chester Racoon and the Big Bad Bully* by Audrey Penn
- *Cock-a-Doodle-Moo!* by Bernard Most
- *Fletcher and the Falling Leaves* by Julia Rawlinson
- *The Grouchy Ladybug* by Eric Carle
- *If You Find a Rock* by Peggy Christian
- *In the Snow: Who's Been Here?* by Lindsey Barrett George
- *In the Woods: Who's Been Here?* by Lindsey Barrett George
- *Jayden's Impossible Garden* by Mélina Mangal
- *Jump, Frog, Jump!* by Robert Kalan
- *The Kissing Hand* by Audrey Penn
- *Leaf Man* by Lois Ehlert
- *Make Way for Ducklings* by Robert McCloskey
- *Natsumi's Song of Summer* by Robert Paul Weston
- *Not a Stick* by Antoinette Portis
- *Our Tree Named Steve* by Alan Zweibel
- *Over in the Meadow* by Olive A. Wadsworth
- *Rocket Says Clean Up!* by Nathan Bryon
- *The Salamander Room* by Anne Mazer
- *Scaredy Squirrel* by Melanie Watt
- *Seasonal Adventures* by Johnny Ray Moore
- *Silly Sally* by Audrey Wood
- *Ska-Tat!* by Kimberley Knutson
- *The Snail's Spell* by Joanne Ryder
- *Snowballs* by Lois Ehlert
- *The Snowy Day* by Ezra Jack Keats
- *Stellaluna* by Janell Cannon
- *Story of the Little Mole Who Went in Search of Whodunit* by Werner Holzwarth
- *Summer Days and Nights* by Wong Herbert Yee
- *We're Going on a Bear Hunt* by Michael Rosen
- *When Will It Be Spring?* by Catherine Walters

Item 8: Informational texts represent authentic, local nature aligned with seasonal happenings.

Sometimes pre-K programs struggle to integrate informational texts into the classroom. This is where nature-based programs can shine! There are many opportunities for informational texts, from children's science books on specific topics such as skeletons to natural-history field guides such as bird-identification books to quiz-style books to maps. Higher-rated nature-based programs will ensure these texts primarily focus on accurate facts about nature found at or near the school.

Furthermore, the texts available to children at any given time will primarily focus on the current seasonal events. That is not to say that a book on spring can't be available in winter; after all, there is value in comparison and pattern building over time. However, the majority of books during the winter months should emphasize winter. Also, these books should primarily reflect what the season looks like where the program is located. For example, if you live in southern Texas or Florida, you wouldn't want books that emphasize a snowy winter in the Midwest. These informational texts serve to connect to and build on children's experiences outdoors.

Level 7: Informational texts provided *almost always* represent authentic, local nature and align with current seasonal happenings.

Level 7 pre-K programs are almost always intentional about providing informational texts that accurately represent nature that is found locally and occurring at a given point in time.

Level 5: Informational texts provided *often* represent authentic, local nature and align with current seasonal happenings.

Pre-K programs at Level 5 often provide informational texts that connect to authentic, local, and seasonal nature. There may be inauthentic or far-off nature presented in some texts, but generally texts represent authentic, local, and seasonal happenings. For example, there might be a book about moose in a classroom located near the Saguaro National Park, which does not have moose. Additionally, informational texts may be accurate and frequently available to children in the classroom, but not always. For example, the class does not have field guides available every day, but children are able to borrow one from a shared school library.

Level 3: Informational texts provided sometimes represent authentic, local nature and align with current seasonal happenings.

A Level 3 pre-K program sometimes provides informational texts representing authentic, local, and seasonal happenings. A class at this level is unlikely to have nature-based informational texts on a frequent and regular basis, but they do have them available at times.

Level 1: Informational texts provided *rarely* represent authentic, local nature and align with current seasonal happenings.

Pre-K classes at a Level 1 rarely, if ever, provide informational texts related to nature for children to use in learning.

> ## Tips for Growing: Field Guides as Informational Texts
>
> Field guides can range in topic in terms of location and species. When selecting informational texts, keep things simple by focusing on the most common species found locally and in broad categories. For example, if the class regularly visits the local creek, it might be helpful to purchase a book on mussels found in your state or region. From there, follow the children's interests as much as possible in selecting additional texts. The same group of children might, for example, get very excited about dragonflies near the creek, and that could be the next text to purchase.
>
> When selecting field guides specific to your region, consider topics such as the following:
>
> - Fish
> - Reptiles
> - Amphibians
> - Mammals
> - Birds
> - Bird nests
> - Bird eggs
> - Arthropods
> - Insects, such as butterflies, dragonflies, and caterpillars
> - Spiders
> - Mussels
> - Trees
> - Shrubs
> - Flowers
> - Plant galls
> - Fungi
> - Lichens
> - Seashells

Tips for Growing: Integrating Maps

Maps are valuable informational texts often overlooked in the classroom. Classroom maps can be purchased, printed from online resources, or even created by the children themselves. Ideally, a classroom would have maps from a mix of these sources. When selecting maps for the classroom, it's also useful to provide a mix of maps at different scales and of different types. Specifically, consider the following:

Maps at a range of scales such as:

- School site
- Your town or city
- Your county
- Your country
- The world

Maps of a variety of types:

- Architectural (for example, building plans of the school or schematics of the outdoor play area)
- Physical
- Political (for example, city, county, state or province, or country boundaries)
- Topographical
- Road
- Satellite
- Thematic (such as bird migration patterns)

Item 9: Texts (both fictional and informational) represent diverse audiences having positive outdoor experiences.

One of the goals of nature-based education is to model that all children, no matter their background or ability, deserve and can participate in positive outdoor experiences. Many items throughout the NABERS tools relate to and support this goal. The current item is a prime example. Books, in particular, can act as metaphorical windows, mirrors, or sliding glass doors (Sims Bishop, 1990).

As Sims Bishop explains, books act as windows by offering a view of the world, as mirrors by reflecting human experience back to us, and as sliding glass doors because children can walk through to the outer world in their imaginations. Part of children's ability to connect with the world presented in books is to see themselves reflected in the pages. The characters on the pages should show a variety of identity markers to reflect the diversity of the children in the classroom, school, and community.

In addition, the diversity of people should demonstrate positive outdoor experiences and be written or illustrated by someone with the identity being represented. For example, in her article "Black Kids Camp Too . . . Don't They? Embracing 'Wildness' in Picture Books," Michelle Martin (2019) highlights the book *Where's Rodney?* which portrays Black children enjoying wild spaces and was written by an #OwnVoices author, Carmen Bogan, and illustrator, Floyd Cooper.

Diversity includes both fictional and informational texts. An informational text could, for example, highlight different types of scientists and show a variety of genders and ethnicities working in those professional roles.

Level 7: Texts provided *almost always* represent a diversity of people having positive outdoor experiences.

Pre-K programs at Level 7 are intentional about providing texts that include people with a diverse range of identity markers experiencing and learning with the natural world in a positive way.

Level 5: Texts provided *often* represent a diversity of people having positive outdoor experiences.

Texts in Level 5 pre-K programs often represent a large diversity of people enjoying and learning with nature. There may be a few texts that include negative stereotypes about groups of people in the outdoors, but generally the texts include representations of all people having positive outdoor experiences. For example, the classroom might include a book or two that describe a particular ethnic group having fears of or a general dislike for the natural world. However, books like this are rare, and most represent groups having positive experiences.

Level 3: Texts provided *sometimes* represent a diversity of people having positive outdoor experiences.

Pre-K programs that sometimes represent a diversity of people having positive outdoor experiences in texts are rated a Level 3 on this item.

Level 1: Texts provided *rarely* represent a diversity of people having positive outdoor experiences.

Texts in a Level 1 pre-K program rarely represent a diversity of people having positive outdoor experiences or do not show people connecting to nature at all.

Tips for Growing: Consideration for Including Diverse Books

Contributed by Michelle H. Martin, PhD, and J. Elizabeth Mills, PhD

Take a moment to think about the books that inspired you to be a nature lover when you were a child. What do you notice about the protagonists? More likely than not, the majority of them are White. Today, several organizations create space in the outdoors for Black and Brown folks, such as Black Folks Camp Too, Outdoor Afro, Melanin Basecamp, Black Girls Trekkin', Latino Outdoors, and many, many others. But where are the books that feature Black and Brown children out in nature? Here, we offer insight into our research that contributes to changing the landscape of children's literature through an exploration of African American wildness in picture books.

Our essay "Welcoming Black Children into Literary Wildscapes: Wildness in African American Children's Picture Books," in the journal *Children's Literature*, confronts the dearth of picture books that feature African American children who are having immersive outdoor experiences, and it uses a close analysis of the few that do exist to construct a literary framework of African American wildness that offers both a critical and a creative understanding of these portrayals.

Referencing recent articles about the negative encounters that people of color often have in local, state, and national parks, we argue that "[l]iterature can reflect life both as it is and as it could be" and advocate for increased representation of Black and Brown children having immersive outdoor experiences in children's literature. We use naturalist and scholar Drew Lanham's idea of wildness and sociologist Elijah Anderson's idea of White Space to assert that, in literature and in life, wild outdoor areas have historically been White Spaces. Because Black and Brown people often don't feel welcome in these places, they spend less time there, which has resulted in few children's artists portraying children of color having positive outdoor experiences.

In anticipation of these books becoming more widely available, we explain the conditions necessary for Black children to be able to experience wildness in picture books, and then we explore what effects are possible when those conditions are met.

Books focused on wildness in African American children's picture books and discussed in our essay include the following:

Bogan, Carmen, and Floyd Cooper. 2017. *Where's Rodney?* San Francisco, CA: Yosemite Conservancy.
An African American boy has his first wondrous visit to Yosemite with his class.

Farrell, Alison. 2019. *The Hike.* San Francisco, CA: Chronicle Books.
Three girls and the dog Bean spend a day together in the woods, hiking up Buck Mountain and enjoying the flora and fauna as they go.

Keats, Ezra Jack. 1962. *The Snowy Day.* New York: Viking.
An African American boy, Peter, plays all day in the snow in his urban neighborhood and looks forward to the next snowy day.

> Mann, Jennifer K. 2020. *The Camping Trip.* New York: Holiday House.
> An African American girl goes camping with her cousin and aunt for the first time and can't wait to go back next year.
>
> Nadon, Yves, and Jean Claverie. 2018. *We Are Brothers.* Mankato, MN: Creative Editions.
> Two brothers swim together in a pond near their family's summer home, and the older introduces the younger to a ritual they can now do together.
>
> Oswald, Pete. 2020. *Hike.* Somerville, MA: Candlewick Press.
> A child and father take a day hike to a mountain top to plant a seedling.
>
> Rockwell, Anne, and Lizzy Rockwell. 2018. *Hiking Day.* New York: Aladdin.
> An African American girl and her parents spend the day hiking up Hickory Hill, appreciating the wildlife they encounter.
>
> When you introduce stories that feature Black, Indigenous, and People of Color (BIPOC) children having positive, immersive experiences in the wild, you work to make change in the world by spreading the message that children belong in natural spaces everywhere.
>
> An additional annotated bibliography featuring stories with diverse children in outdoor spaces, sorted by topic, is included in appendix A.

K–3 Category C: Curriculum

About This Category

The items in this category evaluate the extent to which the central organizing concept of the curriculum is nature. This section also evaluates to what extent the experiences supporting these concepts are rooted in children's interests based on their local, seasonal, authentic experiences.

Local nature refers to the climate, plants, and animals found geographically close to the classroom, the nature right outside the classroom door or within the geographic region. *Seasonal* experiences are rooted in what is occurring outdoors at the given time. Conversation about these experiences might compare the present moment with other times of the year, but the experience is primarily based on what is currently happening outdoors. *Authentic nature* means the images, objects, and other materials in the classroom accurately represent what is found in the natural world rather than anthropomorphized or caricature versions of nature. This also includes intentionally disrupting stereotypes of nature, such as "Wolves have red eyes," and, "All pigs are pink." For example, a game might ask children to match a picture of a beaver with a number and picture of that number of logs. This relates to an authentic event in nature. However, if the beavers are wearing overalls and hats, it is suddenly an unnecessary and inauthentic representation of the beavers.

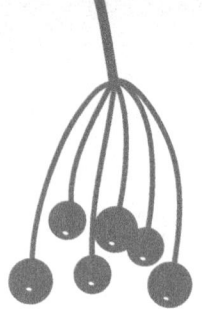

The curriculum section also measures to what extent teachers support and extend children's interests by encouraging play-based learning that is relevant to children's daily lives, using natural materials for teaching, and integrating all developmental domains into activities. When it comes to curriculum, pre-K and K-3 programs are organized differently and are under different regulatory requirements. Thus, the curriculum section of NABERS for K-3 is divided into specific domains. This section also recognizes that the majority of class time in a K-3 classroom is spent in teacher-led activities.

Despite the day being mostly teacher led, teachers in high-quality nature-based programs are intentional in leading activities that not only meet curricular goals (such as those listed in Common Core or Next Generation Science Standards) but also connect to and build on children's nature-related experiences and interests. Although most K-3 classrooms are required to follow predetermined topics or lessons, a nature-based teacher will infuse children's experiences, children's interests, and the natural seasonal events into those lessons.

To be responsive to children's interests, teachers will generally plan no more than a week in advance. This does not mean teachers can't consider natural or social events that will occur in the future and be thinking about activity ideas related to the curricular goals; it means they will not set the specifics of the day's plans beyond a week in advance. For example, a kindergarten teacher might have a math curriculum goal of teaching shapes early in the school year. They might also have a list of climate, plant, and animal events likely to occur in September and October, such as a last flurry of butterflies and insects, flowers going to seed, leaves starting to change colors, and frost in the mornings. If the children seem particularly interested in butterflies, the teacher might plan an activity that connects different shapes with the color patterns of local butterflies.

The K-3 curriculum section includes environmental literacy and connection, literacy, math, science, social studies, and art. These sections should be scored only if they are being taught by the classroom teacher. For example, if the children are engaged in an art activity but it's led by a teacher other than the typical classroom teacher, sometimes referred to as a "specials" teacher, the section would not be scored. We recognize that sometimes a class will engage in activities that are not clearly classified as literacy, math, science, social studies, or art. We find great value in learning that extends beyond these clear categories as well as learning that seamlessly integrates these domains. In these cases, identify the domain or domains that are most dominant in the activity. If this is unclear, observers should ask teachers what their curricular focus or goals were for the activity.

K–3 Curriculum a: Environmental Literacy and Connection

Environmental literacy is often referred to as the outcome of environmental education by which individuals understand their relationship with the natural world and can make responsible decisions for future generations. One foundational philosophy of this NABERS tools is that environmental literacy is not just a cognitive skill but must also include an emotional and spiritual connection to the natural world. This emotional connection is what Ann Pelo refers to as an *ecological identity*, in which children and teachers are in relationship with the natural world (2013).

Deborah Schein (2018) suggests that spiritual moments in nature occur when children experience quality time in and with nature. Whereas most K-3 curricula focus on cognitive development–literacy, math, science, and social studies–to be truly nature based, a program must also include intentional development of children's relationship with the natural world. Thus, the items that follow measure the extent to which teachers support children's development of a relationship with the outdoors. This includes building outdoor skills to safely play and explore outdoors, reflecting on outdoor experiences to make intellectual and emotional connections, and having new experiences that build on past experiences. The development of any relationship takes time, and a relationship with the natural world is no exception.

Item 1: Teachers intentionally develop children's outdoor skills.*

Outdoor skills are those that allow children to have safe, positive outdoor experiences. They include a range of self-care from dressing appropriately for the weather to building a fire to whittling. The types of skills taught will vary depending on the age of the children, the amount of time spent outside, the climate, and the types of activities allowed in the class.

At the very least, high-quality nature-based programs will make explicit connections between the weather and self-care, for example clothing to wear such as rain boots for puddle jumping, places to play such as shaded areas in extreme midday heat, and other techniques such as sitting on fabric cushions instead of a cold rock in cooler times. Other skills might include children picking up their feet when walking through dewy grass, walking quietly through leaves, and identifying hazardous elements such as poison ivy and venomous snakes. The skills taught should be appropriate for children's development and the local place and should minimize impact on the environment. (See other portions of NABERS, such as Section I, Category A, Items 4-6, for these caveats.)

Teachers can explicitly teach outdoor skills, such as having a whole-class discussion before visiting a pond to assess the benefits and the risks. Teachers can also support skill development by interacting with individual children throughout the day–for example, helping children in conducting benefit-risk assessments or discussing appropriate

---

* There are a variety of terms for *outdoor skills,* including *woodcraft, bushcraft,* and even *survival skills.* Whatever term is used, the activities themselves should align with the other quality measures in the NABERS tool, such as *developmentally appropriate* and *environmental impact.*

clothing during free play. Ultimately, whatever specific skills are taught and whether the skills are taught individually or as a whole group, they should allow children to be safe and comfortable while also maximizing connections with nature.

Level 7: Teacher-led activities *almost always* develop children's outdoor skills.

K-3 programs at Level 7 are intentional about developing children's outdoor skills. This is evidenced by explicit discussion and connections to children's behavior and their safety and comfort outdoors. For example, as a teacher helps a child find a dry pair of mittens, they might discuss why it's important to keep hands dry while playing outside in cold weather. Or, when gathering a group for an outdoor circle time, a teacher might say, "Put a cushion under your bottom before you sit down to provide insulation from the ground and help keep you warm."

Level 5: Teacher-led activities *often* develop children's outdoor skills.

Teacher-led activities in Level 5 K-3 programs often develop children's outdoor skills. There may not be daily discussion with children connecting their behavior with their safety and comfort, but it is a regular part of the children's classroom experience.

Level 3: Teacher-led activities *sometimes* develop children's outdoor skills.

K-3 programs that sometimes develop children's outdoor skills are rated a Level 3 on this item. For example, during an observation there might be a few moments during which teachers are developing children's outdoor skills, but these will be few or the moments only occur with a handful of children. If there are several moments, the program would likely score a Level 5.

Level 1: Teacher-led activities *rarely* develop children's outdoor skills.

Level 1 K-3 programs rarely develop children's outdoor skills. The activities focus only on that day's outdoor experiences or do not connect to outdoor experiences at all. For example, the activities at this level will not provide any language related to why something is being done in relation to outdoor skills.

Tips for the Observer: Outdoor Skills

Outdoor skills generally refer to any skills needed to have safe, positive experiences in the outdoors. This includes ways of behaving outdoors that support our basic human needs for food, water, and shelter but also that keep people safe from injury or illness. Among the many different outdoor skills are practices such as these:

- Dressing for the weather
- Staying warm and dry in cold temperatures
- Staying cool and out of the sun in hot temperatures
- Building a fire
- Navigation (with and without a map)
- Knots for different applications
- Pitching a tent or tarp for shelter
- Creating a shelter out of natural materials
- Using the restroom outdoors
- Basic first aid
- Leave No Trace skills (See Section I, Category A for more on this topic.)
- What to do when encountering wildlife
- Whittling

Item 2: Children reflect on their nature experiences.

Ongoing experiences outdoors are core to nature-based education. Although simply having outdoor experiences is valuable, there's even greater value for children's learning in reflecting on those experiences. This item of the NABERS tool is intended to measure teachers' intentionality in reflecting on and connecting nature-based experiences to children's prior experiences and learning while also setting the stage for future connections. This is done through oral, written, and pictorial documentation of children's experiences. Generally, these reflections relate to time in more natural ecosystems, particularly those beyond, but any outdoor experience is relevant to this item.

These reflections can happen in a variety of ways and at different times throughout the class day. For example, at the end of the day a teacher might gather the group in a circle and ask children to share one thing they noticed that day during their outdoor experiences. The teacher might also integrate reflection into the children's daily writing workshops by prompting, "Write about something you are wondering about after our hike today." Teachers might also have children take photos of seeds when outdoors and then use those photos for a whole-group science talk about the different types and purposes of seeds in the natural world. All of these activities open the door for conversation about the children's experiences outdoors.

Children's reflections can happen individually, in a small group, with the entire class, with peers, or with the teacher. For scoring purposes, it's important to capture the extent to which all children in the classroom reflect *rarely, sometimes, often,* or *almost always*. (Note: It is possible to reflect daily even if the class has not visited more natural ecosystems during the observation. For example, the children might discuss the time last week they learned about force and motion by sledding down a hill in the schoolyard.)

Level 7: Children *almost always* reflect on their nature experiences through conversation and documentation.

Level 7 K-3 programs provide opportunities every day for children to reflect on their experiences outdoors. These reflections may vary in format from day to day, but there are opportunities every day. For example, teachers might prompt children during snack, "What was your favorite part of the hike today?" The next day the teacher might gather the group around a large journal to document the "noticings" and wonderings they have about the forest they're playing in. The key for a Level 7 is that reflection about outdoor experiences happens every class day.

Level 5: Children *often* reflect on their nature experiences through conversation and documentation.

K-3 programs at a Level 5 often provide children opportunities to reflect on their experiences outdoors. They don't reflect every day, but reflection is a regular part of the children's classroom experience.

Level 3: Children *sometimes* reflect on their nature experiences through conversation and documentation.

A Level 3 K-3 program sometimes encourages children to reflect on their experiences with nature. The number of days they do not reflect on their experiences with nature is higher than the number of days they do reflect.

Level 1: Children *rarely* reflect on their nature experiences through conversation and documentation.

K-3 programs at a Level 1 rarely provide opportunities for children to reflect on their experiences with nature.

Tips for the Observer: Reflecting on Nature Experiences

Reflecting on experiences with nature can come in many forms, such as in small or large groups, in discussions, or as written documentation. Consider the following examples of evidence to gather and questions to ask as you observe to determine how frequently reflections occur.

Examples of evidence:

- Teacher prompting reflection in conversation with statements such as, "Tell me what it was like seeing that hawk fly over."
- Group gathering around a journal
- Individual journaling prompts

How children react to reflection prompts can indicate consistency or frequency with which the group reflects. For example, a child might say, "What do you mean we should journal?" or, "I want to write the question of the day at the top of the page!" The former suggests journaling is rare—a Level 1 or 3, depending on other evidence—whereas, the latter suggests the children are used to a journaling routine, which indicates a Level 5 or 7.

Question to ask if evidence isn't apparent:

How do you reflect on and document outdoor experiences with the children?

Item 3: Teacher-led activities build on prior nature knowledge and experiences.

While K-3 classrooms may include some free, child-led play time, typically the day is spent mostly in teacher-led activities. Activities usually are organized and directed by the teacher and involve the whole class or a subset of children.

Teachers in high-quality nature-based programs are intentional in introducing activities that build on children's nature knowledge, outdoor experiences, and interests. Teacher-led activities in K-3 classrooms will have specific curricular goals, and one of those goals is to support children's sense-making of outdoor experiences over time. Activity structure and conversations are designed to support children in making connections between ideas. Activities not only reflect the current week's experiences but also connect to previous weeks and months.

For example, during a science lesson the group might be discussing changes in states of matter. The teacher might prompt children to think about the foggy morning several weeks ago when they were in the beyond or the small patches of ice forming on top of the pond last week. As another example, during a writing workshop a teacher might prompt children to compare and contrast the current season to the previous one, highlighting what they notice is similar and different.

Level 7: Teacher-led activities *almost always* build on nature knowledge and experiences *over time*.

K-3 programs at Level 7 are intentional about building on ideas over time. The majority of activities in a Level 7 program connect children's previous knowledge of and experiences with nature.

Level 5: Teacher-led activities *often* build on nature knowledge and experiences *over time*.

Teacher-led activities within Level 5 K-3 programs often build on ideas over time. There may not be connections to experiences from previous days or weeks in every teacher-led activity, but it is a regular part of the children's classroom experience. For example, it is common to hear a teacher say something like, "How is this different from when we visited last week?" or "Wow! The leaves weren't this colorful when we were here a few weeks ago."

Level 3: Teacher-led activities *sometimes* build on nature knowledge and experiences *over time*.

K-3 classes that sometimes build on nature knowledge and experiences over time are rated a Level 3 on this item. These classes may occasionally relate the present learning to previous experiences or knowledge, but these connections are absent more than they are present. For example, a teacher might occasionally ask, "What else in nature does this remind you of?" but will not frequently ask questions, make statements, or create activities to build on concepts or experiences over time.

Level 1: Teacher-led activities *rarely* build on nature knowledge and experiences *over time*.

Level 1 K-3 programs rarely build on nature knowledge and experiences over time. The activities focus only on that day's outdoor experiences or do not connect to outdoor experiences at all.

K-3 Curriculum b: Literacy

Much of the focus on literacy in K-3 is on teaching children how to read and write. For many K-3 educators, the specifics of what to teach are guided by standards such as Common Core. Yet, although children are learning, they must read and write about *something*. Children's experiences learning in, about, and with nature are rich fodder for their writing. Nature not only provides subject matter, but it's also personally meaningful to children–they have stories to share about their own experiences! Further, their curiosities about the natural world can spark a desire to read as a means for discovering more about the outdoors. The following items are intended to measure the extent to which reading and writing activities and materials connect to children's nature-based experiences and learning.

As a reminder, the items in this section, as with all sections in NABERS, are scored separately. For example, if a program does not have ongoing nature-based experiences as a class, it would likely score low on Item 1, but if the literacy activities emerge from children's interests, it could still score high on Item 2.

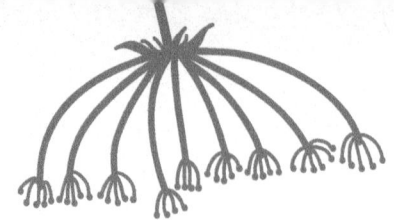

Item 1: Reading and writing activities connect to children's ongoing nature-based experiences.

This item focuses on the extent to which literacy activities relate to children's experiences outdoors. Consider, for example, how often reading and writing activities connect to the ecosystems children have visited outdoors, such as a forest or pond; the animals and birds they have observed; or activities in which they have participated, such as climbing over rocks or fishing. The activities may draw on the nature-based experiences children have had as a group or individual experiences outside of school. Item 2 addresses whether the literacy activities are initiated by the teacher or the children.

Level 7: Reading and writing activities are *almost always* connected to children's ongoing nature-based experiences.

K-3 programs at Level 7 are intentional about connecting reading and writing activities to children's ongoing nature-based experiences. For example, group and individual reading workshops will relate to children's experiences with nature. Writing prompts will also be connected to their nature experiences and might include writing a poem, telling a story of an adventure outdoors, generating a nonfiction piece about an animal they saw and then researched. Level 7 programs are intentional about leveraging nature experiences as topics of or prompts for reading and writing activities.

Level 5: Reading and writing activities are *often* connected to children's ongoing nature-based experiences.

Reading and writing activities in Level 5 K-3 programs often connect to children's ongoing nature-based experiences. For example, there may be activities that are not about nature-based experiences, such as a writing prompt to describe a favorite movie, but generally activities are connected to children's learning about and experiences with nature.

Level 3: Reading and writing activities are *sometimes* connected to children's ongoing nature-based experiences.

K-3 programs that sometimes connect reading and writing activities to children's experiences in and with nature are rated a Level 3 on this item. For example, on Fridays the children might journal about their nature experiences that week, but they don't read or write about their nature experiences at other times of the week.

Level 1: Reading and writing activities are *rarely* connected to children's ongoing nature-based experiences.

Reading and writing activities in a Level 1 K-3 program rarely relate to children's experiences with nature or do not connect to nature at all.

Item 2: Reading and writing activities emerge from children's interest in nature.

In addition to literacy activities being connected to children's ongoing nature-based experiences, it's ideal that activities emerge from children's interests related to those experiences. For example, if children have been asking questions about why leaves change color and the class is currently studying informational texts, the teacher might select a book about trees in autumn. For the same class, the teacher might prompt the children in a writing workshop to write an explanation using evidence as to why they think leaves change color in the fall. (This example involves not only literacy but also the science practices of generating an explanation.) In essence, this item is measuring the extent to which the teaching of reading and writing skills is connected to children's interest in the natural world.

Level 7: Reading and writing activities *almost always* emerge from children's interests in nature.

Level 7 K-3 programs are intentional about planning reading and writing activities that connect to and build on children's interests in nature. In a classroom at this level, teachers provide children with opportunities to read and write about what is of interest to them rather than on a predesignated topic. Children have many choices about what they would like to read or write about.

Level 5: Reading and writing activities *often* emerge from children's interests in nature.

K-3 programs at a Level 5 often provide reading and writing activities that connect to and build on children's interests in nature. There may be occasional activities that do not relate to children's nature-based interests, but generally the activities do connect. Thus, a program like this is scored a Level 5.

Level 3: Reading and writing activities *sometimes* emerge from children's interests in nature.

A Level 3 K-3 program sometimes provides reading and writing activities that are based on children's interests in nature. For example, once a week or every other week children may have opportunities to read or write about something that interests them related to nature.

Level 1: Reading and writing activities *rarely* emerge from children's interests in nature.

K-3 programs at a Level 1 rarely provide reading and writing activities that have emerged from children's interests in nature.

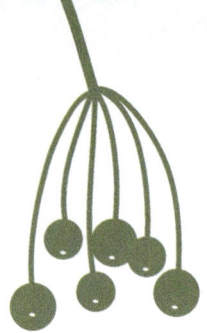

Item 3: Fictional texts represent authentic, local nature and align with seasonal happenings.

Fictional texts, such as picture books and chapter books, provide an opportunity to achieve curricular goals while also connecting with nature concepts and experiences. Many storybooks present anthropomorphized or caricature versions of nature, and although this item isn't suggesting eliminating those texts from the classroom, it is important to be intentional about the balance of messages within the library as a whole. This means intentionally emphasizing texts that provide accurate scientific facts about nature found in the children's geographic place in the world. For example, if a class is located in a temperate rain forest, the storybooks should primarily emphasize temperate rain forest ecosystems and species rather than stories about the desert.

In regard to accuracy, a book might refer to a venomous snake as being *poisonous*. Although teachers don't necessarily need to eliminate this book from the classroom, they should be aware of the error and, in most cases, use this as an opportunity to teach. A text with a factual error should also make a teacher question the accuracy of the rest of the book and analyze what percentage of errors like this occur in all texts within the library. At the very least, texts should not reinforce stereotypes of nature, such as "Wolves have red eyes," or, "All pigs are pink," and should ideally disrupt these stereotypes.

Level 7: Fictional texts provided *almost always* represent authentic, local nature and align with current seasonal happenings.

K-3 programs at Level 7 are intentional about providing fictional texts that accurately represent nature found locally and occurring at a given point in time. An observer looking at the bookshelf will see a collection of fictional texts that are almost entirely focused on natural topics. The nature represented is authentic and local to where the school is located and aligns with the current season.

Level 5: Fictional texts provided *often* represent authentic, local nature and align with current seasonal happenings.

Fictional texts within Level 5 K-3 programs often connect to authentic, local, and seasonal nature. There may be inauthentic nature presented in some texts, but generally fictional texts represent authentic, local, and seasonal happenings.

Level 3: Fictional texts provided *sometimes* represent authentic, local nature and align with current seasonal happenings.

K-3 programs that sometimes provide fictional texts that are authentic and local and align with seasonal happenings are rated a Level 3 on this item. When looking at books in a classroom at this level, there will be more that do not relate to authentic, local, and seasonal nature than those that do.

Level 1: Fictional texts provided *rarely* represent authentic, local nature and align with current seasonal happenings.

Fictional texts in a Level 1 K-3 program rarely represent authentic, local, and seasonal happenings or do not connect to nature at all.

Item 4: Informational texts represent authentic, local nature and align with seasonal happenings.

There are many opportunities for informational texts in the classroom from children's science books on specific topics, such as skeletons; natural-history field guides, such as bird-identification books; quiz-style books; biographies of outdoor enthusiasts and explorers; and maps. Higher-rated nature-based programs will ensure these texts focus primarily on accurate facts about nature found at or near the school.

Further, the texts available to children at any given time primarily focus on the current seasonal events. That is not to say a book on autumn couldn't be available in spring; after all, there is value in comparison and pattern-building over time. However, the majority of books available during the autumn months should emphasize that season. These informational texts serve to connect to and build on children's experiences outdoors.

Level 7: Informational texts provided *almost always* represent authentic, local nature and align with current seasonal happenings.

Level 7 K-3 programs are intentional about providing informational texts that accurately represent nature found locally and occurring at a given point in time.

Level 5: Informational texts provided *often* represent authentic, local nature and align with current seasonal happenings.

K-3 programs at a Level 5 often provide informational texts that connect to authentic, local, and seasonal nature. There may be inauthentic or far-off nature presented in some texts, but generally texts represent authentic, local, and seasonal happenings. For example, there might be a book about moose in a classroom located in the Sonoran Desert, which does not actually have moose. Additionally, informational texts may be accurate and frequently available to children in the classroom, but not always. For example, the class does not have field guides available every day, but children are able to borrow one from a shared school library. Thus, a program like this is scored a Level 5.

Level 3: Informational texts provided *sometimes* represent authentic, local nature and align with current seasonal happenings.

A Level 3 K-3 program sometimes provides informational texts representing authentic, local, and seasonal happenings. When looking at books in a classroom at this level, there will be more that do not relate to authentic, local, and seasonal nature than those that do.

Level 1: Informational texts provided *rarely* represent authentic, local nature and align with current seasonal happenings.

K-3 programs at a Level 1 rarely provide informational texts related to nature for children to use in learning.

Evidence of literacy includes children's writing, which may be outdoors or relate to outdoor activities.

Tips for Growing: Field Guides as Informational Texts

Field guides can range in topic in terms of location and species. When choosing informational texts, keep things simple by focusing on the most common species found locally and in broad categories. For example, if the class regularly visits the local creek, it might be helpful to purchase a book on mussels found in your state or region. From there, follow the children's interests as much as possible in selecting additional texts. The same group of children might, for example, get very excited about dragonflies near the creek, and that could be the next text to purchase.

When selecting field guides specific to your region, consider topics such as the following:

- Fish
- Reptiles
- Amphibians
- Mammals
- Birds
- Bird nests
- Bird eggs
- Arthropods
- Insects, such as butterflies, dragonflies, and caterpillars
- Spiders
- Mussels
- Trees
- Shrubs
- Flowers
- Plant galls
- Fungi
- Lichens
- Seashells

Replacing cartoon images with authentic, local nature can provide more meaning to alphabet lines in the K-3 classroom.

Tips for Growing: Integrating Maps

Maps are valuable informational texts often overlooked in the classroom. Classroom maps can be purchased, printed from online resources, or even created by the children themselves. Ideally, a classroom would have maps from a mix of these sources. When selecting maps for the classroom, it's also useful to provide a mix of maps at different scales and of different types. Specifically, consider the following.

Maps at a range of scales such as:

- School site
- Your town or city
- Your county
- Your country
- The world

Maps of a variety of types:

- Architectural (for example, building plans of the school or schematics of the outdoor play area)
- Physical
- Political (for example, city, county, state or province, or country boundaries)
- Topographical
- Road
- Satellite
- Thematic (such as bird migration patterns)

Item 5: Texts represent diverse audiences having positive outdoor experiences.

One of the goals of nature-based education is to model that all children, no matter their background or ability, deserve and can participate in positive outdoor experiences. Many items throughout this tool relate to and support this goal. The current item is a prime example. Books, in particular, can act as metaphorical windows, mirrors, or sliding glass doors (Sims Bishop, 1990).

As Sims Bishop explains, books act as windows by offering a view of the world, as mirrors by reflecting human experience back to us, and as sliding glass doors because children can walk through to the outer world in their imaginations. Part of children's ability to connect with the world presented in books is to see themselves reflected in the pages. The characters should show a variety of identity markers to reflect the diversity of the children in the classroom, school, and community. In addition, the diversity of people should demonstrate positive outdoor experiences and be written or illustrated by someone with the identity being represented.

For example, in her article "Black Kids Camp Too . . . Don't They? Embracing 'Wildness' in Picture Books," Michelle Martin (2019) highlights the book *Where's Rodney?* which portrays Black children enjoying wild spaces and is written by an #OwnVoices author, Carmen Bogan, and illustrator, Floyd Cooper.

Diversity includes both fictional and informational texts. An informational text could, for example, highlight different types of scientists and show a variety of genders and ethnicities working in those professional roles. (Be sure to check out "Considerations for Including Diverse Books" by Michelle H. Martin and J. Elizabeth Mills on page 78.)

Level 7: Texts provided *almost always* represent a diversity of people having positive outdoor experiences.

K-3 programs at Level 7 are intentional about providing texts that include people with a diverse range of identity markers, experiencing and learning with the natural world in a positive way.

Level 5: Texts provided *often* represent a diversity of people having positive outdoor experiences.

Texts in Level 5 K-3 programs often represent a large diversity of people enjoying and learning with nature. There may be a few texts that include negative stereotypes about groups of people in the outdoors, but generally the texts include representations of all people having positive outdoor experiences. For example, the class might include a book or two that describe a particular racial group having fears or a general dislike for the natural world. However, books like this are rare, and most represent groups having positive experiences. Further, there are many books representing a diversity of people having positive outdoor experiences.

Level 3: Texts provided *sometimes* represent a diversity of people having positive outdoor experiences.

K-3 programs that sometimes represent diversity of people having positive outdoor experiences in texts are rated a Level 3 on this item.

Level 1: Texts provided *rarely* represent a diversity of people having positive outdoor experiences.

Texts in a Level 1 K-3 programs rarely represent a diversity of people having positive outdoor experiences or do not show people connecting to nature at all.

K-3 Curriculum c: Math

Most K-3 educators are required to follow specific math standards, such as Common Core. Yet, most standards do not specify how these math standards are to be taught. The following items are intended to measure the extent to which math activities and materials connect to children's nature-based experiences and learning.

For example, a teacher might be focused on developing children's subitizing skills (the ability to instantly recognize the number of objects without actually counting them). This can be done using plastic objects or dots on a card, but the class could also practice grouping pine cones or with images of birds.

Additionally, nature should be authentically represented during math activities. If, for example, there are printed images of deer to count, the deer should not be dancing on their hind legs but, rather, appear like they would in the wild.

The items in this category, as with all categories in NABERS, are scored separately. As an example, if a program does not have ongoing nature-based experiences as a class, it would likely score low on Item 1, but if the teacher brings natural objects into the classroom, the program could score high on Item 3.

Item 1: Math activities are connected to children's ongoing nature-based experiences.

This item focuses on the extent to which math activities relate to children's experiences outdoors. Consider how often math activities connect to the ecosystems children have visited outdoors, such as a meadow or wetland; the plants and animals they have observed, such as pine trees and birds; or activities they have participated in, such as climbing trees or searching for frogs. The activities may draw on the nature-based experiences children have had as a group or children's individual experiences outside of school. Whether these math activities are related to children's interests is addressed in Item 2.

Evaluating Natureness: Measuring the Quality of Nature-Based Classrooms in Pre-K through 3rd Grade

Section I: Program Goals and Curriculum Practices

Level 7: Math activities are *almost always* connected to children's ongoing nature-based experiences.

K-3 programs at Level 7 are intentional about connecting math activities to children's ongoing nature-based experiences. At this level, teachers take advantage of the natural world to bring to life and make tangible the math concepts they are teaching. For example, when in the beyond, children might collect different seeds and create a graph to represent the numbers of each type they collected. At this level, virtually every math lesson has a connection to children's experiences in nature.

Level 5: Math activities are *often* connected to children's ongoing nature-based experiences.

Math activities in Level 5 K-3 programs often connect to children's ongoing nature-based experiences. There may be activities that are not about nature-based experiences, such as counting trucks, but generally activities are connected to children's learning about and experiences with nature—for example, patterns in nature and putting acorns into groups of ten.

Level 3: Math activities are *sometimes* connected to children's ongoing nature-based experiences.

K-3 programs that sometimes connect math activities to children's experiences in and with nature are rated a Level 3 on this item. For example, a teacher might connect math lessons to children's experiences in nature once a week but not every day or even multiple times a week.

Level 1: Math activities are *rarely* connected to children's ongoing nature-based experiences.

Math activities in a Level 1 K-3 program rarely relate to children's experiences with nature or do not connect to nature at all.

Item 2: Math activities are connected to children's interests in nature.

In addition to math activities being connected to children's ongoing nature-based experiences, it is ideal if the activities emerge from children's interests related to those experiences. Story problems are a great example of an easy way to connect math to children's interests. Imagine that the children have been observing and asking questions about squirrels gathering nuts outside. The teacher could generate a story problem related to squirrels and walnuts rather than one about something unrelated to children's lives. In essence, this item is measuring the extent to which teaching math skills is connected to children's interest in the natural world, thus making the math learning more relevant and meaningful to the children.

Level 7: Authentic math activities are *almost always* connected to children's interests in nature.

Level 7 K-3 programs are intentional about planning math activities that connect to and build on children's interests in nature. For example, children might be interested in the many dragonflies they've seen emerging at a nearby pond. At this level, a teacher might connect their math lessons of addition and subtraction to the numbers of dragonflies emerging and being added to the adult population each day. Or if the children are really interested in the pond, the teacher might take the group outside to measure the boundaries of the pond. At this level, teachers will make extensive connections between math lessons and what children are expressing interest in outdoors.

Level 5: Authentic math activities are *often* connected to children's interests in nature.

K-3 programs at a Level 5 often provide math activities that connect to and build on children's interests in nature. There may be occasional activities that do not relate to children's nature-based interests, but generally the activities do connect. Thus, a program like this is scored a Level 5.

Level 3: Math activities are *sometimes* connected to children's interests in nature.

A Level 3 K-3 program sometimes provides math activities that are based on children's interests in nature.

Level 1: Math activities are *rarely* connected to children's interests in nature.

K-3 programs at a Level 1 rarely provide math activities that have emerged from children's interests in nature.

Item 3: Math materials represent authentic, local nature aligned with seasonal happenings *and* consist of objects found in nature.

Math manipulatives are often used in the classroom to help teach math concepts. These materials provide concrete ways for children to make sense of abstract mathematical concepts. In most K-3 classrooms, these manipulatives are made of primary-colored plastic. Yet, it's possible for math manipulatives to be made from or at least to represent authentic, local nature. For example, rather than using plastic cubes in a ten-frame, the children could use leaves or seeds. As another example, rather than measuring circles on a worksheet indoors, the class might also go outside to discuss and measure the diameter, radius, and circumference of trees. The authenticity of the math activities increases when materials are real and local—ultimately making the learning more personal and meaningful to the children's lived experiences.

Section I: Program Goals and Curriculum Practices

Level 7: Math materials *almost always* represent authentic, local nature aligned with seasonal happenings *and* consist of objects found in nature.

Level 7 K-3 programs are always intentional about providing math materials that accurately represent and include nature that is found locally and occurring at a given point in time. For example, a teacher might have children count the petals of an aster flower during the late summer and fall months when the flowers are blooming outside.

Level 5: Math materials *often* represent authentic, local nature aligned with seasonal happenings *and* consist of objects found in nature.

K-3 programs at a Level 5 often provide math materials that connect to authentic, local, and seasonal nature. There may be inauthentic nature manipulatives, such as plastic replicas of natural objects, but generally materials represent authentic, local, and seasonal happenings. Additionally, those materials include objects found in nature rather than simply representations of nature.

Level 3: Math materials *sometimes* represent authentic, local nature aligned with seasonal happenings *or* consist of objects found in nature.

A Level 3 K-3 program sometimes provides math materials found in nature or representing authentic, local, and seasonal happenings. For example, a teacher might have children count the petals of a plastic sunflower rather than an actual flower, even if flowers are blooming outside when the activity is happening.

Level 1: Math materials *rarely* represent authentic, local nature aligned with seasonal happenings *or* consist of objects found in nature.

K-3 programs at a Level 1 rarely provide math materials made of or related to nature for children to use in learning.

Natural objects can be used in math for counting, sorting, making patterns, and so on.

> ### Tips for Growing: Natural Materials to Consider for Math and Science Activities
>
> Natural materials are powerful for learning in all domains, and there are many different options to include. This is particularly true in choosing materials to use as math manipulatives or in science lessons. Although any natural material is useful, the ideal materials will be local to your place. (And children can help collect materials when outside or in the beyond.)
>
> - Pine cones
> - Seed pods, such as milkweed pods
> - Acorns
> - Dry corn kernels
> - Rocks
> - Seashells
> - Tree "cookies" (a thin cross-section of a log)
> - Stumps
> - Leaves
> - Logs
> - Sticks
> - Soil
> - Sand
> - Snow
>
> *When collecting natural materials, be aware of other parts of the NABERS tool, such as Section I, Category A, Item 6, by selecting items that are "dead and down."

K–3 Curriculum d: Science

Whether a K-3 program follows the Next Generation Science Standards or another set of science standards, the children should have direct experiences with natural phenomena. They should also have many opportunities to make sense of those phenomena through *doing* science, which involves both science and engineering practices such as conducting investigations and exploring crosscutting concepts such as cause and effect (National Research Council, 2012). Nature-based programs strive for children to experience firsthand natural phenomena in the outdoors. This means teachers are intentional about identifying local, authentic, and seasonally based phenomena, materials, or connections to support children's science sense-making. Children's interests should also guide which natural phenomena they explore.

Item 1: Science activities are connected to children's ongoing nature-based experiences.

This item focuses on the extent to which science activities relate to children's experiences outdoors. Consider how often science activities connect to the ecosystems children have visited outdoors, such as a forest or pond; the plants and animals they have observed, such as deer and birds; the soil they have interacted with, such as by digging tunnels; and any other phenomena, such as ponds icing over. The activities may draw on the nature-based experiences children have had as a group or children's

Section I: Program Goals and Curriculum Practices

individual experiences outside of school. Item 2 addresses whether the science activities are connected to children's interests.

Level 7: Science activities are *almost always* connected to children's ongoing nature-based experiences.

Level 7 K-3 programs are intentional about planning science activities that connect to children's ongoing nature-based experiences. The science activities are almost always grounded in phenomena the children have experienced firsthand or directly relate to experiences they've had. For example, the children might have seen a hen turkey and her young while out on a hike. Based on that experience, the teacher might help them explore the needs of the turkey. In a Level 7 classroom, the majority of science activities will connect to the natural world in some way. This could be a direct example of an idea being discussed, or it could be an example for comparing or contrasting.

Level 5: Science activities are *often* connected to children's ongoing nature-based experiences.

K-3 programs at a Level 5 often provide science activities that connect to and build on children's ongoing nature-based experiences. There may be occasional activities that do not relate to children's nature-based experiences, but generally the activities do connect. Thus, a program like this is scored a Level 5. For example, the class might have few science activities throughout the week that are not connected to children's outdoor experiences, but the majority of the science lessons do explicitly connect in some way.

Level 3: Science activities are *sometimes* connected to children's ongoing nature-based experiences.

A Level 3 K-3 program sometimes provides science activities that are based on children's experiences in and with nature. Classes at this level, for example, might connect science activities to children's nature experiences once a week, but most of the lessons do not relate to children's experiences in the outdoors.

Level 1: Science activities are *rarely* connected to children's ongoing nature-based experiences.

K-3 programs at a Level 1 rarely provide science activities that have emerged from children's experiences in and with nature.

Item 2: Science activities emerge from children's interests in and questions about nature.

While science activities should be grounded in phenomena children have experienced firsthand outdoors, they should also support sense-making specific to children's questions about and interests related to those experiences. For example, some children may have been investigating how birds create nests to raise their young but then begin asking many questions about bird beaks. Why are they different shapes? Are the beak shapes to help them build the different nests or something else? If a teacher supports this line of questioning through additional experiences or research, they are connecting to and building on children's interests. This item is measuring the extent to which the science teaching is meaningful to the children by connecting directly to their interests.

Level 7: Science activities *almost always* emerge from children's interests in and questions about nature.

K-3 programs at Level 7 are intentional about connecting science activities to children's interests in nature. Teachers at this level provide extensive opportunities for children to investigate science ideas and phenomena based on what they are curious about. Activities that are determined or planned by the teacher build on the questions children have about the phenomena they have been experiencing outdoors. Science activities are only planned a few days in advance because they are responsive to the science ideas children are interested in figuring out.

Section I: Program Goals and Curriculum Practices

Level 5: Science activities *often* emerge from children's interests in and questions about nature.

Science activities in Level 5 K-3 programs often connect to children's interests in nature. There may be activities that are not connected to the phenomena children are curious about, but generally activities are connected to children's questions about and interests related to nature.

Level 3: Science activities *sometimes* emerge from children's interests in and questions about nature.

K-3 programs that sometimes connect science activities to children's interests in and questions about nature are rated a Level 3 on this item. For example, most science activities will be planned well in advance, but there may be a few times a month when a teacher adapts the science plans to respond to children's interests.

Level 1: Science activities *rarely* emerge from children's interests in and questions about nature.

Science activities in a Level 1 K-3 program rarely relate to children's interests in nature.

Item 3: Authentic, local, and seasonal natural materials are used to explore seasonally aligned science phenomena.

In addition to science activities being rooted in phenomena children have experienced outdoors and related to their interests, ideally, the activities include real materials and objects that are found locally and seasonally.

Level 7: Authentic, local, and seasonal natural materials are *almost always* used to explore seasonally aligned science phenomena.

K-3 programs at Level 7 intentionally use materials available outdoors to help children make sense of phenomena happening in nature at that time. Classes at this level take advantage of the natural phenomena right outside the classroom door to help children make sense of science ideas. For example, if a class is having a group discussion inside to develop an explanation about the needs of plants, teachers might have a variety of plant parts present for the children to look at, use as props in their explanation, or simply refer to. As another example, if the class is exploring changes in state during the fall or winter, the children might investigate how ice is forming on the pond nearby.

Level 5: Authentic, local, and seasonal natural materials are *often* used to explore seasonally aligned science phenomena.

Science materials in Level 5 K-3 programs often align with authentic, local, and current seasonal happenings. Authentic, local, or current seasonally based materials may not be included in every activity, but they are a regular part of the children's classroom experience.

Level 3: Authentic, local, and seasonal natural materials are *sometimes* used to explore seasonally aligned science phenomena.

K–3 programs that sometimes use authentic, local, and seasonal materials to explore seasonally aligned science phenomena are rated a Level 3 on this item. In classrooms at this level, most of the science activities are not related to local or seasonal phenomena, but it is not entirely uncommon for activities to relate to nature happening outside the classroom walls.

Level 1: Authentic, local, and seasonal natural materials are *rarely* used to explore seasonally aligned science phenomena.

Level 1 K–3 science materials rarely align with authentic, local, and current seasonal happenings. The materials primarily focus on nature found elsewhere in the world or from a season different than the current one or include representations of the phenomena rather than the real event.

K–3 Curriculum e: Social Studies

A social studies curriculum is intended to develop knowledge, skills, and dispositions so children can be engaged citizens—both now and in the future. Just as the natural world is diverse and interconnected, so too is our social world. The items in this category specifically look at the interconnectedness between humans and the nonhuman world, such as plants, animals, weather, and climate.

In a high-quality nature-based program, nature is central to social studies activities. This is the case whether a program adheres to the *College, Career, and Civic Life (C3) Framework for Social Studies State Standards* (National Council for the Social Studies, 2013) or other standards. Even when teachers are focused on civics, economics, geography, or history, the activities relate back to the natural world in some way. For example, if the class is focused on map symbols and scale related to geography, the children might create their own maps of the outdoor play area or the beyond space.

Disciplinary concepts aren't the only place where teachers can integrate nature into social studies. Nature and experiences with nature can be incorporated when using and teaching the framework dimensions of evaluating sources and using evidence or communicating conclusions and taking informed action. For example, after finding a turtle's nest while out exploring, the children might create signs on the school grounds encouraging visitors to stay away for the safety of the baby turtles. This is a developmentally appropriate way for the children to take informed action in their local place related to the natural world around them.

The goal of intentional integration of nature into social studies is to highlight the ways in which humans influence and are influenced by the natural world—to bring focus to the interconnectedness of humans and nature. As such, social studies activities connect to or build on children's authentic, place-based experiences with the natural world.

Item 1: Social studies activities are connected to children's ongoing nature-based experiences.

This item focuses on the extent to which social studies activities relate to children's experiences outdoors. Consider, for example, how often social studies activities connect to the ecosystems children have visited outdoors, such as a meadow or wetland; the plants and animals they have observed, such as pine trees and birds; or activities they have participated in, such as climbing trees or searching for frogs. The activities may draw on the nature-based experiences children have had as a group or children's individual experiences outside of school. Whether these social studies activities are related to children's interests is addressed in Item 2.

Level 7: Social studies activities are *almost always* connected to children's ongoing nature-based experiences.

K-3 programs at Level 7 are intentional about connecting social studies activities to children's ongoing nature-based experiences. At this level, teachers recognize the interconnectedness of humans and nature and are explicit in making those connections in lessons. For example, often towns are established in a particular location based on a natural resource or feature. This can be connected to children's own experiences by asking questions such as, "Why might it be useful for a lumber mill to be built along the river?"

Level 5: Social studies activities are *often* connected to children's ongoing nature-based experiences.

Social studies activities in Level 5 K-3 programs often connect to children's ongoing nature-based experiences. There may be activities that are not about nature-based experiences, such as structures of government, but generally activities are connected to children's learning about and experiences with their local natural world.

Level 3: Social studies activities are *sometimes* connected to children's ongoing nature-based experiences.

K-3 programs that sometimes connect social studies activities to children's experiences in and with nature are rated a Level 3 on this item. Teachers may make some connections between children's experiences and their social studies, such as comparing human communities to communities in the natural world, but these connections are not predominant at this level.

Level 1: Social-studies activities are *rarely* connected to children's ongoing nature-based experiences.

Social studies activities in a Level 1 K-3 program rarely relate to children's experiences with nature or do not connect to nature at all.

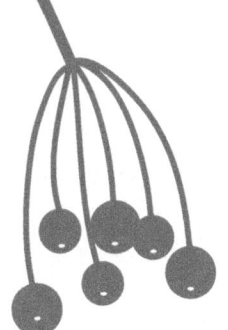

Item 2: Social studies activities are connected to children's interests in nature.

Not only should social studies activities connect to children's ongoing nature-based experiences, but ideally the activities also will emerge from children's interests related to those experiences. The children might, for example, be curious about the history of the bridge they cross every time they visit the creek. Who built it? When? Why did they build it? By helping children to evaluate sources as they gather evidence to answer these questions, a teacher is connecting the learning directly to children's interests. In essence, this item is measuring the extent to which the teaching of social studies builds on and extends children's interest in the natural world—making the social studies learning more relevant and meaningful to the children.

Level 7: Social studies activities are *almost always* connected to children's interests in nature.

Level 7 K-3 programs are intentional about planning social studies activities that connect to and build on children's interests in nature. Teachers in classrooms at this level will provide extensive opportunities for children to connect the social studies concepts to things they are interested in. For example, a child might be interested in all the places water is found, including aquifers, so the class might do a comparison of aquifer maps with settlement maps. At Level 7, this kind of flexibility to follow children's lead and interests will be extensive.

Level 5: Social-studies activities are *often* connected to children's interests in nature.

K-3 programs at Level 5 often provide social studies activities that connect to and build on children's interests in nature. There may be occasional activities that do not relate to children's nature-based interests, but generally the activities do connect. For example, a teacher may provide a lesson on the branches of government without making any connections to nature, but almost all of the other social studies lessons that week do connect to nature. Thus, the program is scored a Level 5.

Level 3: Social-studies activities are *sometimes* connected to children's interests in nature.

A Level 3 K-3 program sometimes provides social studies activities that are based on children's interests in nature. This means teachers may provide a few lessons a month that connect to children's interests in nature, but predominantly the lessons are disconnected from children's interests.

Level 1: Social studies activities are *rarely* connected to children's interests in nature.

K-3 programs at a Level 1 rarely provide social studies activities which have emerged from children's interests in nature.

Item 3: Social studies activities are connected to local history, culture, and natural resources.

Place is a critical component to nature-based education. This means understanding the history of local culture, the natural resources present, and human interactions with those resources. Some social studies lessons will inevitably be about people and places in other parts of the world. As much as possible, a nature-based teacher connects those lessons to children's local place–comparing and contrasting to what is more personally relevant and, in some cases, even more tangible to children. For example, if a lesson is focused on what food a culture typically eats, the teacher could connect that to the local growing seasons, locations, and crops by asking how these two cultures are similar or different. How the children answer will be greatly influenced by the local factors related to living organisms and nonliving factors.

Level 7: Social studies activities are *almost always* connected to local history, culture, and natural resources.

Level 7 K-3 programs are intentional about connecting social studies activities to the local history, culture, and natural resources of the school community. Human interaction with and dependence on the natural world is universal. So, although a culture in another part of the world may have a different climate, there are opportunities to compare and contrast to the local situation. Teachers at Level 7 make extensive efforts to make these connections to highlight the relationship between humans and nature.

Level 5: Social-studies activities are *often* connected to local history, culture, and natural resources.

K-3 programs at a Level 5 often connect social studies activities to the local history, culture, and natural resources of the school community. There may be times when lessons do not reference or connect locally, but generally lessons connect to local place.

Level 3: Social studies activities are *sometimes* connected to local history, culture, and natural resources.

Although not a predominant practice, a Level 3 K-3 program sometimes connects social studies activities to the local history, culture, and natural resources of the school community. For example, teachers may provide a few lessons a month that connect social studies concepts to the children's own lives and the history, culture, and natural resources of the place where they live.

Level 1: Social studies activities are *rarely* connected to local history, culture, and natural resources.

K-3 programs at a Level 1 rarely connect social studies activities to the local history, culture, and natural resources of the school community.

K–3 Curriculum f: Arts

For all of human history, it seems nature has been an inspiration for creative expression. Whether in dance, media arts, music, theater, or visual arts, the natural world has inspired creative work. Sometimes the art reflects what is present in the natural world–the wonder, beauty, ruggedness, harshness, and so on. Other times art is a way to express human connection to the natural world–both nature's impact on humans and humans' impact on nature.

A high-quality nature-based program recognizes the artistry nature can inspire. As such, arts activities intentionally connect to children's ongoing nature-based experiences, allow children's interests related to nature to guide the expression, and often include natural materials in the work. This could include taking art materials outdoors to create based on what children are observing or are inspired by outdoors. Art activities might also involve taking natural materials indoors.

Item 1: Arts activities are connected to children's ongoing nature-based experiences.

This item focuses on the extent to which arts activities relate to children's experiences outdoors and how often a program's arts activities connect to the ecosystems (including both living and nonliving components of those ecosystems) children have visited outdoors. The activities may draw on the group's nature-based experiences or on individual children's experiences in and out of school. Whether the arts activities are connected to children's interests related to these nature-based experiences is addressed in Item 2.

Level 7: Arts activities (for example, performing and visual arts) are *almost always* connected to children's ongoing nature-based experiences.

Level 7 K-3 programs are intentional about planning arts activities that connect to children's ongoing nature-based experiences. The arts activities are almost always grounded in children's firsthand experiences with the natural world. Nature-based experiences may be the source of inspiration for their creations, the art may document their experiences, or the materials used to create the art may come from or be inspired by their nature-based experiences. For example, teachers might prompt children to create an illustration of a bird they observed while in the beyond. At this level, almost every art prompt will be related in some way to children's nature-based experiences.

Level 5: Arts activities are *often* connected to children's ongoing nature-based experiences.

K-3 programs at Level 5 often provide arts activities that connect to and build on children's ongoing nature-based experiences. There may be occasional activities that do not relate to children's nature-based experiences, but generally the activities are connected. For example, the class might design t-shirts and posters for a school fundraiser that is unrelated to nature, but the other art activities that week are connected to nature. Thus, this program is scored a Level 5.

Level 3: Arts activities are *sometimes* connected to children's ongoing nature-based experiences.

A Level 3 K-3 program sometimes provides arts activities that are based on children's experiences in and with nature.

Level 1: Arts activities are *rarely* connected to children's ongoing nature-based experiences.

K-3 programs at Level 1 rarely provide arts activities that have emerged from children's experiences in and with nature.

Item 2: Arts activities are connected to children's interests in nature.

While arts activities should be grounded in children's firsthand experiences outdoors, they should also support children's expression of the thoughts and feelings they had or have related to those experiences. This item measures the extent to which art instruction is meaningful to the children by connecting directly to their interests.

Level 7: Arts activities are *almost always* connected to children's interests in nature.

K-3 programs at Level 7 are intentional about connecting arts activities to children's interests in nature. Art is an expression of human creativity, skill, and imagination. At this level, teachers recognize the power nature has to inspire creativity and imagination and that each child will be inspired by something different. Thus, teachers will provide open-ended art prompts that allow children to explore their own interests in an artistic way.

Level 5: Arts activities are *often* connected to children's interests in nature.

Arts activities in Level 5 K-3 programs often connect to children's interests in nature. There may be art activities that are not connected to outdoor experiences or phenomena children are curious about, but generally activities are connected to children's questions about, thoughts, feelings, and interests related to nature.

Level 3: Arts activities are *sometimes* connected to children's interests in nature.

K-3 programs that sometimes connect arts activities to children's interests in nature are rated a Level 3 on this item. For example, there may be a few times a month when children are allowed to express their creativity related to their nature-based interests, but the other art activities are directed and determined by the teacher.

Level 1: Arts activities are *rarely* connected to children's interests in nature.

Arts activities in a Level 1 K-3 program rarely relate to children's interests in nature.

Item 3: Art materials consist of objects found in nature.

Natural materials are useful in artistic expression as tools for creation or as part of the end product. Including natural objects in art creation provides young children another, more detailed way to explore natural materials in regard to form, texture, and so forth. In addition, natural materials are much more sustainable than plastic objects such as beads or chenille sticks. (Programs should be mindful of the Leave No Trace Seven Principles when gathering materials for art projects.)

Level 7: Art materials *almost always* consist of objects found in nature.

Level 7 K-3 programs are always intentional about providing natural arts materials found locally as tools for creation or the final product. There may be some times when natural materials are not available for creation, but those times are rare. For example, at this level the class may create their own paints, paintbrushes, charcoal, and crayons using materials found in nature. The children might also create prints, stamps, rubbings, or stencils using natural materials.

Section I: Program Goals and Curriculum Practices

Level 5: Art materials *often* consist of objects found in nature.

K-3 programs at a Level 5 often provide natural arts materials found locally as tools for creation or the final product. Although not every art activity at this level will include materials that can be found locally in nature, many of the activities will. It is more unusual for an activity to not include natural materials than it is to include them.

Level 3: Art materials *sometimes* consist of objects found in nature.

A Level 3 K-3 program periodically provides natural arts materials that are found locally as tools for creation or final artistic product.

Level 1: Art materials *rarely* consist of objects found in nature.

K-3 programs at a Level 1 rarely provide natural arts materials found locally as tools for creation or the final product.

Tips for Growing: Art Integration

When it comes to art, nature can serve as a space to create, inspiration for creative expression, or even as a tool for creating art. When thinking about ways to integrate nature and art, be sure to consider different types of art and these examples:

- Painting: depicting natural scenery, plants, animals, and so on
- Sculpture: building with clay or snow, creating sculptures that represent nature
- Literature: writing stories or poems inspired by the natural world
- Architecture: designing shelter spaces for staying out of the rain and wind, identifying form and shape in buildings and in the natural world
- Cinema: creating fictional outdoor films, producing documentaries about nature in the community
- Music: writing songs inspired by experiences outdoors, generating music to mimic the sounds of nature
- Theater: creating plays about nature, having theatrical performances outdoors

We also highly recommend the book *The Organic Artist for Kids: A DIY Guide to Making Your Own Eco-Friendly Art Supplies from Nature* by Nick Neddo.

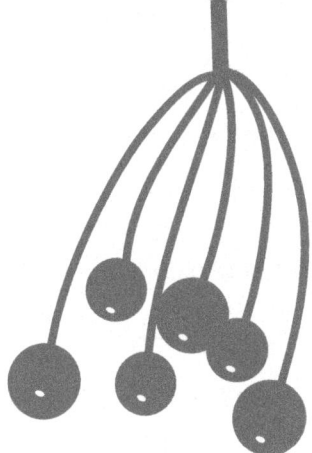

Section II:
Staffing

Characteristics, qualifications, and training of the staff are important factors in providing a high-quality nature-based program. The items in this category relate directly to the role staff members play in planning, supporting, and implementing a nature-based approach. Administrators' and teachers' titles will vary among programs, especially between the pre-K and K-3 schools. Administrators in a public K-3 setting could include the superintendent, assistant superintendent, principal, outdoor learning coordinator, and possibly school board members. In a private school, they might include the head of school or trustees. In a pre-K setting they could include the owner, director, or board members. Their degree of involvement will vary based on the size of the school and their particular role. Most important is their support and advocacy for and incorporation of a nature-based approach. The teachers might include lead teachers, assistant teachers, or coteachers, depending on the setting (public or private) and children's ages, and they directly implement nature-based education in their classes.

A program scoring in the upper range would include teachers whose role is as facilitators and who are trained in both early childhood education and environmental education. Teachers' professional development would be supported, and they would cultivate their own interest in nature. Administrators would be supportive and provide resources for nature-based education. Organizational planning would include intentionally integrating nature-based education, and administrators would publicly advocate for this approach in their schools.

A program scoring in the mid-range would include teachers who are trained in either early childhood education or environmental education, but not both. The teachers in a program scoring in the mid-range would be somewhat enthusiastic

about outdoor time and sometimes show an interest and comfort in interacting with the natural world. Administrators would be somewhat supportive but would not make this approach a priority or publicly advocate for it.

Programs scoring in the low range would be those that have teachers who are not interested or comfortable in the natural world. Teachers may be trained as early childhood educators and teachers but would not be trained in environmental education. Administrators would not be supportive of a nature-based approach.

Category A: Administrators' Role

About This Category

Some of the most important indicators of nature-based program success are the vision, support, and leadership of the administrators of the program or school. Administrators support the teaching staff in implementing a nature-based approach by providing them with planning time, funding for materials, and resources. Examples of resources might include additional support outdoors–whether by the administrator, scheduled volunteers, or part-time staff–and access to natural collections, natural play areas, diverse ecosystems, and animals. Other resources might include outdoor gear for the teachers as well as the students, radios, backpacks with first-aid kits, and opportunities for professional development in conducting outdoor learning. Administrators also include nature-based education in their short- and long-term planning and publicly advocate for the approach. The type of support will vary depending on the type of school and children's age group.

An administrator is anyone involved in or responsible for the operations of the program or schools. The most important indicator of support will be how intentional the administrator is in integrating nature-based approaches in the program by including funding in the budget, making nature-based learning part of long-term plans, advocating publicly for more outdoor time, and hiring teachers with environmental backgrounds.

Item 1: Administrators allocate time, money, and material resources to implement nature-based education.

The degree to which nature-based approaches are supported comes directly from the administrators. Providing a nature-based program requires time for teachers to plan and funding for material resources and professional development. A supportive administrator provides a safe environment in which to implement nature-based education; planning time for teachers; professional-development opportunities, including bringing in experts; and indoor and outdoor materials and outdoor classrooms.

Administrators can support the implementation of nature-based education by allocating material resources, planning time, and professional development to teachers. This includes an appropriate budget for nature-based materials—both capital equipment and tools, as well as consumables. Examples in the classroom might include sensory tables, magnifying glasses, animals, plants, tree blocks, animal artifacts, nature books and field guides, owl pellets, animal puppets, and animal-track sets.

Budgetary support also includes funding for outdoor classrooms and materials such as tents, outdoor structures, stumps, logs, mud kitchens, gardens, loose parts, clipboards, insect nets and containers, garden tools, bird feeders, ponding equipment, and outdoor gear for all students and teachers. The main point is that funds are allocated each year to provide the necessary resources to conduct a nature-based program successfully, replace or repair equipment, and purchase consumable materials.

In addition to financial and material resources, administrators provide paid nonteaching time in the schedule for teachers to plan their nature-based lessons. This might be an extra hour per day or an afternoon per week, paid time in the summer, or planning time during specials. The key is to provide the time needed to plan nature-based lessons and outdoor activities.

Administrators can also show support for nature-based education by allowing and even encouraging professional development. For example, an administrator might provide substitute-teacher support and cover registration fees and expenses to let teachers attend nature-based conferences and workshops. An administrator might also hire an expert to work with the teachers to help set up a gardening or composting program or to assist with integrating nature into the curriculum.

Ideally, administrative allocation of resources is extensive so teachers know they are able to implement nature-based education at the quality level they desire.

Level 7: Administrators *almost always* allocate time, money, and material resources to implement nature-based education (for example, in-classroom materials, planning time, professional development).

A program scoring at Level 7 will have an administrator who supports implementation of nature-based education through the extensive, ongoing allocation of money, time, and material resources. The administration demonstrates a clear desire to ensure teachers always have the resources they need to be successful in implementing nature-based education.

Level 5: Administrators *often* allocate time, money, or material resources to implement nature-based education.

Programs scoring at Level 5 might have an administrator who supports implementation of nature-based education, but time, money, or material resources are not always available or provided. For example, the annual budget may not include funding for nature-based activities, but the administrator might help the teachers apply for grants and may publicly advocate for this approach. In another example, the administrator might encourage teachers to attend professional-development conferences or workshops but may not support them financially or be able to provide paid time off to attend.

Level 3: Administrators *sometimes* allocate time, money, or material resources to implement nature-based education programs.

Programs scoring at Level 3 have little support from administrators to implement nature-based education. At this level, administrators don't provide extensive support, but they are not against the approach. If teachers are willing to spend their own time and resources, they are encouraged to incorporate nature in their curriculum.

Level 1: Administrators *do not* help facilitate a nature-based education.

Level 1 programs do not have administrators who support a nature-based approach and do not provide resources to implement it. Administrators may look down on this idea or even block the teachers from incorporating nature in their program.

Tips for the Observer: Administrator's Support to Implement Nature-Based Education

An administrator's support for outdoor learning may not be easily apparent. Following are some examples of evidence to look for during observations. We have also provided questions an observer might ask if the evidence is not clearly apparent.

Examples of evidence:

- Posted schedule with teacher planning time for nature-based education is apparent.
- An abundance of nature-based materials and equipment—such as sensory tables, wheelbarrows, digging equipment, insect nets, natural materials, animals, field guides, and the like—is in the inside and outside classrooms.
- Materials and equipment (as mentioned above) are in good, working condition.
- Professional-development opportunities have included topics such as planting gardens, setting up compost bins, and creating nature-based integrated lessons.

Questions to ask if evidence isn't apparent:

- When do teachers or teaching teams plan lessons that incorporate nature? Are they paid for this time?
- How much of the budget is allocated to nature-based materials?
- How much of the budget is allocated to teacher professional development (particularly for nature-based education)? What kinds of professional development have the teachers attended in the past year?

> ❊ What types of materials are available to support nature-based education? Are they easily accessible, and are there enough materials for all students to participate?
>
> ❊ How often do paid experts visit to support teachers in planning and implementing nature-based activities?

Item 2: Organizational planning focuses on the intentional integration of nature-based education.

This item examines the extent to which a program or school plans for nature-based education in the future, rather than only for the present moment. High-quality programs and schools integrate nature-based education in their planning, both short- and long-term. As schools plan their yearly schedules, create five-year strategic plans, consider new hires, or choose curricula, they are intentional about integrating nature-based education in their decision making.

Organizational planning might include capital expenditures; organization-wide decisions, such as choosing a curriculum; or plans for hiring additional support staff, such as a nature-based curriculum coordinator. Yearly and daily schedules are clearly thought out to include outdoor time as part of the academic learning day, not just as recess. For example, this might include adjusting the schedule for specials classes in K-3 schools to allow for larger blocks of time outdoors. Family involvement events that include intentional outdoor activities and programs are another example of short- and long-term organizational planning.

The intentional aspect of integrating nature-based education within a short- or long-term organization plan is the key to scoring high on this item.

Level 7: Short- and long-term organizational planning *almost always* focuses on the intentional integration of nature-based education.

To score a Level 7, a program is intentional about including nature-based education in both short- and long-term planning—so much that both short- and long-term planning for nature are almost always present. Documents such as strategic plans and board meeting notes highlight the organization's ongoing intentions to support nature-based education through funding, creating outdoor classrooms, and supporting teachers.

Level 5: Short- or long-term organizational planning *often* includes nature-based education.

A program scoring in this level may not intentionally integrate nature-based education in its organizational planning, but curriculum goals, such as learning about the flora and fauna in a program's local region, provide room for occasionally incorporating activities and materials focused on the natural world. Budgeting and planning may not automatically include nature-based resources and staff, but an attempt to include this approach is apparent in family programs offered or time allotted for going outside for nature play.

Level 3: Short- or long-term organizational planning *sometimes* includes nature-based education.

A program scoring at this level does not intentionally plan for nature-based activities or hire staff with a background in nature education. Nature-based activities used in the curriculum might be supported by administrators when they are connected to natural science topics.

Level 1: Short- or long-term organizational planning *does not* include nature-based education.

A program scoring in this level does not include nature-based education in its organizational planning, either short- or long-term. It is not given any thought or emphasis.

> ### Tips for the Observer: Intentionality of Organization Planning to Integrate Nature-Based Education
>
> Intentional integration of nature-based education in an administrator's organizational planning may be challenging to observe. Following are some examples of evidence to look for during observations. We have also provided questions an observer might ask if the evidence is not clearly apparent.
>
> **Examples of evidence:**
>
> - Elements of strategic plans that focus on nature-based education are posted.
> - The yearly schedule of family activities includes nature programs.
>
> **Questions to ask if evidence isn't apparent:**
>
> - Is there a strategic plan that intentionally includes nature-based education?
> - Is a curriculum chosen that includes nature-based activities? If none is available, are teachers able to include nature-based activities within the plan?

Item 3: Administrators are public advocates for nature-based education.

Being a public advocate for nature-based education can take many forms, and the degree to which administrators publicly advocate determines the program's level on this indicator. Public advocacy for nature-based education might include talking about the school and elements of nature-based education with families during an orientation or open house, presenting how the school includes nature-based education to school boards, writing professional articles or op-eds about how the program includes nature-based education at their school, being interviewed about their school and the place of nature-based education with news media outlets, or supporting a professional learning community (PLC) for nature-based education. For example, advocacy could include presenting on the benefits of nature-based education to professional school administrator conferences, such as the state superintendent conference.

Level 7: Administrators are *almost always* public advocates for nature-based education.

Administrators who support nature-based education publicly and extensively advocate for this approach. For example, administrators post information about nature-based education in prominent places for families to see. They provide family education about the benefits of nature-based education or share examples at professional conferences of how their program integrates nature-based education. Additionally, if there are multiple administrators, they are almost all public advocates. At Level 7, it is rare to *not* hear administrators advocating for the nature-based approach.

Level 5: Administrators are *often* public advocates for nature-based education.

Administrators scoring in this category are favorable to nature-based education but may not make this a focus of their advocacy. They might be positive when the topic comes up at a school board meeting, but they don't necessarily begin the conversation.

Level 3: Administrators are *sometimes* public advocates for nature-based education.

Administrators in this category normally do not publicly advocate for nature-based education. They might be positive in rare cases but as an afterthought. For example, if a teacher takes their class outside to look for insects, the administrator may make a positive comment to families or in a board meeting, but not as a general rule.

Level 1: Administrators are *not* public advocates for nature-based education.

Administrators in this category are not public advocates for nature-based education and, in some cases, react negatively to this approach.

Tips for the Observer: Administrators Are Public Advocates of Nature-Based Education

Public advocacy of nature-based education by an administrator may not be easily observed. Here are some examples of evidence to look for during observations. We have also provided questions an observer might ask if the evidence is not clearly apparent.

Examples of evidence:

- Benefits of nature-based education are included in orientation or open house for families.
- Professional journal articles or op-eds written by administrators promote nature-based education.
- There is involvement in PLCs or other supportive nature-based organizations.
- Presentations are made at school boards or professional conferences on the benefits of nature-based education.

Questions to ask if evidence isn't apparent:

- How do administrators talk about nature-based education publicly? In what settings do they usually talk about nature-based education?
- How do administrators talk about nature-based education in front of teachers, colleagues, and the broader community?
- Have administrators written articles or op-eds on this topic?
- Are administrators involved in a nature-based education administrator's PLC?

Category B: Teacher's Role

About This Category

In nature-based education, the teacher's role is of the utmost importance. Nature-based teachers facilitate open-ended play, demonstrate enthusiasm for being and learning outdoors, and model positive interactions with the natural world.

Teachers facilitate open-ended nature exploration and play by supporting authentic engagement that is child centered in nature. Facilitating, rather than directing, children's connection to nature allows children to spend time exploring and playing in the natural world. No matter what the environment is (natural play space or traditional playground), the teacher can focus on the nature that exists, such as a tree on the playground, gardens, grassy areas, flowers, and looking for animals, and so on.

Additionally, teachers convey a positive attitude about nature experiences in all weather and environments. They do this by expressing and communicating enthusiasm for the natural world and demonstrating a comfort in nature immersion.

The teacher also has an important role in demonstrating or modeling engagement with the natural environment. For high-quality nature-based education to occur, teachers themselves need to be fully engaged with the natural world, such as by lying on the ground, raking leaves, catching insects, picking up worms, turning over logs, or planting or harvesting gardens. This engagement can have a positive effect on children's ability to develop connections with nature.

Item 1: Teachers facilitate open-ended nature exploration and play.

This item focuses on how a teacher facilitates play when they are outside with the children. Does the teacher actively look for ways the children can interact and connect with nature—for example, by suggesting children turn over logs to look for insects, suggesting natural places the children can explore, or allowing children to use natural loose parts in their play? The teacher sets the tone and models appropriate behavior to allow for open-ended nature exploration and play.

Facilitation includes providing opportunities for children to engage in nature exploration that is not highly structured. Teachers encourage children to explore and play in natural areas by modeling curiosity about the natural world. If children are aimlessly moving around, teachers help them to focus on their surroundings by asking open-ended questions, engaging in nature play with the children, or involving them in relevant activities such as looking for insects under logs or observing birds. When children are engaged in exploring or interacting with nature, teachers step back, observe, and wait before stepping in so that children perceive the experience as self-initiated play and unstructured exploration in nature.

Level 7: Teachers *almost always* facilitate open-ended nature exploration and play during outdoor time.

To score at this highest level, teachers are constantly looking for ways to facilitate open-ended nature exploration and play when children are outdoors. For example, the teacher explores the natural world alongside the children, such as by searching for animal tracks or observing birds. The teacher provides materials, such as animal-track field guides, and/or tools, such as insect nets or binoculars, for the children to use when exploring.

Level 5: Teachers *often* facilitate open-ended nature exploration and play during outdoor time.

Teachers scoring in this category spend some time facilitating open-ended nature exploration and play when children are outdoors, but not always. When not facilitating, they may be leading teacher-directed activities or allowing for unstructured time, but not encouraging children to explore the natural world.

Level 3: Teachers *sometimes* facilitate open-ended nature exploration and play during outdoor time.

Teachers scoring in this category rarely spend time facilitating open-ended nature exploration and play when children are outdoors. During rare occasions, they do encourage nature exploration and play, but primarily they lead teacher-directed activities or take children outside for recess but do not actively encourage children to explore the natural world.

Level 1: Teachers *do not* facilitate open-ended nature exploration and play during outdoor time.

Teachers who score in this level do not promote nature exploration and play during outdoor time. Their primary focus is on supervising recess or taking children outside to do a specific activity that is teacher directed.

Tips for the Observer: Teacher's Role in Setting the Tone for Open-Ended Nature Play

Examples of evidence to look for during the observation that show that the teacher encourages open-ended exploration and play are listed below. We have also provided questions that may be asked if evidence is not apparent.

Examples of evidence:

- Children are outdoors engaged in exploration in the natural world. This may be on a traditional built playground, in a natural play space, or beyond in natural ecosystems.

- Teachers are observed exploring nature themselves, such as overturning logs or using exploration equipment.

- Teachers are heard using questions to encourage children's exploration, such as, "How might you investigate that more?" or, "What tools could you use to find out?"

- The teacher is near and with children during children's play in natural areas—for example, standing to the side observing or crouching down on the ground alongside children.

Question to ask if evidence isn't apparent:

How do you see your role as a teacher when you're outdoors with the children?

Item 2: Teachers express and communicate enthusiasm for outdoor time.

Being enthusiastic about taking children outdoors in all types of weather goes a long way toward helping children have positive experiences outdoors in different seasons. When teachers express a positive attitude about going outdoors, the children are more likely to enjoy being outdoors as well. In winter, this might include enthusiasm for looking for animal tracks or excitement to collect snowflakes on black felt to see if each snowflake really is different. Enthusiasm might also include teachers happily catching raindrops on their tongues or talking about how refreshing it is to be outdoors on a rainy day or how much they love jumping in puddles. It is important to note that teachers need to be truly enthusiastic about going outdoors and not faking it. In other words, they need to actively participate with enthusiasm and inquisitiveness and genuinely enjoy being in nature. It is this authentic enjoyment and engagement with the natural world that positively influences young children.

Level 7: Teachers *almost always* express enthusiasm about scheduled outdoor time and communicate this enthusiasm to the children.

In Level 7 programs, teachers are almost always enthusiastic about going outdoors. They express this enjoyment by getting excited about what they might find outdoors, and they communicate this to the children.

Level 5: Teachers *often* express enthusiasm about scheduled outdoor time.

Often teachers at this level express enthusiasm about taking children outdoors. Most likely it would be when the weather is nice and sunny or warm, but they may also express enthusiasm at having fun in the winter time, such as by sledding or building a snowman.

Level 3: Teachers *sometimes* express enthusiasm about scheduled outdoor time.

Teachers at this level rarely express enthusiasm about going outdoors, but when they do it is typically only when the weather is warm and pleasant.

Level 1: Teachers *do not* express enthusiasm about scheduled outdoor time.

To score at this level, teachers may tolerate scheduled outdoor time but are not enthusiastic about taking children outdoors. They may not enjoy time outdoors, especially when the weather is cold or rainy.

Item 3: Teachers interact with natural environments.

This item explores how engaged a teacher is with the natural environment. For high-quality nature-based education to occur, teachers need to be fully engaged with the natural world. Their interactions with nature provide a model for young children. Teachers should interact with natural environments in several ways and, ideally, in at least three different ways within a given class observation. Interacting with the natural environment might include lying on the ground, climbing on rocks, raking leaves, looking at insects with a magnifying glass, turning over logs, planting or harvesting gardens, collecting shells, looking for animal tracks, and so forth. Depending on a program's ability to allow contact with living creatures, picking up worms or catching tadpoles and frogs are also ways teachers can be engaged with the natural environment. After letting the children carefully observe them, the creatures need to be released back into the wild so they are not harmed. Each of these interactions model for children lifelong learning, curiosity, and ways to make sense of the world around them.

Level 7: Teachers are seen to interact with natural environments in *at least three* ways.*

Teachers in Level 7 programs seem to comfortably interact with nature as a regular part of their outdoor time. They are not afraid to pick up small creatures such as insects and worms. They feel comfortable lying down on the ground with the children and getting buried in leaves or looking up at the trees. They enjoy catching tadpoles and frogs at the pond and use nets with ease. They plant gardens with the children and easily get their hands dirty in the process. Teachers model this ease of interactions with nature by providing positive experiences for children outdoors.

---

* For example, by lying on the ground, raking leaves, catching insects, picking up worms, catching tadpoles and frogs, turning over logs, planting and/or harvesting gardens, or tapping maple trees.

Level 5: Teachers are seen to interact with natural environments in *two* ways.*

Teachers at this level interact with the natural world, however, not in as many ways as at Level 7. Although they may be comfortable with some activities, they may feel less so with others. For example, they may enjoy rolling over a log to look for creatures and are comfortable sitting on the ground, but they may find catching insects or tadpoles less appealing.

Level 3: Teachers are seen to interact with natural environments in *one* way.*

Teachers at this level don't interact with natural environments as easily as those at the previous two levels. They may find one way to interact, such as making a pile of leaves, but exhibit squeamishness when a child brings a worm over to them.

Level 1: Teachers *do not* engage with the natural environment.

Teachers at this level do not interact with the natural world at all. They find it difficult and uncomfortable to do so and, therefore, are unable to model positive behavior for children.

* For example, by lying on the ground, raking leaves, catching insects, picking up worms, catching tadpoles and frogs, turning over logs, planting and/or harvesting gardens, or tapping maple trees.

Section II: Staffing

Tips for the Observer: Teachers Interact with Natural Environments

Identifying the level of engagement a teacher has with the natural environment can be observed in several ways. The following examples supplement those already mentioned by providing additional details. It is unlikely that a teacher would be observed within a three-hour window doing all of the items listed. The key to determining whether they are Level 3, 5, or 7 would be based on the types of interactions the teacher is observed having. Are they fully engaged with the natural world and want to continue? Or do they limit the ways they engage with the natural world?

Examples of evidence:

- Teachers rolling over a log and looking for insects and worms with the children and encouraging them to observe what they find and ask questions about what they see.
- Teachers making a pile of leaves with the children and jumping in them.
- Teachers helping children observe tadpoles and other creatures in a pond. This may involve using small nets to catch them, putting them in a small container, and then releasing them.
- Teachers working with children to use insect nets to catch and release insects in a field or prairie.
- Any hands-on activity that teachers do outdoors as they model positive interactions with nature with the children.

Item 4: Teachers are comfortable with nature immersion.

Being comfortable with nature immersion means teachers dress appropriately for the weather and conditions and express enthusiasm for all types of weather. Dressing appropriately might include wearing sun hats and good walking shoes (not sandals) in the spring and summer, donning rain gear when venturing outside in rainy weather, and wearing snow gear when winter snowflakes arrive. Not only does dressing appropriately show their comfort, it also allows teachers to model positive behavior toward being outdoors in all types of weather.

Level 7: Teachers *almost always* are comfortable with nature immersion and show this by dressing appropriately for and communicating positively about the weather (for example, wearing appropriate footwear for the terrain and weather).

At Level 7, teachers dressing appropriately for the weather is a cultural norm within the school. As such, children learn to do the same from seeing their teachers show comfort in nature immersion. Therefore, teachers communicate positively about being outdoors in all weather conditions.

Level 5: Teachers *often* are comfortable with nature immersion and show this by dressing appropriately for and communicating positively about the weather.

In programs at Level 5, teachers are somewhat comfortable with nature immersion but not always. They may dress appropriately for some conditions but may not be comfortable with others. For example, they may be comfortable on warm days when it is sunny or raining, but not when going outside in cold temperatures. This may be because they do not have the right gear to venture out in cold weather. They may not communicate positively to children about going outdoors when the weather is below a certain temperature.

Level 3: Teachers *sometimes* show comfort with nature immersion by dressing appropriately for and communicating positively about the weather.

Teachers at this level don't usually show comfort with nature immersion, as they may not dress appropriately or have the proper gear on days when the weather is not sunny and warm. For example, they may have appropriate walking shoes or sun hats but not rain gear or cold-weather gear.

Level 1: Teachers *do not* show comfort with nature immersion by dressing appropriately for and communicating positively about the weather.

Teachers at this level are not comfortable with nature immersion and don't have appropriate clothing or gear to spend time outdoors in all weather conditions. They don't communicate positively with children about going outdoors when the weather isn't perfect.

> ## Tips for the Observer: Teachers Are Comfortable with Nature Immersion
>
> Observing how comfortable teachers are with nature immersion will vary depending on the weather on the day they are observed. If the teacher is not observed on a cold or rainy day, then the following questions can be asked to better determine their level of comfort.
>
> **Examples of evidence:**
>
> - Teachers dress appropriately for the weather, donning rain pants, raincoats, and rain boots for rainy days and snow pants, warm jackets, snow boots, gloves, and mittens for cold days.
> - Teachers communicate positively with the children about going outdoors in all weather, including on rainy and cold days.
>
> **Questions to ask if evidence isn't apparent:**
>
> - Do you go outside with the children on cold or rainy days? If so, how do you dress for that type of weather?
> - What do you say to children about going outdoors in all weather, including on rainy and cold days?

Pre-K Category C: Staff Qualifications

About This Category

Staff background and training remain two of the most important factors in providing a high- quality nature-based preschool program (Bailie, 2012). In most preschool programs, teachers and directors will have early childhood degrees or, at the least, the early childhood training required to meet state licensing regulations. When staff also have a background or degree in environmental or nature-based education, the ability to offer high-quality nature-based programming increases. Therefore, the best scenario is that program staff, including directors and teachers, are formally trained in both early childhood education (ECE) and environmental education (EE).

Formal training in ECE might be an associate's, bachelor's, or master's degree in early childhood education. Formal training in EE might also be an associate's, bachelor's, or master's degree or a minor in EE.

What is most important for a program is the mix of EC and EE formal training in the whole program, as individual directors and teachers may not have training in both disciplines. Often a director will not have formal training in EE but may hire teachers who do. When teachers who have training in both ECE and EE are not available, hiring two teachers in the classroom (one with ECE training and the other with EE training) is the next best option.

Item 1: The program administrator (for example, the preschool director) has formal training in early childhood education and environmental education.

The following levels are self-explanatory. They describe the formal educational backgrounds of pre-K directors who support nature-based education within their programs.

Level 7: The administrator, in addition to meeting regulatory qualifications for licensing, has a *bachelor's or master's degree* related to nature-based education *or* natural science (for example, environmental education, biology).

Level 5: The administrator, in addition to meeting regulatory qualifications for licensing, has a *bachelor's degree, minor, or university certificate* in a field related to nature-based education *or* natural science.

Level 3: The administrator, in addition to meeting regulatory qualifications for licensing, has an *associate's degree or a nonaccredited certificate* in a field related to nature-based education *or* natural science.

Level 1: The administrator does not meet regulatory qualifications and/or has *no additional degree or certificate* related to nature-based education *or* natural science.

Item 2: The teachers have formal training in ECE and/or EE.

The following levels are self-explanatory. They describe the formal educational backgrounds of pre-K teachers who provide nature-based education to their classes.

Level 7: At least one of the teachers, in addition to meeting regulatory qualifications for licensing, has a *bachelor's or master's degree* related to nature-based education *or* natural science (for example, environmental education, biology).

Level 5: At least one of the teachers, in addition to meeting regulatory qualifications for licensing, has a *bachelor's degree, minor, or university certificate* in a field related to nature-based education *or* natural science.

Level 3: At least one of the teachers, in addition to meeting regulatory qualifications for licensing, has an *associate's degree or a nonaccredited certificate* in a field related to nature-based education *or* natural science.

Level 1: The teachers do not meet regulatory qualifications and/or have *no additional degrees or certificates* related to nature-based education *or* natural science.

> ## Tips for the Observer: Pre-K and K-3 Teacher Qualifications
>
> The following are examples of evidence to look for during the observation. If these examples are not apparent, we provide additional questions to ask.
>
> **Examples of evidence:**
>
> - Degree credentials hanging on a wall in the office or classrooms of the preschool director and/or pre-K or K–3 teachers
> - Training certificates are available in a file or hanging on a wall in the office or classrooms of the preschool director and/or pre-K or K–3 teachers
>
> **Questions to ask if evidence isn't apparent:**
>
> - What is the preschool director's educational background related to early childhood education and/or environmental education? Do they have formal degrees or training in either or both?
> - What are the teachers' educational backgrounds in early childhood education and/or environmental education? Do they have formal degrees or training in either or both?

K–3 Category C: Teacher Qualifications

About This Category

Teachers are some of the most important factors in providing a quality nature-based education. One facet of nature-based teacher development is their formal training in both ECE and EE, which this category focuses on. In addition to being certified to teach, teachers in a nature-based program also have formal training in nature-related topics. Certified K-3 teachers will inherently have training in early childhood education. Teachers who also have environmental education, biology, or a related natural-history degree contribute a substantial benefit for providing nature-based education and will score higher than those who don't have this education.

Item 1: The teacher qualifications include teaching certification and formal training in environmental education.

The following levels are self-explanatory. They describe the formal educational backgrounds of teachers who provide nature-based education to their classes. Although it is not always feasible for teachers to have dual degrees, some do, and programs should be awarded points based on those accomplishments. Having this high degree of experience and natural-history knowledge will enhance the nature-based aspects of the program.

Level 7: The teacher, in addition to being a certified elementary teacher, has a *bachelor's or master's degree* related to nature-based education *or* natural science (for example, environmental education, biology).

Level 5: The teacher, in addition to being a certified elementary teacher, has a *bachelor's degree, minor, or university certificate* in a field related to nature-based education *or* natural science.

Level 3: The teacher, in addition to being a certified elementary teacher, has an *associate's degree or a nonaccredited certificate* in a field related to nature-based education *or* natural science.

Level 1: The teacher, in addition to being a certified elementary teacher, has *no additional degree or certificate* related to nature-based education *or* natural science.

Category D: Professional Development

About This Category

Teachers participate in ongoing professional development to facilitate their interest, skills, and knowledge of nature and nature-based pedagogy, including outdoor safety. There are many nature-based education conferences (local, regional, national, and international) as well as workshops, webinars, master naturalist programs, and wilderness training opportunities available for teachers and administrators to help them stay current in the field. Professional development can also include visiting model programs, having ongoing support from a nature-based curriculum coach, reading pertinent articles, and attending workshops that focus on outdoor safety. For example, informal education organizations such as the National Association of Interpretation (NAI) and the North American Association for Environmental Education (NAAEE) offer relevant trainings. Other professional development might include wilderness first aid, forest-school training, outdoor skills, and so on.

Item 1: Teachers participate in professional development to improve their skills and knowledge of nature-based education.

Professional development is a critical aspect of providing an excellent nature-based program. Several types of professional development are recommended to support both natural-history knowledge and nature-based education pedagogy. Natural-history knowledge includes an understanding of plants and animals in their natural environment. Much of this knowledge can be learned through observation and interaction with the natural world. Nature-based education pedagogy refers to how to work with children outdoors. Teachers need both types of professional development to successfully implement a nature-based curriculum. Scoring levels depend on how often teachers participate and which types of training they attend.

Level 7: Teachers cultivate their own knowledge of and interest in nature by participating at least *twice* a year in professional development (for example, visiting model programs, attending workshops) related to both nature-based education pedagogy *and* natural-history knowledge.

To score at this level, teachers need to attend or participate in some type of training related to both nature-based education pedagogy and natural-history knowledge at least twice during the year. One example would be a master naturalist program offered by a local nature center. This type of program provides not only a great deal of natural-history knowledge but also offers pedagogy on how to share this knowledge with children.

Level 5: Teachers cultivate their own knowledge of and interest in nature by participating *once* a year in professional development related to nature-based education pedagogy *and* natural-history knowledge.

To score at this level, teachers need to attend at least one type of training each year that is related to both nature-based education pedagogy and natural-history knowledge. For example, attending a conference such as the Natural Start Alliance's Nature-Based Early Learning Conference would provide plenty of opportunities to learn more nature-based education pedagogy and about specific natural-history subjects.

Level 3: Teachers cultivate their own knowledge by participating *once* a year in professional development related to nature-based education pedagogy *or* natural-history knowledge.

To score at this level, teachers need to attend at least one training each year related to nature-based education pedagogy or natural-history knowledge. For example, a workshop at a nature center about birds would provide natural-history knowledge but not nature-based education pedagogy.

Level 1: Teachers *do not* participate in professional development related to nature topics.

Programs that score at this level do not have teachers who participate in any type of training related to nature-based education pedagogy or natural-history knowledge.

Tips for the Observer: Pre-K and K-3 Professional Development

Below are examples of evidence to look for during observations. We have also provided questions to ask if evidence is not apparent.

Examples of evidence:

Certificates of completion of attending a conference, workshop, or training related to nature-based education pedagogy (including safety skills) and/or natural-history knowledge are posted on a wall in the classroom or another public place.

Questions to ask if evidence isn't apparent:

- Do the teachers attend conferences, workshops, or trainings that relate to nature-based education pedagogy (including safety skills)? Which ones have they completed and how often?

- Do the teachers attend conferences, workshops, or trainings that relate to natural-history knowledge? Which ones have they completed and how often?

Tips for Growing: Professional Development Opportunities

With the growth of the nature-based education movement, there has been a growing need for professional development opportunities for teachers. The following is a list of universities and colleges that offer degree and/or certification programs. Also, we offer a list of other organizations that provide learning opportunities for teachers and administrators.

Universities and Colleges

- Alverno College, Early Childhood Outdoor Preschool Environmental Education Program
- Antioch University, New England and Santa Barbara, CA, Certificate in Nature-Based Early Childhood Education
- Florida Atlantic University, Early Childhood Environmental Education Certificate
- Hamline University, Certification in Nature-Based Early Learning
- Miami University, Early Childhood Environmental Educator Certification
- North Carolina State University, NC State Natural Learning Initiative, Early Childhood Outdoor Learning Environments Certificate
- Prescott College, Center for Nature and Place
- University of Cincinnati (Online), Bachelor in Early Childhood Education with Concentration in Nature-Based Early Learning
- University of Maine at Farmington, Graduate Certificate in Nature-Based Education
- University of Minnesota, Bachelor of Applied Science in Childhood Nature Studies

Other Professional-Development Opportunities*

- American Forest School Association
- Eastern Region Association of Forest and Nature Schools, http://www.erafans.org/
- Forest School Canada, https://childnature.ca/forest-school-canada/
- Growing up WILD, https://www.fishwildlife.org/projectwild/growing-wild
- Inside-Outside, https://www.insideoutside.org/
- Mindstretchers Academy, https://us.mindstretchers.academy/
- Natural Start Alliance, https://naturalstart.org/
- Nature Explore, https://natureexplore.org/
- NOLS Wilderness Medicine, https://www.nols.edu/en/wilderness-medicine/why-nols/
- Project Learning Tree, https://www.plt.org/
- Samara Early Learning, https://www.samarael.com/

*This list is ever changing. We encourage you to visit Natural Start Alliance (https://naturalstart.org/professional-development) for the most up-to-date list of resources and opportunities.

Section III:
Environment

The environment of a nature-based program generally consists of three distinct spaces—inside, outside, and beyond—that are provided to meaningfully integrate nature among the physical environments.

The inside classroom is a space most early childhood educators are familiar with. However, in a nature-based program, in addition to the typical licensing or school rules that apply to a pre-K or K-3 class, the indoor space should also include various materials and design features that provide connections to nature.

Natural play areas, or outside spaces, are covered by licensing or school rules and usually are fenced. But instead of, or in addition to, typical playground equipment, outdoor spaces include more natural elements that provide opportunities for children to explore natural areas, balance on natural loose parts such as logs, and dig in natural materials such as sand or soil. These outside areas are created and maintained by the school staff and are thus sometimes referred to as *managed outdoor spaces* (Merrick, 2019).

The third environment that supports a nature-based program is composed of the wilder areas beyond the fence. Sometimes this environment is referred to as *wild outdoor spaces*, *natural ecosystems*, or simply *the beyond*. In NABERS, we generally use *natural ecosystems* and *the beyond* to be more inclusive of a variety of spaces that may not be seen as wild. In doing so, we hope to disrupt the human-nature divide and the typical definition of what counts as nature. Thus, the beyond space may be a forest, prairie, wetland, or neighborhood park. Depending on the program's geographic location, this area may be within walking distance or may require transportation to get there. These natural ecosystems are not managed, so safety protocols are an important part of taking children to these areas (see Program Practices on pages 44-48 and 56-59).

Some programs may not have an indoor space. In that case, score only the Alternate Item under Category A below, and then complete Categories B and C.

Category A: Indoor Classroom (Inside)

About This Category

In a high-quality nature-based classroom, nature is infused into all areas of the space, giving the classroom a nature-like feel and appearance. This category provides examples of a natural environment including natural light and views of outdoors, natural furnishings and colors, means of access directly to the outdoors, natural materials that are realistic and represent local nature, and classroom plants and animals.

For programs that do not have an indoor classroom space or have an indoor space that is only used as emergency shelter, score the following Alternate Item 1-3 in place of Items 1, 2, and 3. Items 4-7 may be found in an outdoor classroom and should be scored if applicable.

Alternate Item 1-3 (for classes without an indoor classroom space): Need for an Emergency Shelter

This item pertains to programs that are held nearly 100 percent of the time outdoors. To provide a safe environment, an emergency shelter should be in close proximity and available in case of inclement weather or other life-threatening emergencies.

Level 7: The class has an emergency shelter in close proximity at *all* times.

To score at this level, programs that are primarily outdoors have an indoor space that is located within walking distance of the outdoor space and is available in case of inclement weather.

Level 5: The class has an emergency shelter in close proximity *some* of the time.

To score at this level, the emergency shelter is nearby, when possible, but not necessarily all of the time. This might be the case for an outdoor program that meets at different places throughout the week and in some locations has an indoor space nearby but at others does not.

Level 3: The class has an emergency shelter, but it is *not* in close proximity.

To score at this level, an outdoor program has an indoor space that is available but not within walking distance.

Level 1: The class *does not have* an emergency shelter.

An outdoor program that has no indoor space to use for inclement weather will score at this level. Teachers or administrators would need to cancel classes when conditions are not safe for children to be outdoors.

Item 1: The indoor classroom has natural lighting and views of outdoors.

Natural light and views of natural green spaces can have beneficial effects for children (Faber Taylor, Kuo, and Sullivan, 2001). Windows that are low enough for children to be able to look outside are preferred over high windows or skylights, but all will let in natural light. Views of natural spaces (trees, bushes, gardens, or green spaces) are preferred over views of nonnatural spaces such as parking lots or buildings.

Level 7: The indoor classroom has *extensive* natural light with child-level views to a *natural space* outdoors.

To score at the highest level, the classroom contains plenty of windows (and possibly skylights) that let natural light into the room. Windows are low enough for children to be able to look outdoors easily, and the view out the windows is of a natural green space.

Level 5: The indoor classroom has *some* natural light with child-level views to *any outdoor space*.

Classrooms that have some natural light and views of outdoor spaces that are not natural would score at this level. For example, the windows look out to a city street or parking lot.

Level 3: The indoor classroom has *some* natural light *without* child-level views to the outdoors.

Classrooms at this level have some natural light but don't contain windows that allow children to view the outdoors.

Level 1: The indoor classroom *has no* windows.

The program would score at the lowest level if there are no windows, which means no natural light and no views of the outdoors are available.

Section III: Environment

Tips for the Observer: Indoor Classroom Natural Light and Views of the Outdoors

The following list contains examples of evidence to support the levels in this item. We also include questions to ask if you are unable to observe the indoor classroom.

Examples of evidence:

- Windows are low enough for children to look outside and big enough to provide natural light; windows are also oriented to let in light (not in shadow)
- Skylights let in natural light
- Views out the windows of green spaces, trees, bushes, gardens, and so on

Questions to ask if evidence isn't apparent:

- Are there windows in the classroom? If so, how big are they? Do they allow natural light to come in?
- Are there skylights that provide natural light?
- What is the view out of the windows? Are views natural or human-made?

Item 2: The indoor classroom has natural furnishings and colors.

Early childhood environments can have an impact on children's learning and development (Curtis and Carter, 2015; Greenman and Lindstrom, 2017). The purpose of this item is to establish how natural the classroom environment appears to be by taking a look at the furnishings, textures, and colors inside. For example, wood furnishings have a more natural appearance as compared to plastic ones. Earth-based colors (neutral, earthy greens, tans, browns) are more aesthetically pleasing and calming than bright primary colors in large quantities. This doesn't mean there are no accents of bright colors, but primarily earth-based colors are used. A variety of natural textures provides sensory experiences for children that are authentic and realistic, giving the children opportunities to feel different surfaces such as textured wood flooring and smooth, leather-type couches.

Level 7: The indoor classroom has an *extensively* natural look and feel (for example, natural furnishings, diverse textures, earth-based colors).

To score at this level, classrooms are beautiful environments containing natural elements such as wood furnishings, textured wood floors, and woven rugs and are full of neutral, earthy colors such as brown, tan, off-white, muted yellow, and light green or blue, with accents of brighter or deeper colors such as brick red or forest green.

Level 5: The indoor classroom has *some* natural look and feel (for example, a mix of natural and plastic furnishings, diverse textures, earth-based colors).

To score at this level, teachers make an effort to provide an environment that has a natural look and feel (wood furnishings, earthy colors, and interesting textures) but the classroom may contain some plastic furnishings, such as tables and chairs, and bright colors.

Level 3: The indoor classroom has a *limited* natural look and feel (for example, mix of natural and plastic furnishings, diverse textures, primary colors).

To score at this level, teachers do not try to provide an environment that has a natural look and feel. Very few wood furnishings, earthy colors, or interesting textures are present in the classroom. Most of the furnishings are plastic, and there may be an excess of bright colors.

Level 1: The indoor classroom has *no* natural look and feel (for example, plastic furnishings, primary colors).

To score at this lowest level, the classroom does not have a natural look or feel. Furnishings are typically plastic and have no variety of textures. Primary colors are used throughout the classroom.

The indoor classroom environment should include natural lighting, views to the outdoors, and a more natural appearance with earth-based colors.

Tips for the Observer: Natural Look and Feel of the Indoor Classroom

The following are examples of evidence to look for during observations.

Examples of evidence:

- Furniture, such as tables and chairs, bookshelves, sensory tables, is made of wood.

- The classroom has various textures throughout, such as wood floors, woven rugs, tile floors or walls, and fabric wall hangings.

- The classroom is painted in earthy tones, such as tan, brown, greens, blues, and off-white. If bright or deep color is used, it is with accents of colors such as brick red and forest green that don't overwhelm the space, but supply areas of focus.

Item 3: The indoor classroom affords children access and movement between indoors and outdoors.

One of the characteristics that makes a nature-based early childhood program successful is the ease of access to the outdoors. This is usually a door that opens from the classroom directly to an outdoor play area. Of even greater importance is the ability to have children be indoors or outdoors during class time or free-choice time. This free-range movement is possible when more than one teacher is present, enabling one teacher to be inside the classroom and the other outside. A transition space, such as a porch or sunroom, enables children to easily move between indoor and outdoor spaces.

Level 7: The indoor classroom has immediate access to the outdoors, *and* children have free-range movement between the indoor and outdoor classroom through a transition space (for example, a porch or sunroom).

To score in this level, a door to the outside play area is available directly from the classroom. Children are able to move from indoors to outdoors as part of their classroom time because adults are available in both spaces. Transition spaces are available to help with this movement.

Level 5: The indoor classroom has immediate access through a door to the outdoor classroom.

To score at this level, the classroom has a door to the outside directly from the classroom. Children do not have a choice of being indoors or outdoors during class or free choice time.

Level 3: The indoor classroom has an easy, but not direct, transition to the outdoors.

To score at this level, the classroom does not have a door directly to the outdoors, but there is an easy access to the outdoors–for example, a door to the outdoors is down a hallway just around the corner, or a porch is available to stage outdoor transitions.

Level 1: The indoor classroom has a difficult transition to the outdoors.

Classrooms that have no door from the classroom directly outdoors and a difficult transition (for example, no hallway that is close by with a door to the outdoors) will score at this level.

Tips for the Observer: Transition between Indoors and Outdoors

Look for the following evidence during the observation to support this item. Additional questions are included if the evidence is not apparent.

Examples of evidence

- There is a door in the classroom that opens up directly to the outdoors.
- There is a transitional space, such as a porch, outside the classroom.
- Children are observed being indoors and outdoors during class time or free-choice time.
- If there is not a door in the classroom that opens directly to the outdoors, there is easy access to the outdoors from the classroom, such as through a hallway and door to the outdoors nearby.

Questions to ask if evidence isn't apparent:

- Is there a door in the classroom that opens directly to the outdoors? If not, is there easy access to the outdoors nearby?
- Is there a transitional space such as a porch outside the classroom?
- Do the children have a choice of being indoors or outdoors during class time or free-choice time?

Item 4: Natural materials are present and reflect local nature.

Natural materials are an important part of bringing nature inside, and many different materials can be used throughout the classroom (for example, sunflower seeds in the sensory table, tree cookies in the block area, acorns for counting, evergreen branches as paintbrushes). Other natural materials might be from collections or brought in by the children from home, such as feathers and other bird parts, bird's nests, animal bones, owl pellets, animal pelts, shells, or a paper-wasp nest (after it was outside all winter and the wasps are not alive in it anymore). One positive aspect of having natural materials in the classroom is that they are from the local environment and typically what children can find in the area.

If you are evaluating a class that spends all of its time outdoors, look for natural materials in areas of the outdoor space that are available for various activities, such as building, dramatic play, art, science, and math. (Note: See Pre-K and K-3 Category C Tips for Growing on pages 71 and 101 for ideas of natural materials to include.)

Level 7: Natural materials (for example, bird parts, animal bones, bird nests, tree seeds) are present in *all* areas of the indoor classroom and reflect a variety of local nature.

To score at the highest level, natural materials need to be found in all areas of the classroom (for example, in sensory tables, block areas, art areas, and the dramatic play center) and not just on the science table. They should also reflect items that would be found in the local area, such as pelts of local animals, bird's nests found in areas around the school, sunflower-seed heads grown in the school garden, and so on.

Level 5: Natural materials are present in *most* areas of the indoor classroom and reflect a variety of local nature.

To score in the mid-range, not all areas of the classroom need to have natural materials, but most of them do. For example, the classroom might offer natural materials in the sensory table, science area, and art area, but none in dramatic play or the library area. Most should reflect what can be found locally.

Level 3: Natural materials are present in *some* areas of the indoor classroom and reflect a variety of local nature.

When some areas of the classroom include natural materials, such as sand in the sensory table and bird's nests on the science table but no natural materials in the math or art areas, the program would score at this level. The materials should still reflect what is local to the area to score at this level.

Level 1: Natural materials are *not* present.

A classroom would score at the lowest level if it did not contain any natural materials.

Tips for the Observer: Natural Materials Found in the Indoor Classroom

Examples of evidence for this item are provided below. Additional questions are listed if evidence is not apparent.

Examples of evidence:

- Natural materials are found throughout the classroom, such as in the sensory table (sand, soil, sunflower seeds, leaves, and so on), materials used for sorting and counting (acorns, rocks, shells, and so on), tree cookies in the block area, and feathers or evergreen branches used as paintbrushes in the art area.

- Collections of animal artifacts are evident in the classroom, such as bird's nests, animal pelts, insect collections, skeletons, and animal skulls.

- The types of natural materials are items that would be found in the local area.

Questions to ask if evidence isn't apparent:

- What types of natural materials are used in the classroom?

- Do the animal artifacts and natural materials reflect local nature?

Item 5: Indoor classroom materials are realistic and representative of local nature.

Providing materials that are representative of nature that children would find in their own backyard or neighborhood provides a more place-based approach. Realistic materials, such as books that show local animals as they appear in nature, offer children opportunities to connect them with the natural world and local environment. Materials included in this item are things such as animal puppets, nature-based books, and materials used in dramatic play.

Level 7: Indoor classroom materials (for example, puppets, books, dramatic play materials) *almost always* represent realistic and local nature.

Programs that score at the highest level will almost always have materials that look realistic and represent local nature. Animal puppets would be of animals that are local to the school or program that children would find if they explored in their own neighborhood. Examples include puppets of birds that come to the bird feeders outside the classroom windows or puppets of animals the children see often. Books in the classroom represent animals and plants in realistic ways and do not show animals dressed up like people but show them as you would see them in the wild.

Level 5: Indoor classroom materials *often* represent realistic and local nature.

To score at this level, materials such as animal puppets and books don't always represent realistic and local nature, but do often. For example, rain-forest animals (in programs that are not in a rain forest) or books that anthropomorphize animals are more prevalent.

Level 3: Indoor classroom materials *sometimes* represent realistic and local nature.

At this level, materials such as animal puppets and books are not very realistic—for example, they have animals wearing clothes, or they don't represent local nature. Most of the materials represent animals and plants from other regions of the world and are not specific to the region where the school or program is located.

Level 1: No indoor classroom materials represent realistic and local nature.

To score at the lowest level, programs do not have any materials that are realistic or represent what is found in the local environment.

Tips for the Observer: Indoor Classroom Materials and Books Are Realistic and Representative of Local Nature

Examples of evidence to look for during observations are provided below. Additional questions are provided if evidence is not apparent.

Examples of evidence:

- Realistic puppets representing local animals are in easy-to-access spaces and available for children's play.

- Children's books that provide realistic images and information about animals, plants, and nature are included throughout the classroom and/or in the book area. There is a combination of nonfiction and fiction children's books that depict animals realistically.

- Children's field guides with excellent photos are plentiful and available throughout the classroom.

Questions to ask if evidence isn't apparent:

- What types of puppets are found in the classroom?

- Is there a mix of fiction and nonfiction children's nature picture books in the classroom?

Item 6: Indoor classroom materials reflect the human diversity of the local community having positive outdoor experiences.

Implicit in nature-based education is the idea that all children, no matter their background or ability, are not only able to but have a right to experience positive outdoor experiences. As discussed in Section I: Program Goals and Curriculum Practices, this includes two key components: "all children, no matter their background or ability" and "positive outdoor experiences" and can be demonstrated in a myriad of ways. This item focuses on the materials in the indoor classroom, including displays, informational texts, fictional texts, toys, games, and dramatic play materials. These materials should reflect the full range of human diversity present in both the school and the broader community. Further, the materials should show these people having positive, asset-based outdoor experiences.

Level 7: Indoor classroom materials *almost always* reflect the human diversity of the local community having positive outdoor experiences.

Level 7 programs are intentional about providing classroom materials that reflect the core nature-based education belief that *all* people have the right to experience positive outdoor experiences. As a result, the program materials reflect a wide range of human diversity–including race, ethnicity, and ability–enjoying outdoor experiences.

Level 5: Indoor classroom materials *often* reflect the human diversity of the local community having positive outdoor experiences.

Early childhood programs at a Level 5 often provide materials that reflect some diverse people enjoying outdoor experiences. The materials may represent some diversity but may not reflect the full range of human diversity within the local community. For example, materials in the program may reflect a range of races enjoying the outdoors but do not reflect people of different physical abilities enjoying the outdoors. A program like this is scored a Level 5.

Level 3: Indoor classroom materials *sometimes* reflect the human diversity of the local community having positive outdoor experiences.

A Level 3 program may display some images, books, and other materials that reflect a wide diversity of people enjoying the outdoors, but these materials are the exception rather than the rule.

Level 1: No indoor classroom materials reflect the human diversity of the local community having positive outdoor experiences.

Programs at Level 1 rarely provide materials in the classroom that reflect a range of human diversity enjoying the outdoors. For example, most of the books include physically able White people hiking outdoors, but not other ethnicities or abilities.

Item 7: The indoor classroom has plants and animals.

Animals and plants in the classroom provide opportunities for children to have positive experiences with living things, including caring for them, which helps children develop empathy. The types of animals a classroom might have will depend on local licensing and/or school rules. Any allergies that children in the classroom may have must be considered as well–for example, children with asthma may have allergies to animals with fur. Often, licensing rules do not allow reptiles or amphibians in the classroom due to possible salmonella infections resulting from handling these animals. Local plants and animals are best to have, if possible. Sometimes collecting local animals to keep for a couple of weeks and then letting them go is a great way for children to experience animals and plants they might see in their neighborhood. Scoring in this category is based on the quantity of living plants and animals found in the classroom. Be careful to make sure the plants are not toxic to children.

Level 7: The indoor classroom has *three or more* living plants and/or animals (if allergies allow).

Level 7 programs will have at least three living plants and/or animals present in the classroom. These might include potted plants the children water, caged animals such as rabbits or guinea pigs, child-created terrariums with local

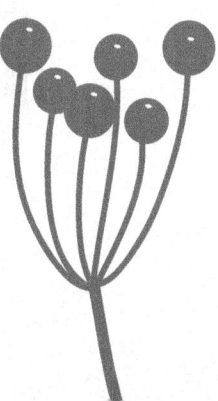

Ideally, calendars and other documentation on the walls of the indoor classroom will represent authentic, local nature rather than cartoon versions or far-off nature.

Section III: Environment

149

plants, child-collected local insects in aquariums with child-created habitats, or fish in an aquarium.

Level 5: The indoor classroom has *two or more* living plants and/or animals (if allergies allow).

Level 5 programs will have at least two living plants and/or animals in the classroom.

These would include similar plants and animals to those mentioned in Level 7, but fewer numbers of them.

Level 3: The indoor classroom has *one or more* living plants and/or animals in the indoor classroom (if allergies allow).

To score at this level, the classroom should include at least one living plant or animal. This would be only a plant or an animal, but not both.

Level 1: There are *no* living plants and/or animals in the indoor classroom.

If there are no living plants or animals in the classroom, a program would score at this level.

Tips for the Observer: The Indoor Classroom Has Plants and Animals

Examples of evidence:

- Animals are found in the classroom and are local to the region. They are housed in appropriate habitats or containers.
- Potted plants are found in the classroom. These are appropriate for young children and do not include toxins that might be harmful to the children.

> ### Tips for Growing: Plants and Animals
>
> The following resource books provide guides for teachers on selecting safe and appropriate plants and animals for children's environments.
>
> Kramer, David C. 1989. *Animals in the Classroom.* Boston, MA: Addison-Wesley Educational.
>
> Moore, Robin C. 1993. *Plants for Play: A Plant Selection Guide for Children's Outdoor Environments.* Berkeley, CA: MIG Communications.
>
> Selly, Patty Born. 2014. *Connecting Animals and Children in Early Childhood.* St. Paul, MN: Redleaf.

Category B: Natural Play Area (Outside)

About This Category

The *managed outdoor space* includes numerous human- and nature-made loose parts and a variety of features for nature-based play. It is often a fenced-in space with several areas that support child development. This category focuses on the elements that make the outdoor space a natural play area. The *Nature-Based Preschool Professional Practice Guidelines* suggest that the "landscape features [of a natural play area should] promote connections to nature and support growth in all developmental domains" by "maximizing affordances for play and learning" (Merrick, 2019). Some of the features that afford opportunities in natural environments include the following:

- Open ground
- Sloping terrain, such as hills and grassy knolls
- Shielded places, such as forts, willow structures, and bushes
- Rigid fixtures, such as trees, logs, and boulders
- Moving fixtures, such as swings, hammocks, and suspension bridges
- Loose objects, such as logs, sticks, rocks, and stones
- Loose material, such as sand, soil, mud, and dirt
- Water
- Creatures (local wildlife)
- Fire

(Greenman and Lindstrom, 2017; Keeler, 2008; Lerstrup and Konijnendijk van den Bosch, 2017). Different features afford different opportunities for play and learning in natural environments.

The degree to which a program includes a wide and deep variety of these different opportunities will influence the score it receives on this item. Although the NABERS tools provide a list of features, not every possible feature is listed. If the program has features not listed, those can be counted toward the total. The more a program includes these features, the higher score it receives. During observations it may be helpful to photograph the play area(s) to refer to when scoring.

Other items that reflect a high-quality, natural play area include the look and feel of the space, natural materials that reflect local nature, and the extent to which human-made materials represent realistic and local nature.

Evaluating Natureness: Measuring the Quality of Nature-Based Classrooms in Pre-K through 3rd Grade

Item 1: The natural play area has a natural look and feel.

One of the aspects of a natural play area is that it has a natural look and feel. This includes the colors used (earth-based rather than bright), types of materials (natural rather than plastic), and whether a variety of textures are included. Examples of natural materials that might be used include wood structures, grass surfaces, boulders, rocks, soil, and sand. These materials also produce diverse textures for children to experience, and earth-based colors can be used for furnishings and features.

Level 7: The natural play area has an *extensive* natural look and feel (natural materials, diverse textures, earth-based colors).

Natural play areas that score at this level have extensive natural materials, such as wood, used for the structures and furnishings throughout the play space. Earth-based colors, such as greens, blues, and browns, are used, and a diversity of textures, such as sand, water, rocks, trees, flowers, wooden benches, and logs, are found throughout.

Level 5: The natural play area has *some* natural look and feel (mix of natural and plastic furnishings, diverse textures, earth-based colors).

Natural play areas that score at this level have a mix of natural materials, earth-based colors, and textures that make up some of the structures and furnishings. However, these are not necessarily used throughout the play area, and some plastic might be used as well.

Level 3: The natural play area has *limited* natural look and feel (mix of natural and plastic furnishings, diverse textures, primary colors).

Play areas that score at this level have less of a natural look and feel than those at higher levels, as more plastic furnishings and primary colors are apparent. Ground surfaces might be artificial turf rather than grass.

Section III: Environment

Level 1: The natural play area has *no* natural look and feel (plastic furnishings, primary colors).

Play areas at this level have no natural look and feel, as their outdoor area primarily is made up of plastic furnishings and primary colors.

Item 2: The natural play area contains a variety of natural features.

The following levels describe the presence of a variety of natural features that should be found in a natural play area to support children's development. The variety and number of features that support nature play define each level.

Level 7: The natural play area includes *at least seven* of the following: loose parts, a variety of vegetation, a vegetable or herb garden, sand and soil, a water feature, opportunities for active motor play, opportunities for less-active play, a variety of terrain, a mix of sunny and shady areas, a variety of gathering spaces, a variety of features, and a variety of seating and tables.

Natural play areas at this level offer at least seven of the following:

- Loose parts, such as logs, sticks, rocks
- Variety of vegetation, such as trees, shrubs, flowers
- Vegetable or herb garden
- Sand and soil
- Water feature
- Opportunities for active motor play: balancing, climbing, swinging, rolling, and so on
- Opportunities for less-active play: creating, watching, reading, and so on
- Variety of terrain, such as hills, open spaces, grassy areas
- Mix of sunny and shady areas
- Variety of gathering spaces: whole group, such as a circle of stumps, and small group, such as a structure built out of sticks
- Variety of features, such as hideouts, pathways, stages
- Variety of seating and tables, such as stump tables and chairs, logs, wooden benches, picnic tables

Level 5: The natural play area includes *at least five* of the following: loose parts, a variety of vegetation, a vegetable or herb garden, sand and soil, a water feature, opportunities for active motor play, opportunities for less-active play, a variety of terrain, a mix of sunny and shady areas, a variety of gathering spaces, a variety of features, and a variety of seating and tables.

Natural play areas at this level offer five or six of the following:

- Loose parts, such as logs, sticks, and rocks
- Variety of vegetation, such as trees, shrubs, and flowers
- Vegetable or herb garden
- Sand and soil
- Water feature
- Opportunities for active motor play: balancing, climbing, swinging, rolling, and so on
- Opportunities for less-active play: creating, watching, reading, and so on
- Variety of terrain, such as hills, open spaces, and grassy areas
- Mix of sunny and shady areas
- Variety of gathering spaces: whole group, such as a circle of stumps, and small group, such as a structure built out of sticks
- Variety of features, such as hideouts, pathways, and stages
- Variety of seating and tables: stump tables and chairs, logs, wooden benches, and picnic tables

Section III: Environment

Level 3: The natural play area includes *at least three* of the following: loose parts, a variety of vegetation, a vegetable or herb garden, sand and soil, a water feature, opportunities for active motor play, opportunities for less-active play, variety of terrain, a mix of sunny and shady areas, a variety of gathering spaces, a variety of features, and a variety of seating and tables.

Natural play areas at this level offer three or four of the following:

- Loose parts, such as logs, sticks, rocks
- Variety of vegetation, such as trees, shrubs, and flowers
- Vegetable or herb garden
- Sand and soil
- Water feature
- Opportunities for active motor play: balancing, climbing, swinging, rolling, and so on
- Opportunities for less-active play: creating, watching, reading, and so on
- Variety of terrain, such as hills, open spaces, and grassy areas
- Mix of sunny and shady areas
- Variety of gathering spaces: whole group, such as a circle of stumps, and small group, such as a structure built out of sticks
- Variety of features, such as hideouts, pathways, and stages
- Variety of seating and tables: stump tables and chairs, logs, wooden benches, picnic tables

Level 1: The outside play area is a traditional playground (for example, climbing structures, sandbox) with few natural features.

Play areas at this level offer no more than one or two of the features listed in higher levels.

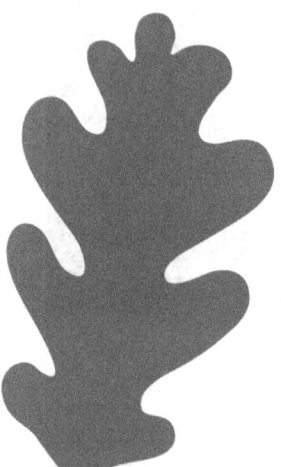

Tips for the Observer: Natural Play Area Features

The following list provides examples of evidence for features that can be observed in the natural play area.

Examples of evidence:

- Gardens and digging areas are available in the outdoor area. These might be raised beds or other types of plantings to which children have access.

- Water features—such as water pumps, hoses, rain barrels, small ponds, and streams—are available for children's exploration and experimentation.

- Natural loose parts—such as logs, stumps, tree cookies, and sticks—are available for children to use in their play.

- Trees are available for children to climb.

- Exposed soil and sand are provided, along with tools for digging.

- A variety of topography, such as hills and open spaces, are placed throughout the natural play area.

- Quiet spaces where children can play alone or in small groups are readily available for children to use to reflect and be peaceful.

Questions to ask if evidence isn't apparent:

- Are there other materials you bring outdoors, in addition to what is here today?

- Tell me about how this play area changes from season to season. For example, are there different materials or features at other times of the year?

- Do children have access to natural materials? If so, what kinds?

Section III: Environment

Tips for Growing: Creating Positive Outdoor Experiences for All Children

If a program has a low score for this item, consider sharing ideas to increase positive outdoor experiences.

Natural loose parts to consider*:

Pine cones	Stumps
Seed pods, such as milkweed pods	Leaves
Acorns	Logs
Rocks	Sticks
Seashells	Soil
Tree cookies (a thin cross-section of a log)	Sand

*When collecting natural materials, be cognizant of Section I, Category A, Item 6 by selecting items that are "dead and down."

Human-made loose parts to consider:

Buckets	PVC pipes
Shovels	Spoons
Rakes	Whisks
Cups	Strainers
Bowls	Buttons
Muffin tins	Nuts and bolts
Bundt pans	Crates
Ropes	Boxes
Pulleys	Art supplies

Item 3: The natural play area includes natural materials that reflect a variety of local nature.

Natural materials are an important part of bringing a natural play area to life and can be used throughout the outside space. These materials should be from the local environment and reflect what children can find in the area, including, for example, tree seeds, bird's nests, sunflower heads grown in the school garden, and local animal pelts

or other animal artifacts. The key to scoring high in this item is that these materials are local and are found throughout the outdoor area.

Level 7: Natural materials (for example, bird parts, animal bones, bird's nests, tree seeds) are present in *all* areas of the natural play area and reflect a variety of local nature.

To score at the highest level, natural materials need to be found in all areas of the natural play area. Materials should also reflect items that would be found in the local area: pelts of local animals, bird's nests found in areas around the school, sunflower seed heads grown in the school garden, and others.

Level 5: Natural materials are present in *most* areas of the natural play area and reflect a variety of local nature.

To score in the mid-range, not all areas of the outdoor play area need to have natural materials, but most of them do. Most should reflect what can be found locally.

Level 3: Natural materials are present in *some* areas of the natural play area and reflect a variety of local nature.

When some areas of the natural play area include natural materials, but most do not, the program would score at this level. The materials should still reflect what is local to the area to score at this level.

Level 1: Natural materials are *not* present.

A program would score at the lowest level if the classroom does not contain any natural materials.

Item 4: Natural play area materials represent realistic and local nature.

Providing materials, whether natural or human made, that are representative of nature that children would find in their own backyard or neighborhood offers a more place-based approach. Realistic materials provide children opportunities to connect with the natural world and local environment. These materials might include animal puppets, books, and dramatic play materials that can be used outside and represent local nature. Realistic tools, such as shovels, buckets, baskets, and so on, are also included.

Level 7: Natural play area materials (for example, puppets, books, dramatic play materials) *almost always* represent realistic and local nature.

Programs that score at the highest level will almost always have outdoor materials that represent realistic and local nature. Puppets would be of animals that children might find if they explored in their own neighborhood; examples include puppets of birds and animals children often see outside. Books represent animals and plants in realistic ways. Tools, such as metal shovels and bamboo rakes, are realistic and work.

Level 5: Natural play area materials *often* represent realistic and local nature.

To score at this level, outdoor materials, such as animal puppets and books, don't always represent realistic and local nature, but they do often. Rain-forest animals (in programs that are not in a rain forest) or books that anthropomorphize animals are more prevalent. Some tools are made out of plastic rather than metal and may not be sturdy enough to use for real, meaningful work.

Level 3: Natural play area materials *sometimes* represent realistic and local nature.

At this level, outdoor materials, such as animal puppets and books, are not very realistic or representative of local nature. Most of the materials represent animals and plants from other regions of the world and are not specific to the region where the school or program is located. If tools are included, they are made out of plastic.

Level 1: No materials represent realistic and local nature.

To score at the lowest level, programs do not have any materials outside that are realistic or represent what is found in the local environment.

Section III: Environment

Category C: Natural Ecosystems (Beyond)

About This Category

This category refers to areas of natural ecosystems for exploration outside the play area. Natural ecosystems are communities rich with living and nonliving components, such as soil and sun. Natural ecosystems may include ponds, rivers, wetlands, marshes, meadows, fields, prairies, lake/beach, vernal pools, or woodlands. They can also include spaces that have been cultivated by humans, such as parks, arboretums, gardens, or ponds. A hallmark of a nature-based program is children's opportunities to explore natural ecosystems, some of which may be wilder. These areas beyond the fenced outdoor play area may be just outside the fence or miles away. Programs may access these beyond spaces by walking or transporting children to them. Ideally, the areas beyond the fence will include a diversity of natural ecosystems so children can experience the uniqueness and richness of a variety of ecosystems. The ecosystems are healthy in that they are rich in biodiversity and have a minimum of exotic and invasive species and thus are rich with natural loose parts and natural features.

Item 1: The class has access to natural ecosystems.

This item focuses on the variety of natural ecosystems available to children to access or visit throughout the year. High-quality nature-based programs provide opportunities for children to access multiple different natural ecosystems, such as hiking in a forest, looking for insects in a prairie, and catching frogs at a pond. The variety of natural places for children to explore provides rich experiences with opportunities to connect and build concepts in multiple contexts and over periods of time. For example, children are able to compare and contrast the areas, such as which one gets more sun, which has more water, which has tall plants, and what types of animals live there. How often programs visit these natural ecosystems is covered under Program Practices on pages 40-41 and 52.

Beyond spaces will come in many forms. Here the school has a wooded section of property adjacent to the more manicured schoolyard.

Level 7: The class accesses *at least three* natural ecosystems (for example, a pond, river, wetland, marsh, meadow, field, prairie, lake/beach, vernal pool, woodland, park) throughout the year.

It's ideal for programs to visit as many different ecosystems as possible throughout the year, but to score a Level 7, programs must visit at least three. For example, at this level a class might visit a lakeshore, a forest, a prairie, and a pond.

Level 5: The class accesses *two* natural ecosystems throughout the year.

To score a Level 5, programs must visit two different natural ecosystems. This might, for example, be a forest and a pond or a park and a field.

Level 3: The class accesses *one* natural ecosystem throughout the year.

Sometimes natural ecosystems are hard to access, but visiting one natural space beyond the fence is always better than none. Thus, programs must visit at least one natural ecosystem to score a Level 3.

Level 1: The class has no access to natural ecosystems outside the natural play area.

Programs that have no access to natural ecosystems will be rated Level 1.

Tips for the Observer: Natural Ecosystems

To distinguish among the ecosystems the group visits, consider the variety of plants, animals, water, and terrain. The following list provides examples of evidence.

Examples of evidence:

- A class visits a forest that contains many different types of trees, possibly some wildflowers (depending on the time of year), a blanket of leaves, squirrels carrying acorns, birds chirping in the trees, and so on.

- A class visits a pond that is teaming with frogs and fish, cattails and other water plants, macroinvertebrates such as crayfish, and others.

- A class visits a beach with seaweed, seashells, hermit crabs, sea glass, driftwood, and so on.

- There are several more types of ecosystems a class might visit, including a prairie, river, lake, or park. (See Tips for Growing on page 167 for more ideas.)

Questions to ask if evidence isn't apparent:

- Where do you go to access natural ecosystems outside the fenced play area?
- How often do classes visit these natural ecosystems?

Tips for Growing: Finding the Beyond Sites

Sometimes, finding sites to explore beyond can be tricky. We particularly hear this challenge from programs in more urban areas. The following are a few places to consider when looking for beyond spaces to visit.

- Apartment-building courtyards
- City parks
- Community gardens
- County parks
- Hiking or biking trails
- Land conservancies
- Rooftop gardens
- State parks
- National parks
- Other private land
- Public or private nature centers
- Public schools
- Sidewalks with trees and planters

Please note, you should always inquire about permits or other permissions that may be needed.

Item 2: The natural ecosystems are healthy.

Whereas the previous item focused on the number of ecosystems a class or school visits, this item focuses on the health of those ecosystems. What makes an ecosystem healthy? A healthy natural ecosystem has rich biodiversity of both plants and animals and lacks exotic and invasive species. Although it is often not possible to have these types of settings available close to a school, when there is a choice of places to visit, preference should be given to healthy spaces over the unhealthy ones. Visiting ecosystems rich with biodiversity gives children opportunities to see how animals and plants rely on each other to survive. They can begin to understand the needs of the plants and animals and how each different type of ecosystem provides those needs and, therefore, why plants and animals make that space their home.

Level 7: The natural ecosystems are *almost always* healthy (rich biodiversity and minimal exotic and invasive species).

At a Level 7, classes visit ecosystems that are rich in biodiversity, allowing children to explore and discover the variety of plants and animals that live there. For example, visiting a river, pond, or lake to study macroinvertebrates, such as crayfish, dragonflies, and snails, can help the children identify the health of the ecosystem. The types of organisms found in the water provide clues as to how clean the water is, as some types of larvae can only survive in clean water.

Level 5: The natural ecosystems are *often* healthy.

Classes scoring at a Level 5 have some healthy ecosystems for children to visit, but not always. For example, children might visit a forest that has few invasive plants but also visit a city park that contains several invasive species. One way to determine invasive species is to take a field guide along. The children can help identify the plants and keep track of the number of different species they find.

Level 3: The natural ecosystems are *sometimes* healthy.

Classes that score at this level visit natural ecosystems that are rarely healthy. This means the places are full of invasive plants and exotic species, not species that are local. The ecosystems will have all the same types of plants, such as a forest with no variety of trees and with invasive plants such as garlic mustard growing rampant. To help children identify an invasive plant, refer to a field guide. If the plant is not toxic or potentially harmful, they can help to pull it out as a service project. But not being able to see a diversity of species and how they interact is unfortunate.

Level 1: The natural ecosystems are *never* healthy *or* they are nonexistent.

Level 1 classes may visit a natural ecosystem, but the condition of the ecosystem is not healthy, or they do not visit natural ecosystems.

Healthy or Not?

Determining whether an ecosystem is healthy is difficult, even for well-trained ecologists. Local conservation organizations can help you find healthy ecosystems in your region. Consider reaching out to your state's department of natural resources, state extension offices, native plant societies, local Nature Conservancy chapters, local land conservancies, or similar organizations for assistance.

Item 3: The natural ecosystem includes loose parts and natural features.

In addition to the number and health of ecosystems, it's important to consider the number of loose parts and natural features found there. Natural loose parts, such as logs, boulders, sticks, rocks, and tree stumps, provide materials children can explore and use for building. Natural features might include trees, flowers, and wildlife that children can see when visiting the area. The extent to which an area has loose parts and natural features may determine how the area is used and how engaging it is for children. For example, loose parts allow children opportunities for dramatic play such as building forts. When wildlife is abundant, children will seek it by, for example, turning a log over to find insects or watching a butterfly sip nectar from a flower. If an area has no natural features to explore, the children may become bored and not find an interest in their surroundings. Thus, ecosystems rich with a variety of loose parts and natural features are best suited for nature-based programs.

Level 7: There are *many* loose parts and natural features to interact with (for example, trees, flowers, wildlife).

Classes scoring at this level will have extensive loose parts and natural features for children's exploration and engagement. For example, visiting a prairie, children will find many loose parts to interact with, such as grasses, seeds, dried flowers, sticks, and milkweed pods. Natural features might include paths through the grasses, birds, nests, and insects.

Level 5: There are *some* loose parts and natural features to interact with (trees, flowers, wildlife).

Classes scoring at this level will have some loose parts and natural features, but not a huge variety. As a result, children may be engaged but not for as long as they would be if there were more loose parts and features. For example, a sandy beach that has been cleared of its driftwood and sticks could be a boring place for children to interact with the natural world.

Level 3: There are *few* loose parts and natural features to interact with.

Classes scoring at this level have little in terms of loose parts or natural features available in the ecosystem.

Level 1: There are *no* loose parts and natural features to interact with, *or* there is no ecosystem available to visit.

Classes scoring at this level do not have any loose parts or natural features available, or there is no ecosystem available to visit.

Tips for Growing: Materials to Take to the Beyond

Field guides	Aquaria
Mirrors	Sheets/tarps
Magnifiers	Ropes
Spoons	Books
Buckets	Art supplies

Tips for the Observer: Loose Parts and Natural Features Available in Different Ecosystems

The following list provides examples of evidence for this item. Additional questions are provided to ask if evidence isn't apparent.

Examples of evidence:

- In a woodland or forest, natural features might include boulders, large logs, rooted tree stumps, trees, wildflowers, and easily seen wildlife such as squirrels, deer, birds, and insects under a log.

- In a woodland or forest, loose parts might include logs, loose tree stumps, sticks, and rocks that can be manipulated and used in dramatic play or building forts.

- In a prairie or meadow, natural features might include prairie plants, grasses, and easily seen wildlife such as butterflies, grasshoppers, and snakes.

- In a prairie or meadow, loose parts might include seed pods such as milkweed, sticks, dried plants, and dandelion seeds. (See page 160 for more examples of loose parts.)

Questions to ask if evidence isn't apparent:

- Describe the natural ecosystems you visit with the children. What types of features are there? What types of loose parts are available for the children to use when in the ecosystem?

- Talk a bit about children's engagement in the different places they visit beyond the fence. Do they get bored and find it difficult to interact with the space, or do they get deeply lost in play?

Section IV:
Community Partnerships and Resources

Strong relationships between a school and the outside community not only help support academic achievement in children but also help to contribute to the sustained success of a program (Epstein, 2010), as well as the community organization. In addition, building partnerships with the community can help families learn more about local nature-based resources. This section focuses on how programs use local nature-based organizations, the resources they have available on site, and how additional programs are incorporated into the ongoing curriculum.

Category A: Nature Educator

About This Category

The items in this category are related to the presence of a nature educator and the role the nature educator plays in the current program. A nature educator is an expert in natural history, ecology, outdoor education, interpretation, or a related field; examples might include a naturalist from a nature center who visits the classroom regularly, a nature or science specialist or coach who supports nature-based education in the school or district, or a child's family member with nature-based expertise.

Regular visits from a nature educator allow children to form a personal relationship with the educator in which they feel comfortable asking questions and sharing their thoughts. Such visits also provide opportunities for the educator to build on nature concepts previously discussed with the children. In addition, a nature educator can model best practices in nature-based education for the teachers, thus building their capacity to lead interactions with nature as part of the regular class day.

High-scoring nature programs will demonstrate a strong ongoing relationship with a nature educator through regular visits to the classroom. Programs scoring in the medium range will have a nature educator who visits monthly or seasonally, or the nature educator may be a different person every visit. Programs scoring low in this category may not have a nature expert visit the classroom at all.

Item 1: The nature educator visits frequently.

This item focuses on how often a nature educator visits a classroom. The more often a nature educator is present in the classroom, the more opportunities both children and teachers have to learn *with* and *about* nature.

Level 7: Nature educator visits at least *once a week*.

The highest scoring classrooms have frequent access to a nature educator. This is demonstrated through at least weekly visits to the classroom, but the visits could be as frequent as every day. The nature educator may be the classroom teacher, if they have training in nature-based education. (See the category on teacher qualifications.)

Level 5: Nature educator visits at least *once a month*.

To score at this level, classrooms will have a nature educator visit at least once every month. For example, a class that has a nature educator visit two times per month would score a Level 5.

Level 3: Nature educator visits *seasonally*.

To score at this level, classrooms will have a nature educator visit three to four times a year. These visits may or may not align with the seasons exactly, but the emphasis here is multiple times a year and less than monthly.

Level 1: Nature educator visits *once per year or less*.

To score at this level, classrooms will have a nature educator visit once a year or less. If a classroom does not have a nature educator visitor, it would earn a score of Level 1.

Tips for the Observer: Nature Educator Visits Frequently

Depending on when an observation takes place, the observer may not have an opportunity to interact with the nature educator. If a nature educator is not present during the observation, the observer can look for the following evidence:

Examples of evidence:

- Look at the classroom schedule or monthly calendar to see if a nature educator is listed.
- Children might mention a nature educator with statements like, "Remember last week when Maya came and took us on the trail to the pond?"
- Photos are displayed of a nature educator working with children in the class.

Questions to ask if evidence isn't apparent:

- Do you have a relationship with a nature educator or environmental education expert? If so, do they visit your classroom? How often?
- What is the role of a nature educator in your classroom?

Item 2: The program has a strong, supportive relationship with the same nature educator.

In addition to a nature educator visiting frequently, it is helpful if the nature educator is the same person from visit to visit. This encourages an ongoing relationship between the nature educator and the students. Having the same nature educator visit allows the educator to build a deeper relationship with the children and the teacher, which in turn supports learning that builds over time while also connecting to each individual's strengths and interests. The ongoing relationship also helps the nature educator provide more individualized instruction. Instead of spending time every visit getting to know the children, the nature educator can pick up where a previous lesson ended and more easily tailor instruction to the current curriculum topic.

Level 7: Nature educator is *almost always* the same individual.

To score at this level, classrooms will have a strong, ongoing relationship with a nature educator. As with any teacher, there may be occasions when the nature educator has to be absent, but this is rare. Generally, the classroom teacher and children expect the same person to visit each time.

Level 5: Nature educator is *often* the same individual.

A program may earn a Level 5 score if the nature educator is often the same individual, but at times it may be a different person. Evidence for this might include children asking the classroom teacher if the nature educator today will be, for example, Marcus or Lauren.

Level 3: Nature educator is *sometimes* the same individual.

In a Level 3 classroom, the nature educator is occasionally the same individual but often is a different person.

Level 1: The program has *no* relationship with a nature educator.

A classroom will earn this score if there is no evidence of a relationship with a nature educator.

> ### Tips for the Observer: Ongoing Relationship with the Same Nature Educator
>
> Depending on when an observation takes place, the observer may not have an opportunity to interact with the nature educator. If a nature educator is not present during the observation, the observer can look for the following evidence of an ongoing relationship.
>
> **Examples of evidence:**
>
> - Pictures in the classroom show multiple experiences with a nature educator.
> - There is a schedule of visits by a nature educator.
> - Children ask the classroom teacher in advance if "X" or "Y" educator will be attending.
> - Children use the nature educator's name.
> - The nature educator, teacher, and children refer to prior experiences together.
>
> **Questions to ask if evidence isn't apparent:**
>
> - Do you have a nature educator who visits regularly?
> - How often is the nature educator the same person? How often is it a different person?

Category B: Artifacts/Resources—On-Site

About This Category

The items in this category refer to a class's access to artifacts and resources that support a nature-based curriculum but cannot be stored inside the classroom. These might include live animals such as raptors, gardens for growing food, a greenhouse, an apiary, a sugarhouse for making maple syrup, or diverse habitats for discussing healthy ecosystems. These artifacts might be stored on the school property at all times for teacher and children's use, but they could also be shared between community organizations.

Classrooms scoring high in this category will have a variety of artifacts, resources, and animals available for classroom use whenever they are needed to support the ongoing curriculum. Classrooms scoring in the mid-range may have access to a variety of artifacts, resources, and animals, but they are not readily available. For example, a class might need to coordinate with a local museum to use their skins and skulls artifacts. A program scoring low on this category will not have access to artifacts, resources, or animals.

Item 1: The program has access to artifacts and resources.

This item highlights the importance of programs having access to a variety of artifacts and resources to support and enrich the nature-based curriculum. Ideally, programs will have regular and immediate access to a variety of artifacts and resources. However, there are times when a program or school may share resources with another classroom in the school building or with another community organization, such as a local nature center.

Level 7: The class *almost always* has access to a variety of artifacts and resources on the school grounds (for example, diverse habitats, greenhouses, apiary, raptors, sugarhouse, gardens).

Classrooms earn this score if they have a variety of resources available and easily accessible to help support the ongoing curriculum. Classrooms are able to access these resources immediately when they fit in with the ongoing curriculum; classes don't have to wait weeks to access the resource. For example, if children notice large birds circling overhead, the teacher could explain the birds are called *turkey vultures* and could take the children on a trip to the on-site raptor center to give them a closer look at the birds they observed in the sky. A class at this level could also take a trip to the greenhouse or gardens on the property when classrooms are discussing where food comes from.

Level 5: The class *often* has access to a variety of artifacts and resources on the school grounds.

Classrooms scoring at this level have a variety of artifacts and resources available to use, but these need to be coordinated with other classrooms or programs. For example, the class might have its own set of animal skulls but must borrow animal pelts from a shared library.

Level 3: The class *sometimes* has access to a variety of artifacts and resources on the school grounds.

Classrooms scoring at this level rarely have access to a variety of artifacts and resources. They may need to coordinate with a local community organization to access resources. For example, a class might coordinate with a local nature center or museum to borrow an insect collection for an activity. In this example, the class does not have immediate access to the artifacts. Community organizations may have waiting lists for artifacts and resources that could delay when a program can use the materials.

Level 1: The class *does not* have access to a variety of artifacts and resources on the school grounds.

Classrooms scoring at this level do not have artifacts or resources available for classroom use.

Tips for the Observer: Access to Artifacts and Resources

Classrooms might have special collections displayed around the indoor classroom, outdoor play area, or around the school. If it is not apparent that artifacts are available or clear how classrooms acquire them, the observer might look for the following evidence.

Examples of evidence:

- Special natural or historical collections are available for use, such as animal skins and skulls and bird-egg replicas.
- Unique or seasonal artifacts are apparent, such as a sugarhouse for turning sap into syrup or an apiary for caring for bees.

Questions to ask if evidence isn't apparent:

- Where are resources and artifacts stored?
- What types of collections do you use with your teaching?
- Do you need to make a special request for resources or artifacts?
- Do you share resources and artifacts with other programs or community organizations?

> ## Tips for Growing: Artifacts and Resources
>
> Here are some ways to increase access to artifacts and resources.
>
> - Contact a local nature center to rent or borrow materials.
> - See if families have expertise, artifacts, and/or resources to contribute.
> - Hold a fundraiser to purchase artifacts.
> - Share the purchase and use of artifacts with other programs or organizations.

Item 2: Wild and/or domestic animals are available to support nature-based learning.

Animals provide wonderful opportunities for children's learning. This item examines the availability of wild and/or domestic animals to support topics and the curriculum overall. Although having access to both wild and domestic animals is encouraged, this item focuses on a classroom's access to any animals available to support nature-based learning. Wild animals may include rehabilitated wildlife such as raptors, oppossums, turtles, and snakes. The animals may be housed on-site, or the school might work with a rehabilitation specialist who conducts educational programs and visits the school periodically.

Ideally, wild animals available in the program will be ones that can be found in the local community. However, given that wild animals will primarily be rehabilitated animals, they may not be native to the program's location. Domestic animals might include rabbits, guinea pigs, chinchillas, fish, Madagascar hissing cockroaches, snakes, turtles, goats, and chickens. For classrooms looking to incorporate more animals into their program, please see Tips for Growing: Plants and Animals (page 151) for suggested resources. (Note: Programs should adhere to all local and federal laws regarding the housing of both wild and domestic animals, including securing all necessary permits. Additionally, some states' licensing regulations have limits on what animals are acceptable in a classroom.)

Level 7: Wild and/or domestic animals are *almost always* available to support programs (for example, wildlife rehab education animal or a class pet).

To score at this level, a classroom will have regular access to wild and/or domestic animals and use these animals to support the curriculum. For example, children can interact with a classroom pet rabbit by feeding it or giving it water. Or the program may have raptors kept on site the class can visit whenever they choose.

Level 5: Wild and/or domestic animals are *often* available to support programs.

To score at this level, a program may have animals present, but classes are unable to access them regularly. For example, a class that is part of a nature center may have to

schedule a month in advance to see animals. If classes do not have a class pet or other regular access to animals, then the program would score a Level 5.

Level 3: Wild and/or domestic animals are *sometimes* available to support programs.

To score at this level, a class may have animals present on the school property, but the class is unable to or chooses not to use them to support the curriculum.

Level 1: Wild and/or domestic animals are *not* available to support programs.

A program that does not have access to any animals to support the curriculum will score at this level.

> ## Tips for the Observer: Wild and/or Domestic Animals
>
> To determine to what extent animals are used in the classroom, observers should look for the following evidence.
>
> **Examples of evidence:**
>
> - Animal cages, aquaria, and so on, inside the classroom
> - Pictures in the classroom of children visiting or engaging with animals
> - Language by teachers and/or children referencing animals they have encountered
>
> **Questions to ask if evidence isn't apparent:**
>
> - Tell me about your classroom pets or other animals children interact with during the day.
> - How often, if ever, do you have visitors bring animals into the classroom?

Category C: Special Programs—Field Trips

About This Category

The natural world is vast, and it comes in many different forms. It's nearly impossible for a school to have all of the different forms on-site. Thus, many programs organize field trips to other locations, such as a nature center, zoo, arboretum, children's garden, apple orchard, or dairy farm. Nature-based field trips help promote environmental awareness and a closer connection to nature in children (Dopko et al., 2019; Heras, Medir, and Salazar, 2020). In addition, they have been shown to promote children's social and emotional development (Dopko et al., 2019; Heras, Medir, and Salazar, 2020).

However, for these field trips to be the most beneficial, they need to be integrated into the ongoing curriculum. Research has shown that more positive student outcomes are associated with the extent to which a field trip has been introduced to children and with the subsequent classroom follow up (Lee, Stern, and Powell, 2020). For example, before a trip to an apple orchard, teachers might talk with children about where food comes from. After the field trip, the children might discuss what foods they would like to grow in their classroom garden and begin to plant and care for a garden of their own.

A program may be part of one of these locations, but classes might be required to schedule a time to visit for the trip to be considered a "field trip." This category examines how frequently a program has access to nature-based programs that occur at another location (i.e., field trips) and the extent to which these programs are integrated into the ongoing curriculum. Higher-quality nature-based programs will take multiple field trips in a school year, and these experiences will be integrated into the ongoing classroom curriculum. Mid-range programs may only take one nature-based field trip a school year, and it may or may not be integrated into the ongoing curriculum. A low-scoring program will not go on any nature-based field trips.

Item 1: The program attends nature-based field trips that are integrated into the curriculum.

Level 7: Children attend special nature-based programs (for example, nature center, zoo, arboretum, apple orchard, dairy farm) away from the school (field trips) at least *two* times per year, *and* these experiences <u>are</u> integrated into the classroom curriculum.

To earn a Level 7, a program will take at least two nature-based field trips each year. These could be to different places or to the same place multiple times a year. Additionally, there are classroom activities leading up to and after the field-trip experience. If a classroom is part of a typical field-trip location, such as a nature center or zoo, an experience above and beyond the typical day needs to be scheduled for the trip to count as a field trip. For example, a typical day at a zoo-based program may be walking around and seeing the animals, but a field trip could include a scheduled time for the zoologist to talk with the children.

Level 5: Children attend special nature-based programs at least *one* time per year *and* these experiences <u>are</u> integrated into the classroom curriculum.

To earn a Level 5, a program will attend at least one nature-based field trip a year, and this experience is part of the ongoing curriculum, with classroom activities leading up to and after the experience. For example, a class might discuss plants—what they need to survive, which plants grow in certain areas,

and so on–prior to a field trip to a children's garden. After the field trip, the children might discuss invasive plants and work to safely remove them from a local area.

Level 3: Children attend special nature-based programs at least *one* time per year *but* experiences <u>are not</u> integrated into the classroom curriculum.

In contrast to Level 5, programs at Level 3 also attend at least one nature-based field trip a year, but this experience is a standalone activity and is not part of the ongoing curriculum. An example of this could be a class going to a pumpkin patch in the fall, with no classroom activities pre- or post-field trip related to pumpkins.

Level 1: Children take no nature-based field trips during the school year.

If a program does go on field trips, but they are not nature based, such as going to the movies, it would earn a Level 1.

Tips for the Observer: Nature-Based Field Trips

Because we encourage observations on typical days, it is unlikely that an observation will take place when a classroom is on a field trip. Therefore, the observer will need to look for examples or ask the teacher for evidence related to field trips. Here are some suggestions.

Examples of evidence:

- Photos of field trips that are not part of the nature-based classroom
- A schedule of upcoming field trips
- Teachers refer to previous trips, saying something like, "Remember, when we went to visit the goat farm?"

Questions to ask if evidence isn't apparent:

- Have you gone on any field trips this year? Where have you gone?
- Do you have any field trips planned? Where will you go?
- How do you prepare for field trips?
- What, if any, follow-up activities do you plan related to the field trip?

Section V:
Family Engagement

It is important to engage and build connections with the families whose children attend nature-based programs. Not only do families need to be kept up to date on what is going on in the classroom, but building connections with them helps a program to be inclusive to all who attend. Research has shown that strong home and school connections are associated with positive outcomes for children (Galindo and Sheldon, 2012). Finally, nature-based classrooms have an additional responsibility of communicating the benefits of a nature-based approach to families and other stakeholders.

Category A: Family Communication and Education

About This Category

Clear communication with and education for families about the benefits of nature experiences for young children is an important component of a quality nature-based program. This communication happens both formally, through written communication with families such as in newsletters or mission statements, orientations, and program philosophy, and informally, through posting pictures, student work, and whole-class artifacts of nature-based learning.

Highest-rated nature-based classrooms will demonstrate strong connections between the school and home environments by communicating frequently with families. This communication will include nature-related content that includes the benefits of nature, nature-based activities to do at home, and even nature-related community activities. Additionally, communication with families should provide information and documentation about the various nature-based activities that are happening in their child's classroom. This allows families to talk about, connect to, and build on learning that is happening in the classroom when children are out of school.

Item 1: The program shares nature-related content to families through formal communication.

This item focuses on the extent to which nature-related content is shared with families through formal communication. It is important that programs share with families their approach to nature and how it is embedded within the classroom and curriculum. This should be done in multiple methods of communication throughout the school year.

Level 7: Nature-related content (benefits of nature, activities to do at home, appropriate clothing) is embedded in *all* of these communication methods: family handbook, family orientation, family newsletter, reports of classroom activities to families, and family-teacher conferences.

Classrooms scoring at this level will communicate with families about nature-related content in all of the methods listed above. The family handbook should include the program's mission statement and overall philosophy related to nature and have a section on appropriate clothing for children to wear (or pack) for the weather. This information can be part of a nature-specific handbook or the entire-school handbook, or it might be included in separate letters to families, but all methods need to be used with families to score a Level 7 in this category.

Level 5: Nature-related content is embedded in *most* of these communication methods: family handbook, family orientation, family newsletter, reports of classroom activities to families, and family-teacher conferences.

Programs scoring at this level will communicate with families about nature-related content in most of the methods listed above. For example, if a program's handbook, newsletters, reports, and conferences all contain nature-related information, but they do not have a family orientation or the family orientation does not discuss nature-related content, the program would earn a score of Level 5 on this item.

Level 3: Nature-related content is embedded in *some* of these communication methods: family handbook, family orientation, family newsletter, reports of classroom activities to families, and family-teacher conferences.

Programs scoring at this level will share nature-related content with families through some of the methods listed above. For example, the family handbook and weekly newsletters may discuss nature-related activities, but nature is not part of other methods of communication.

Level 1: No nature-related content in family communication.

Programs scoring at this level may communicate regularly with families, but this communication lacks any information about nature-related content.

Tips for the Observer: Nature-Related Communication

During a classroom observation, the observer may notice evidence of nature-related communication throughout the room. If not, they should look for the following evidence.

Examples of evidence:

- Handbook shared with families
- Newsletters
- Weekly schedules posted around the classroom
- Template or form used for planning family-teacher conferences

Questions to ask if evidence isn't apparent:

- In what ways do you communicate with the families in program? May I see some examples?
- Does your program offer a family orientation? What does that consist of?
- Do you hold family-teacher conferences? If so, to what extent is nature-related content discussed during conferences?

Item 2: The program documents its nature-based activities and shares documentation with families.

An important element of any early childhood classroom is communication with families about the activities and learning their children are engaging with each day. Nature-based programs are no different. This communication allows families to ask deeper questions about their children's day and make learning connections when children are out of school. This item addresses the extent to which documentation of nature-based learning happening in the classroom is shared with families. Documentation might include photos or videos of children's play, samples of children's drawings, samples of children's writing, group or individual journal entries, and more. This documentation can be shared on an ongoing basis through classroom displays, school hallway and lobby displays, printed or emailed newsletters, texts, online document-sharing programs, and so on. Documentation can also be shared during periodic family-teacher conferences.

Level 7: *Extensive* documentation of nature-based activities and/or projects is posted.

Classrooms earning this score will display extensive evidence of nature-based activities, projects, and additional elements of the ongoing curriculum throughout the classroom. For example, a classroom might have an ongoing chart posted on which the class keeps track of a plant's growth for a science activity, children's drawings of nature are posted throughout the classroom, class-created books about nature are in the book area, and journals are available for children to record their experiences in nature.

Level 5: *Moderate* documentation of nature-based activities and/or projects is posted.

Classrooms earning this score will display a moderate amount of evidence of nature-based activities, projects, or additional elements of the ongoing curriculum throughout the classroom. This could mean some activities are displayed, but not a majority. For example, children's artwork may be displayed throughout the classroom and a monthly newsletter is sent to families about the nature activities within the classroom.

Level 3: *Minimal* documentation of nature-based activities and/or projects is posted.

Classrooms earning this score will display a minimal amount of evidence of nature-based activities, projects, or additional elements of the ongoing curriculum throughout the classroom. For example, there might be photos displayed from a previous field trip, but no child work is displayed.

Level 1: *No* documentation of nature-based activities and/or projects is posted.

Classrooms earning this score will display no evidence of nature-based activities, projects, or additional elements of the ongoing curriculum in the classroom. In addition, classrooms may earn this score if they display evidence of children's work, but it is not related to the nature-based curriculum.

Tips for the Observer: Documentation of Nature-Based Activities

Throughout an observation, the observer should look for the following evidence of nature-based activities:

Examples of evidence:

- Posters of classroom nature activities
- Displays of children's writing or art
- Baskets of journals
- Group journal
- Newsletters
- Photos or videos of nature activities

Questions to ask if evidence isn't apparent:

- How do you share with families the nature-based activities that occur as part of the class?
- Do you use a document-sharing system for communicating with families? If so, what do you typically share with them?

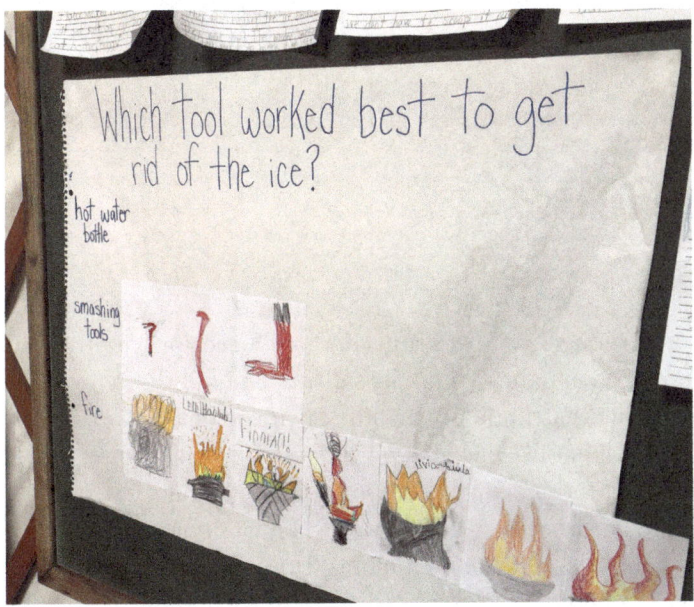

Section V: Family Engagement

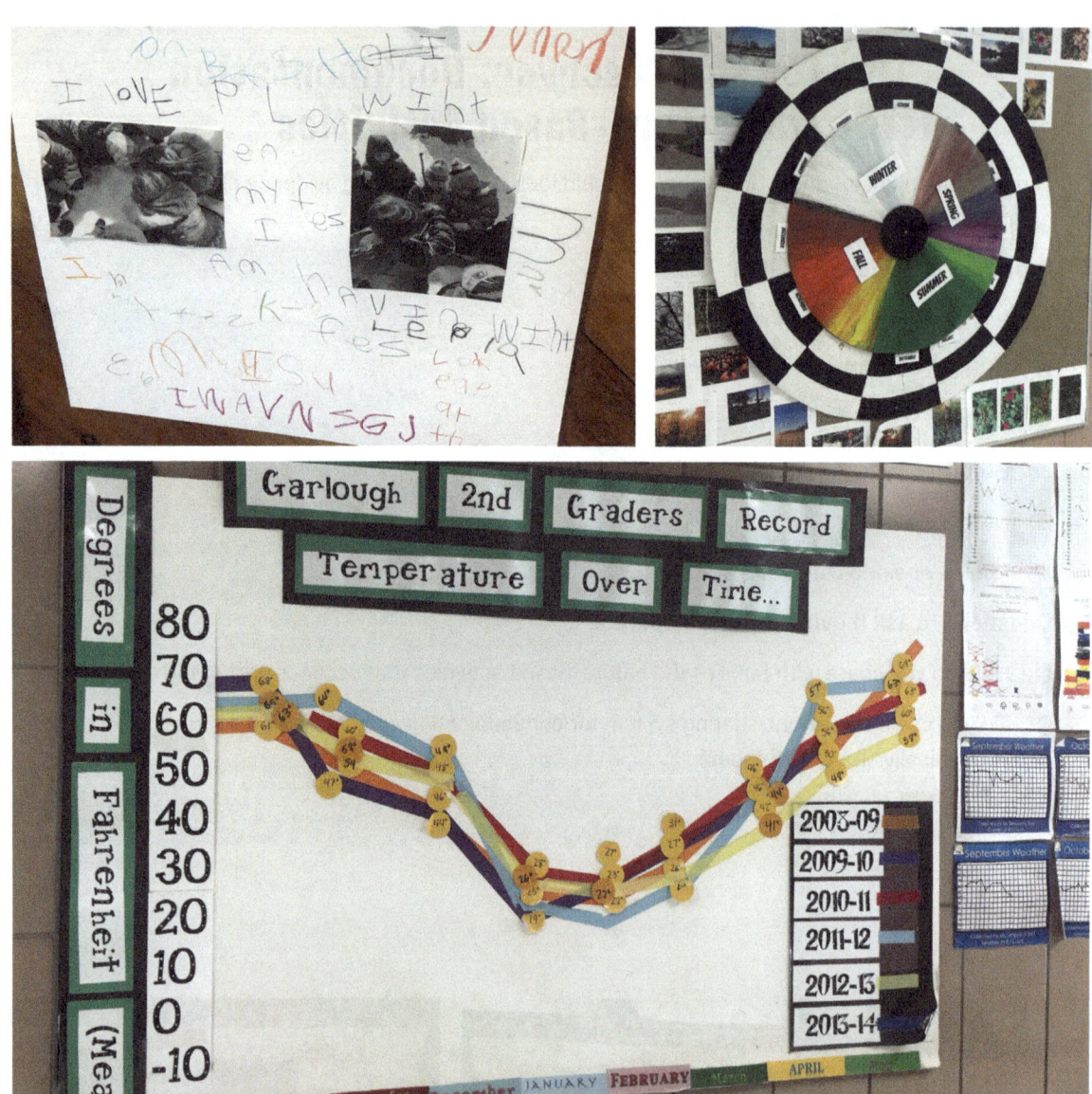

Category B: Family Nature Experiences

About This Category

This category focuses on the types and frequency of programs and resources provided to families to facilitate positive experiences in nature. A family's attitude about the environment is a strong predictor of a child's attitude toward the environment (Eagles and Demare, 1999). Providing families with nature-based experiences and resources allows them to develop a more positive attitude toward their environment, while also stimulating a deeper connection to nature. These experiences help support environmental awareness, not only in children but also in families (Dopko et al., 2019; Heras, Medir, and Salazar, 2020). When children are able to share nature-based experiences with their families, it helps to reinforce their understanding of nature-based topics. In addition, families are more likely to adopt lasting conservation practices when they are offered follow-up resources around a nature-based experience (Hughes et al., 2011), which school-supported activities usually do.

Programs scoring high in this category will offer numerous opportunities for families to engage in nature-based programs and will share resources available in the community for families to access. Programs earning a medium score will occasionally offer nature-based programs and share nature-based activities available within the community. Programs scoring low in this category will not offer nature-based activities for families; nor will they provide community resources to families related to nature.

Item 1: The program offers nature-based family programs.

This item focuses on the frequency with which nature-based programs are offered to families. Programs may be designed for the whole family, or they may be adult-only programs to help adults cultivate their own appreciation for nature. To be counted in this item, an activity must be related to nature. For example, an indoor family meet and greet would not count, but an outdoor campfire meet and greet would. Examples of programs offered about nature include owl hikes; camping excursions; scavenger hunts on the school property; bird watching; catching frogs or insects; sunrise/sunset watching; learning about composting, recycling, or urban farming; and excursions to local parks, farms, or nature centers. These activities could be offered by the classroom or for the entire program or school (if applicable).

Level 7: At least *three* seasonal, nature-based family programs (for example, owl hikes, camping, catching frogs or insects) are offered annually.

To score at this level, a program must offer three or more nature-based programs for adults or families each year. This could include three different programs or one program offered at three different times per year. For example, a program might offer an adult night hike in the fall and spring (two times a year) and a sunset drawing activity for families. This program would earn a score of Level 7.

Level 5: At least *two* seasonal, nature-based family programs are offered annually.

To score at this level, a program must offer two nature-based programs for adults or families each year. This might include two different programs or one program offered two different times per year. For example, a program might hold a yearly family camping night and schedule one day a year when families can volunteer to clean up a local natural area.

Level 3: At least *one* seasonal, nature-based family program is offered annually.

To score at this level, a program must offer one nature-based program for adults or families per year.

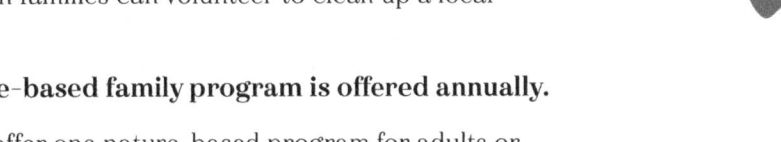

Level 1: No nature-based family programs are offered either inside or outside of the school.

A program that offers no additional nature-based programs will score at this level.

> ### Tips for the Observer: Nature-Based Family Programs
>
> An observer may see evidence of nature-based family programs offered throughout the classroom. If not, they may need to ask to see examples such as the following.
>
> **Examples of evidence:**
>
> - School calendar, including family/adult-only nature-based events
> - Newsletter promoting or reporting on events
> - Poster on family bulletin board announcing upcoming events
>
> **Question to ask if evidence isn't apparent:**
>
> Do you offer any family or adult-only events that are nature based?

Item 2: The program shares community resources and events about nature with families.

This item focuses on the frequency in which community events are shared with families. Sharing community nature-based events not only gives families opportunities to interact with nature but also helps build connections within the community. These connections to the community can help promote positive educational outcomes and also help ensure a program's longevity (NAAEE, 2019). Community events can be shared with families through a newsletter, bulletin board, or conversations.

Level 7: Community resources for family experiences in nature are *almost always* included in family newsletters and/or weekly reports.

To earn this score, teachers will regularly communicate community nature-based events to families. Families will be updated weekly on local events about nature.

Level 5: Community resources for family experiences in nature are *often* included in family newsletters and/or weekly reports.

To earn this score, teachers will sometimes communicate community nature-based events to families. This may include sharing local events once a month or less often.

Level 3: Community resources for family experiences in nature are *sometimes* included in family newsletters and/or weekly reports.

To earn this score, teachers will rarely communicate community nature-based events to families. This may include sharing local events once or twice a year.

Level 1: No community resources are shared with families.

To earn this score, teachers will not share community events with families.

Tips for the Observer: Community Resources and Events

The following can be used to determine to what extent community resources are shared with families.

Examples of evidence:

- Community events section in family newsletter
- Bulletin board on community events

Question to ask if evidence isn't apparent:

Do you share community events with families? If so, how do you share these events?

Tips for Growing: Finding Community Resources and Events

Here are some ideas of places to look for upcoming community events and resources to share with families.

- Local nature center, watershed, or community park
- Local, state, or federal department of parks and recreation
- Local, state, or federal department of natural resources
- Nature conservatory organizations

Category C: Family Involvement

About This Category

The focus of this category is the extent to which families are involved in nature-based classroom activities. Families are a vital part of children's education and are often referred to as children's first teachers. Research has shown that families' involvement in their children's education is associated with more positive outcomes, including improvements in social skills and declines in problem behaviors (El Nokali, Bachman, and Votruba-Drzal, 2010). Nature-based education provides an opportunity for families not only to volunteer their time but also to share any nature-based expertise they have.

A classroom scoring high on this category will actively try to encourage families to be involved in the classroom. A classroom scoring in the mid-range might ask families to sign up to visit the classroom only a few times per school year. A classroom scoring low in this category might not ask families to be involved in the classroom.

Item 1: Families are encouraged to share their expertise and experiences in nature-based activities with the class.

The focus of this item is on how often families are encouraged to share their experiences and expertise with nature with the class. This can include a family sharing home nature-based practices, such as farming or beekeeping, or a nature-based experience such as a recent camping trip or a day spent picking up litter on a local trail. It could also include a family member sharing their nature-based profession or hobby, such as taking the class birdwatching or creating art with nature.

Level 7: Families are *almost always* encouraged to share their expertise and experiences in nature-based activities with the class.

To score at this level, teachers will encourage families to share their interests in nature with the class. Teachers can offer an ongoing sign-up sheet or approach families about sharing with the class. For example, a family could be asked to share about their family farm or a recent trip to a national park.

Level 5: Families are *often* encouraged to share their expertise and experiences in nature-based activities with the class.

To score at this level, teachers will encourage families to share their nature-based experiences, but they may not do this regularly. For example, a sign-up sheet might be available once every few months. Or a program might offer an after-school event with family members sharing their expertise.

Level 3: Families are *sometimes* encouraged to share their expertise and experiences in nature-based activities with the class.

At this level, teachers rarely encourage families to share their interests in nature with the class. For example, teachers may mention to families the class would be interested in hearing about their expertise but might not follow up with families to schedule a time to share with the class.

Level 1: Families are *not* encouraged to share their expertise and experiences in nature-based activities with the class.

At this level, families do not share nature-based activities with the class. Families might be involved in other areas of the classroom, but this is not related to nature-based activities. For example, a family may share about a recent trip to an amusement park.

Tips for the Observer: Family Expertise and Experiences

Given that observations are scheduled on typical days, it will be unusual for an observer to see a family member sharing their nature expertise or experience with the class. With that in mind, an observer may look for the following evidence to determine the extent to which families are encouraged to share their nature-based expertise and experiences with the class.

Examples of evidence:

- Family volunteers are mentioned in the family handbook.
- There is sign-up sheet for family presentations.
- Photos of family members interacting with the class are displayed in the classroom.

Questions to ask if evidence isn't apparent:

- Do you have families share their nature-based expertise with the class?
- If so, how often? What do these events look like?

Item 2: The program encourages family volunteers to participate in nature-based classroom activities.

The focus of this item is on how often families are encouraged to volunteer within the nature-based classroom. Having families volunteer not only provides the teachers with an extra pair of hands but also allows families to actively engage in their children's learning. (Note: Families are often very busy and can have difficulty finding time to volunteer in the classroom. This item is focused on the efforts the teacher makes to elicit family involvement, not to the number of times or amount of time families are able to volunteer.)

Level 7: Families are *almost always* encouraged to volunteer to participate in nature-based classroom activities.

To score at this level, teachers will regularly, such as each month, encourage families to volunteer in the classroom. For example, at the end of every newsletter, the teacher could mention they are always looking for classroom volunteers. See Tips for Growing (page 193) for examples of activities for which families can volunteer.

Level 5: Families are *often* encouraged to volunteer to participate in nature-based classroom activities.

To score at this level, teachers will encourage family members to volunteer but may not do so regularly. For example, a sign-up sheet may be offered every few months but then taken down after a week.

Level 3: Families are *sometimes* encouraged to volunteer to participate in nature-based classroom activities.

Programs in which teachers sometimes encourage families to volunteer in the classroom will score at this level. For example, at orientation the teacher may share that they welcome family volunteers but then never follows up with families to ask them to volunteer.

Level 1: Families are *not* encouraged to volunteer to participate in nature-based classroom activities.

Programs in which families are not encouraged to volunteer as part of the classroom will score at this level.

Tips for the Observer: Family Volunteers

During an observation, family volunteers may or may not be present. An observer should look for the following evidence of family volunteers within the classroom.

Examples of evidence:

- A family sign-up sheet is on display.
- There is mention in the class newsletter or family handbook of volunteer opportunities.

Questions to ask if evidence isn't apparent:

- How often, if ever, do families volunteer in your classroom?
- When volunteers are here, what do they typically do?

Tips for Growing: Family Volunteer Opportunities

Following are some ideas of activities families can volunteer to do as part of the classroom.

- Interacting, playing, and engaging with children in nature
- Chaperoning excursions to the beyond
- Maintaining trails
- Helping gather materials for an upcoming nature-based activity
- Repairing classroom field guides or fiction books about nature as needed
- Sharing a nature-based experience with the class
- Taking photos of classroom nature activities to share with families or display
- Putting together posters of classroom nature activities or field trips (can be done at home)

NAture-Based Education Rating Scale (NABERS) for Pre-K Education: Comprehensive Assessment Rubric

The NABERS for Pre-K is organized into five sections. Within each section are multiple categories. Each category has multiple items with descriptors, Level 1 through Level 7, for each item. There are anywhere from 1 to 9 items for each category, and these differences in the number of items are accounted for in the scoring process.

SECTION I: Program Goals and Curriculum Practices
D. Program Goals
E. Program Practices
F. Curriculum

SECTION II: Staffing
A. Administrator's Role
B. Teacher's Role
C. Staff Qualifications
D. Professional Development

SECTION III: Environment
A. Indoor Classroom (Inside)
B. Natural Play Area (Outside)
C. Natural Ecosystems (Beyond)

SECTION IV: Community Partnerships
A. Nature Educator
B. Artifacts/Resources–On-Site
C. Special Programs–Field Trips

SECTION V: Family Engagement
A. Family Communication and Education
B. Family Nature Experiences
C. Family Involvement

Guidance for Observations and Scoring

Step 1: Observe the classroom and/or conduct teacher interviews as appropriate to document supporting evidence.

- NABERS is designed to rate individual classrooms. Some items may apply to all classrooms in a building or program, but the majority will be specific to a particular classroom setting.

- Observations should last at least 3 hours on a typical day. With this in mind, try to avoid using the tool within the first or last four weeks of the school year. "Typical" days should avoid special events, guest teachers, and extreme weather events.

- Observers should minimize their impact on the classroom as much as possible. This means not inferring with or participating in classroom activities— including talking with teachers or children during the class session.

- Supporting evidence includes observation, teacher reports to the assessor, children's work products, and documents such as lesson plans and strategic plans. Supporting evidence may be relevant in multiple sections or subsections of the tool. If there is a question about whether a particular practice is present, the assessor should ask the teacher about this after the observation.

- If there are multiple teachers in the classroom as coteachers, the scores should reflect the practices of all teachers.

Step 2: Read each item and check one box for the descriptor that best describes the classroom.

❋ Once you have observed and collected supporting evidence, score each item by placing a check mark in one of the boxes in the columns labeled 1, 3, 5, and 7. If a category does not apply, make a note to that effect. This will be relevant in Step 3.

❋ When scoring, keep in mind these clarifications of the terms *almost always/all, often/most, sometimes/some,* and *rarely/no/does not*. *Almost always* is every day children are present at school. Generally speaking, *often* would be more than 60 percent of the time, *sometimes* would be 30-60 percent of the time, *rarely* would be less than 30 percent of the time, and *no/does not* is never.

Step 3: Determine the score for each category.

Circle the corresponding level (1, 2, 3, 4, 5, 6, or 7) at the top of the category. The score for each category is determined using the following criteria:

For categories with **three or more items**:

Level 1: Half or more of the Level 1 boxes are checked (regardless of the Level 3, 5, or 7 boxes that may be checked).

Level 2: Fewer than half of the Level 1 boxes are checked, some of the Level 3 boxes are checked, and no Level 5 or 7 boxes are checked.

Level 3: All Level 3 boxes are checked or one Level 1 box is checked, and the remaining boxes are checked at Level 5 or 7.

Level 4: No Level 1 boxes are checked, half or fewer of the Level 3 boxes are checked, and the remaining boxes are checked at Level 5 or 7.

Level 5: All Level 5 boxes are checked or one Level 3 box is checked, and the remaining boxes are checked at Level 7.

Level 6: No Level 1 or 3 boxes are checked, half or fewer of the Level 5 boxes are checked, and the remaining boxes are checked at Level 7.

Level 7: All Level 7 boxes are checked.

For categories with **two items**:

Level 1: Both Level 1 boxes are checked.

Level 2: One Level 1 box and one Level 3 box are checked.

Level 3: Both Level 3 boxes are checked or one Level 1 box is checked, and the remaining box is checked at Level 5 or 7.

Level 4: One Level 1 or 3 box is checked and one Level 5 box is checked.

Level 5: Both Level 5 boxes are checked or one Level 3 box is checked, and the remaining box is checked at Level 7.

Level 6: One Level 5 box is checked, and the remaining box is checked at Level 7.

Level 7: Both Level 7 boxes are checked.

If a category does not apply or cannot be observed, compute the quality level based on the number of subcategories completed for that category.

Section I: Program Goals and Curriculum Practices

This section addresses the dual goals of developmentally appropriate early childhood and environmental education in which nature is the central organizing concept. The program goals, daily structure, and curriculum reflect the intentional implementation of nature-based education.

A. Program Goals: The program demonstrates dual goals of both child development and environmental stewardship based on high-quality practices of early childhood education (ECE) and environmental education (EE)

Item 1: The program has a mission or purpose statement that indicates dual goals of both child development and environmental stewardship.

1	2	3	4	5	6	7	Supporting Evidence
☐ Program has no mission or purpose statement.		☐ Program has a mission or purpose statement that indicates a goal of child development with no mention of nature.		☐ Program has a mission or purpose statement that indicates a goal of child development with mention of nature as a tool to accomplish that goal.		☐ Program has a mission or purpose statement that indicates dual goals of both child development *and* environmental stewardship.	

Item 2: The program models that all children, no matter their background or ability, deserve and can participate in positive outdoor experiences.

1	2	3	4	5	6	7	Supporting Evidence
☐ Program *does not* model that all children, no matter their background or ability, deserve and can participate in positive outdoor experiences.		☐ Program *sometimes* models that all children, no matter their background or ability, deserve and can participate in positive outdoor experiences.		☐ Program *often* models that all children, no matter their background or ability, deserve and can participate in positive outdoor experiences.		☐ Program *almost always* models that all children, no matter their background or ability, deserve and can participate in positive outdoor experiences.	

Item 3: Emphasis is placed on learning with nature.

1	2	3	4	5	6	7	Supporting Evidence
☐ No integration of nature in learning.		☐ Learning primarily emphasizes learning *in* nature.		☐ Learning primarily emphasizes learning *about* nature.		☐ Emphasis is placed on learning *with* nature versus learning in or about nature (i.e., integration of nature in learning).	

Item 4: Learning topics and scope are developmentally appropriate.

1	2	3	4	5	6	7	Supporting Evidence
☐ Learning topics and scope are above children's understanding (e.g., abstract aspects of climate change, faraway places).		☐ Learning topics and scope are *sometimes* developmentally appropriate (e.g., concrete, locally focused).		☐ Learning topics and scope are *often* developmentally appropriate (e.g., concrete, locally focused).		☐ Learning topics and scope are *almost always* developmentally appropriate (e.g., concrete, locally focused).	

Item 5: Sustainable practices are evident.

1	2	3	4	5	6	7	Supporting Evidence
☐ *No* sustainable practices are evident in the program.		☐ At least *1* sustainable practice* is evident in the program.		☐ At least *2* sustainable practices* are evident in the program.		☐ At least *3* sustainable practices* are evident in the program.	

*Examples of sustainable practices include using real plates, utensils, cloth napkins, recycling, composting, rain barrels, and so on.

SCORING NOTE:
Almost always: every day, or nearly every day, children are present; *often:* more than 60 percent of the time; *sometimes:* 30–60 percent of the time; *rarely:* less than 30 percent of the time; *no/does not:* never.

Item 6: Program implements Leave No Trace® principles in natural ecosystems.

1	2	3	4	5	6	7	Supporting Evidence
☐ The program *does not* practice Leave No Trace principles in natural ecosystems.		☐ The program *sometimes* practices Leave No Trace principles in natural ecosystems.		☐ The program *often* practices Leave No Trace principles in natural ecosystems.		☐ The program *almost always* practices Leave No Trace principles in natural ecosystems.	

B. Program Practices: The class demonstrates a value for ongoing experiences in nature through daily class structure.

Item 1: The class day starts outdoors.

1	2	3	4	5	6	7	Supporting Evidence
☐ The class *does not* start the day outdoors.		☐ The class *sometimes* starts the day outdoors.		☐ The class *often* starts the day outdoors.		☐ The class *almost always** starts the day outdoors.	

Item 2: A majority of the class time is spent outdoors.

1	2	3	4	5	6	7	Supporting Evidence
☐ Daily outdoor time is less than that required by regulations.		☐ Daily outdoor time in the natural play area and/or beyond of up to 30 percent of class time is equivalent to or greater than that required by regulations.		☐ Thirty to fifty percent (30–50 percent) of total daily class time is spent outdoors in the natural play area and/or beyond.		☐ At least 50 percent of total daily class time is spent outdoors in a natural play area and/or beyond.	

Item 3: The class regularly visits natural ecosystems.

1	2	3	4	5	6	7	Supporting Evidence
☐ The class visits natural ecosystems less than once a month.		☐ The class visits natural ecosystems at least once a month.		☐ The class visits natural ecosystems at least once a week.		☐ The class visits natural ecosystems daily.	

* A rare exception would be days when the weather is dangerous and, as a result, the program adjusts the schedule for that day. For example, on an extremely cold morning, teachers might shift the schedule so outdoor time occurs an hour later than normal to allow the sun and temperatures to rise. It will be evident that this is an unusual event when children and families comment or appear visibly surprised that the class is not starting outdoors.

SCORING NOTE:
Almost always: every day, or nearly every day, children are present; *often:* more than 60 percent of the time, *sometimes:* 30–60 percent of the time, *rarely:* less than 30 percent of the time; *no/does not:* never.

Item 4: Extensive daily class time is unstructured nature play.

1	2	3	4	5	6	7	Supporting Evidence
☐ No outdoor class time is spent in unstructured nature play.		☐ Up to 30 percent of the outdoor class time is spent in unstructured nature play.		☐ Thirty to fifty (30–50) percent of the outdoor class time is unstructured nature play.		☐ At least 50 percent of the outdoor class time is unstructured nature play.	

Item 5: Safety-related policies and procedures based on ongoing site and benefit-risk assessments are in place.

1	2	3	4	5	6	7	Supporting Evidence
☐ *No* safety-related policies and procedures based on ongoing site and benefit-risk assessments are in place for activities.		☐ Safety-related policies and procedures based on ongoing site and benefit-risk assessments are in place for *some* activities.		☐ Safety-related policies and procedures based on ongoing site and benefit-risk assessments are written for *most* activities.		☐ Safety-related policies and procedures based on ongoing site and benefit-risk assessments are written for *almost all* activities.	

Item 6: Safety-related policies and procedures are followed.

1	2	3	4	5	6	7	Supporting Evidence
☐ Safety-related policies and procedures *are not* followed.		☐ Safety-related policies and procedures are *sometimes* followed.		☐ Safety-related policies and procedures are *often* followed.		☐ Safety-related policies and procedures are *almost always* followed.	

C. Curriculum: This category evaluates the extent to which nature is the central organizing concept of the program's curriculum and to what extent the experiences supporting this concept are based on children's interests in their local natural environment.

Item 1: Teachers intentionally develop children's outdoor skills.*

1	2	3	4	5	6	7	Supporting Evidence
☐ Teacher-led activities *rarely* develop children's outdoor skills.		☐ Teacher-led activities *sometimes* develop children's outdoor skills.		☐ Teacher-led activities *often* develop children's outdoor skills.		☐ Teacher-led activities *almost always* develop children's outdoor skills.	

Item 2: Activities emerge from children's interests in nature.

1	2	3	4	5	6	7	Supporting Evidence
☐ Activities are *rarely* connected to children's interests in nature.		☐ Activities are *sometimes* connected to children's interests in nature.		☐ Activities are *often* connected to children's interests in nature.		☐ Activities *almost always* emerge from children's interests in nature.	

Item 3: Activities and experiences align with authentic, local, and current seasonal happenings.

1	2	3	4	5	6	7	Supporting Evidence
☐ Activities and experiences *rarely* align with authentic, local, and current seasonal happenings.		☐ Activities and experiences *sometimes* align with authentic, local, and current seasonal happenings.		☐ Activities and experiences *often* align with authentic, local, and current seasonal happenings.		☐ Activities and experiences *almost always* align with authentic, local, and current seasonal happenings.	

*There are a variety of terms for outdoor skills, including *woodcraft*, *bushcraft*, and even *survival skills*. Whatever term is used, the activities themselves should align with the other quality measures in the NABERS tool, such as developmentally appropriate and environmental impact.

SCORING NOTE:
Almost always: every day, or nearly every day, children are present; *often*: more than 60 percent of the time; *sometimes*: 30–60 percent of the time; *rarely*: less than 30 percent of the time; *no/does not*: never.

Item 4: Children reflect on their nature experiences through conversation and documentation.

1	2	3	4	5	6	7	
☐ Children *rarely* reflect on their nature experiences through conversation and documentation.		☐ Children *sometimes* reflect on their nature experiences through conversation and documentation.		☐ Children *often* reflect on their nature experiences through conversation and documentation.		☐ Children *almost always* reflect on their nature experiences through conversation and documentation.	Supporting Evidence

Item 5: Teacher-led activities build on nature knowledge and experiences.

1	2	3	4	5	6	7	
☐ Teacher-led activities *rarely* build on nature knowledge and experiences *over time*.		☐ Teacher-led activities *sometimes* build on nature knowledge and experiences *over time*.		☐ Teacher-led activities *often* build on nature knowledge and experiences *over time*.		☐ Teacher-led activities *almost always* build on nature knowledge and experiences *over time*.	Supporting Evidence

Item 6: Natural materials are used as tools for teaching curricular domains.

1	2	3	4	5	6	7	
☐ Natural materials are *rarely* used as tools for teaching curricular domains (literacy, math, science, social studies, and art).		☐ Natural materials are *sometimes* used as tools for teaching curricular domains (literacy, math, science, social studies, and art).		☐ Natural materials are *often* used as tools for teaching curricular domains (literacy, math, science, social studies, and art).		☐ Natural materials are *almost always* used as tools for teaching curricular domains (literacy, math, science, social studies, and art).	Supporting Evidence

Item 7: Fictional texts represent authentic, local nature and align with seasonal happenings.

1	2	3	4	5	6	7	
☐ Fictional texts provided *rarely* represent authentic, local nature and align with current seasonal happenings.		☐ Fictional texts provided *sometimes* represent authentic, local nature and align with current seasonal happenings.		☐ Fictional texts provided *often* represent authentic, local nature and align with current seasonal happenings.		☐ Fictional texts provided *almost always* represent authentic, local nature and align with current seasonal happenings.	Supporting Evidence

Item 8: Informational texts represent authentic, local nature aligned with seasonal happenings.

1	2	3	4	5	6	7	
☐ Informational texts provided *rarely* represent authentic, local nature and align with current seasonal happenings.		☐ Informational texts provided *sometimes* represent authentic, local nature and align with current seasonal happenings.		☐ Informational texts provided *often* represent authentic, local nature and align with current seasonal happenings.		☐ Informational texts provided *almost always* represent authentic, local nature and align with current seasonal happenings.	Supporting Evidence

Item 9: Texts (both fictional and informational) represent diverse audiences having positive outdoor experiences.

1	2	3	4	5	6	7	
☐ Texts provided *rarely* represent a diversity of people having positive outdoor experiences.		☐ Texts provided *sometimes* represent a diversity of people having positive outdoor experiences.		☐ Texts provided *often* represent a diversity of people having positive outdoor experiences.		☐ Texts provided *almost always* represent a diversity of people having positive outdoor experiences.	Supporting Evidence

SCORING NOTE:
Almost always: every day, or nearly every day, children are present; *often*: more than 60 percent of the time, *sometimes*; 30–60 percent of the time, *rarely*; less than 30 percent of the time; *no/does not*: never.

Section II: Staffing

The teachers' roles are as facilitators, and they are trained in both early childhood education and environmental education. Administration supports professional development, and teachers cultivate their own interest in nature.

A. Administrators' Role: Administrators support teaching staff in implementing a nature-based approach. (Note: administrators can include a director, owner, or board members.)

Item 1: Administrators allocate time, money, and material resources to implement nature-based education.

1	2	3	4	5	6	7	Supporting Evidence
☐ Administrators *do not* help facilitate a nature-based education.		☐ Administrators *sometimes* allocate time, money, or material resources to implement nature-based education programs.		☐ Administrators often allocate time, money, or material resources to implement nature-based education.		☐ Administrators *almost always* allocate time, money, and material resources to implement nature-based education (e.g., in-classroom materials, planning time, professional development).	

Item 2: Organizational planning focuses on the intentional integration of nature-based education.

1	2	3	4	5	6	7	Supporting Evidence
☐ Short- or long-term organizational planning *does not* include nature-based education.		☐ Short- or long-term organizational planning *sometimes* includes nature-based education.		☐ Short- or long-term organizational planning *often* includes nature-based education.		☐ Short- and long-term organizational planning *almost always* focuses on the intentional integration of nature-based education.	

Item 3: Administrators are public advocates for nature-based education.

1	2	3	4	5	6	7	Supporting Evidence
☐ Administrators are *not* public advocates for nature-based education.		☐ Administrators are *sometimes* public advocates for nature-based education.		☐ Administrators are *often* public advocates for nature-based education.		☐ Administrators are *almost always* public advocates for nature-based education.	

SCORING NOTE:
Almost always: every day, or nearly every day, children are present; *often:* more than 60 percent of the time; *sometimes:* 30–60 percent of the time; *rarely:* less than 30 percent of the time; *no/does not:* never.

B. Teacher's Role: Teachers play a critical role in setting the tone and appropriate behavior to allow for and encourage open-ended nature exploration and play.

Item 1: Teachers facilitate open-ended nature exploration and play.

1	2	3	4	5	6	7	Supporting Evidence
☐ Teachers *do not* facilitate open-ended nature exploration and play during outdoor time.		☐ Teachers *sometimes* facilitate open-ended nature exploration and play during outdoor time.		☐ Teachers *often* facilitate open-ended nature exploration and play during outdoor time.		☐ Teachers *almost always* facilitate open-ended nature exploration and play during outdoor time.	

Item 2: Teachers express and communicate enthusiasm for outdoor time.

1	2	3	4	5	6	7	Supporting Evidence
☐ Teachers *do not* express enthusiasm about scheduled outdoor time.		☐ Teachers *sometimes* express enthusiasm about scheduled outdoor time.		☐ Teachers *often* express enthusiasm about scheduled outdoor time.		☐ Teachers *almost always* express enthusiasm about scheduled outdoor time and communicate this enthusiasm to the children.	

Item 3: Teachers interact with natural environments.

1	2	3	4	5	6	7	Supporting Evidence
☐ Teachers *do not* engage with the natural environment.		☐ Teachers are seen to interact with natural environments in *1 way.**		☐ Teachers are seen to interact with natural environments in *2 ways.**		☐ Teachers are seen to interact with natural environments in *at least 3 ways.**	

Item 4: Teachers are comfortable with nature immersion.

1	2	3	4	5	6	7	Supporting Evidence
☐ Teachers *do not* show comfort with nature immersion by dressing appropriately for and communicating positively about the weather (e.g., wearing appropriate footwear for the terrain and weather).		☐ Teachers *sometimes* show comfort with nature immersion by dressing appropriately for and communicating positively about the weather (e.g., wearing appropriate footwear for the terrain and weather).		☐ Teachers *often* are comfortable with nature immersion and show this by dressing appropriately for and communicating positively about the weather (e.g., wearing appropriate footwear for the terrain and weather).		☐ Teachers *almost always* are comfortable with nature immersion and show this by dressing appropriately for and communicating positively about the weather (e.g., wearing appropriate footwear for the terrain and weather).	

*For example, by lying on the ground, raking leaves, catching insects, picking up worms, catching tadpoles and frogs, turning over logs, planting and/or harvesting gardens, or tapping maple trees.

SCORING NOTE:
Almost always: every day, or nearly every day, children are present; *often*: more than 60 percent of the time, *sometimes*; 30–60 percent of the time, *rarely*; less than 30 percent of the time; *no/does not*: never.

C. Staff Qualifications: Program staff (e.g., directors and teachers) are formally trained in both early childhood education (ECE) and environmental education (EE).

Item 1: The program administrator (e.g., preschool director) has formal training in ECE and EE.

1	2	3	4	5	6	7	Supporting Evidence
☐ The administrator does not meet regulatory qualifications and/or has *no additional degree or certificate* related to nature-based education or natural science (e.g., EE, biology).		☐ The administrator, in addition to meeting regulatory qualifications for licensing, has *an associate's degree or a nonaccredited certificate* in a field related to nature-based education or natural science (e.g., EE, biology).		☐ The administrator, in addition to meeting regulatory qualifications for licensing, has a *bachelor's degree, minor, or university certificate* in a field related to nature-based education or natural science (e.g., EE, biology).		☐ The administrator, in addition to meeting regulatory qualifications for licensing, has a *bachelor's or master's degree* related to nature-based education or natural science (e.g., EE, biology).	

Item 2: The teachers have formal training in ECE and/or EE.

1	2	3	4	5	6	7	Supporting Evidence
☐ Teachers do not meet regulatory qualifications and/or have *no additional degrees or certificates* related to nature-based education or natural science (e.g., EE, biology).		☐ At least one of the teachers, in addition to meeting regulatory qualifications for licensing, has an *associate's degree or a nonaccredited certificate* in a field related to nature-based education or natural science (e.g., EE, biology).		☐ At least one of the teachers, in addition to meeting regulatory qualifications for licensing, has a *bachelor's degree, minor, or university certificate* in a field related to nature-based education or natural science (e.g., EE, biology).		☐ At least one of the teachers, in addition to meeting regulatory qualifications for licensing, has a *bachelor's or master's degree* related to nature-based education or natural science (e.g., EE, biology).	

D. Professional Development: Teachers participate in ongoing professional development to facilitate their interests, skills, and knowledge of nature and nature-based education pedagogy.

Item 1: Teachers participate in professional development to improve their skills and knowledge of nature-based education.

1	2	3	4	5	6	7	Supporting Evidence
☐ Teachers *do not* participate in professional development related to nature topics.		☐ Teachers cultivate their own knowledge by participating *once a year* in professional development (e.g., visiting model programs, attending workshops) related to nature-based education pedagogy or natural-history knowledge.		☐ Teachers cultivate their own knowledge of and interest in nature by participating *once a year* in professional development (e.g., visiting model programs, attending workshops) related to nature-based education pedagogy *and* natural-history knowledge.		☐ Teachers cultivate their own knowledge of and interest in nature by participating at least *twice a year* in professional development (e.g., visiting model programs, attending workshops) related to both nature-based education pedagogy *and* natural history knowledge.	

SCORING NOTE:
Almost always: every day, or nearly every day, children are present; *often:* more than 60 percent of the time; *sometimes:* 30–60 percent of the time; *rarely:* less than 30 percent of the time; *no/does not:* never.

Section III: Environment

Three distinct spaces—inside, outside, and beyond—are provided to meaningfully integrate nature among the physical environments.

A. Indoor Classroom (Inside): Nature is infused into all areas of the classroom. The classroom generally has a nature-like feel and appearance (e.g., plenty of natural light, wood and natural materials, animals, and plants).

Alternate Item 1–3 (for classes without an indoor space): Need for an Emergency Shelter

1	2	3	4	5	6	7	Supporting Evidence
☐ The class *does not* have an emergency shelter.		☐ The class has an emergency shelter, but it is *not* in close proximity.		☐ The class has an emergency shelter in close proximity *most* of the time.		☐ The class has an emergency shelter in close proximity *at all* times.	

Item 1: The indoor classroom has natural lighting and views of outdoors.

1	2	3	4	5	6	7	Supporting Evidence
☐ The indoor classroom has no windows.		☐ The indoor classroom has *some* natural light *without* child-level views to the outdoors.		☐ The indoor classroom has *some* natural light *with* child-level views to *any outdoor space*.		☐ The indoor classroom has *extensive* natural light *with* child-level views to a *natural space* outdoors.	

Item 2: The indoor classroom has natural furnishings and colors.

1	2	3	4	5	6	7	Supporting Evidence
☐ The indoor classroom *does not* have a natural look and feel (e.g., plastic furnishings, primary colors).		☐ The indoor classroom has a *limited* natural look and feel (e.g., mix of natural and plastic furnishings, diverse textures, primary colors).		☐ The indoor classroom has *some* natural look and feel (e.g., mix of natural and plastic furnishings, diverse textures, earth-based colors).		☐ The indoor classroom has an *extensively* natural look and feel (e.g., natural furnishings, diverse textures, earth-based colors).	

Item 3: The indoor classroom affords children access and movement between indoors and outdoors.

1	2	3	4	5	6	7	Supporting Evidence
☐ The indoor classroom has a difficult transition to the outdoors.		☐ The indoor classroom has an easy, but not direct, transition to the outdoors.		☐ The indoor classroom has immediate access through a door to the outdoor classroom.		☐ The indoor classroom has immediate access to the outdoors, *and* children have free-range movement between the indoor and outdoor classroom through a transition space (e.g., a porch or sunroom).	

SCORING NOTE:
Almost always: every day, or nearly every day, children are present; *often:* more than 60 percent of the time, *sometimes;* 30–60 percent of the time, *rarely;* less than 30 percent of the time; *no/does not:* never.

NAture-Based Education Rating Scale (NABERS) for Pre-K Education: Comprehensive Assessment Rubric

Item 4: Natural materials are present and reflect local nature.

1	2	3	4	5	6	7	Supporting Evidence
☐ Natural materials *are not* present.		☐ Natural materials are present in *some* areas of the indoor classroom and reflect a variety of local nature.		☐ Natural materials are present in *most* areas of the indoor classroom and reflect a variety of local nature.		☐ Natural materials (e.g., bird parts, animal bones, bird nests, tree seeds) are present in *all* areas of the indoor classroom and reflect a variety of local nature.	

Item 5: Indoor classroom materials are realistic and representative of local nature.

1	2	3	4	5	6	7	Supporting Evidence
☐ No indoor classroom materials represent realistic and local nature.		☐ Indoor classroom materials *sometimes* represent realistic and local nature.		☐ Indoor classroom materials *often* represent realistic and local nature.		☐ Indoor classroom materials (e.g., puppets, books, dramatic play materials) *almost always* represent realistic and local nature.	

Item 6: Indoor classroom materials reflect the human diversity of the local community having positive outdoor experiences.

1	2	3	4	5	6	7	Supporting Evidence
☐ No indoor classroom materials reflect the human diversity of the local community having positive outdoor experiences.		☐ Indoor classroom materials *sometimes* reflect the human diversity of the local community having positive outdoor experiences.		☐ Indoor classroom materials *often* reflect the human diversity of the local community having positive outdoor experiences.		☐ Indoor classroom materials *almost always* reflect the human diversity of the local community having positive outdoor experiences.	

Item 7: The indoor classroom has plants and animals.

1	2	3	4	5	6	7	Supporting Evidence
☐ The indoor classroom *does not* have living plants and/or animals.		☐ The indoor classroom has *1 or more* living plants and/or animals in the indoor classroom (if allergies allow).		☐ The indoor classroom has *2 or more* living plants and/or animals (if allergies allow).		☐ The indoor classroom has *3 or more* living plants and/or animals (if allergies allow).	

SCORING NOTE:
Almost always: every day, or nearly every day, children are present; *often*: more than 60 percent of the time; *sometimes*: 30–60 percent of the time; *rarely*: less than 30 percent of the time; *no/does not*: never.

B. Natural Play Area (Outside): The natural play area (outside) includes numerous human- and nature-made loose parts and a variety of features for nature-based play.

Item 1: The natural play area has a natural look and feel.

1	2	3	4	5	6	7	Supporting Evidence
☐ The natural play area *does not* have a natural look and feel (e.g., plastic furnishings, primary colors).		☐ The natural play area has *limited* natural look and feel (e.g., mix of natural and plastic furnishings, diverse textures, primary colors).		☐ The natural play area has *some* natural look and feel (e.g., mix of natural and plastic furnishings, diverse textures, earth-based colors).		☐ The natural play area has an *extensive* natural look and feel (e.g., natural materials, diverse textures, earth-based colors).	

Item 2: The natural play area contains a variety of natural features.

1	2	3	4	5	6	7	Supporting Evidence
☐ The outside play area is a traditional playground (e.g., climbing structures, sandbox) with few natural features.		☐ The natural play area includes *at least 3* of the following: loose parts, a variety of vegetation, a vegetable or herb garden, sand and soil, a water feature, opportunities for active motor play, opportunities for less-active play, a variety of terrain, a mix of sunny and shady areas, a variety of gathering spaces, a variety of features, and a variety of seating and tables.		☐ The natural play area includes *at least 5* of the following: loose parts, a variety of vegetation, a vegetable or herb garden, sand and soil, a water feature, opportunities for active motor play, opportunities for less-active play, a variety of terrain, a mix of sunny and shady areas, a variety of gathering spaces, a variety of features, and a variety of seating and tables.		☐ The natural play area includes *at least 7* of the following: loose parts, a variety of vegetation, a vegetable or herb garden, sand and soil, a water feature, opportunities for active motor play, opportunities for less-active play, a variety of terrain, a mix of sunny and shady areas, a variety of gathering spaces, a variety of features, and a variety of seating and tables.	

Item 3: The natural play area includes natural materials that reflect a variety of local nature.

1	2	3	4	5	6	7	Supporting Evidence
☐ Natural materials *are not* present.		☐ Natural materials (e.g., bird parts, animal bones, bird's nests, tree seeds) are present in *some* areas of the natural play area and reflect a variety of local nature.		☐ Natural materials (e.g., bird parts, animal bones, bird's nests, tree seeds) are present in *most* areas of the natural play area and reflect a variety of local nature.		☐ Natural materials (e.g., bird parts, animal bones, bird's nests, tree seeds) are present in *all* areas of the natural play area and reflect a variety of local nature.	

Item 4: Natural play area materials represent realistic and local nature.

1	2	3	4	5	6	7	Supporting Evidence
☐ *No* materials represent realistic and local nature.		☐ Natural play area materials (e.g., puppets, books, dramatic play materials) *sometimes* represent realistic and local nature.		☐ Natural play area materials (e.g., puppets, books, dramatic play materials) *often* represent realistic and local nature.		☐ Natural play area materials (e.g., puppets, books, dramatic play materials) *almost always* represent realistic and local nature.	

SCORING NOTE:
Almost always: every day, or nearly every day, children are present; *often*: more than 60 percent of the time; *sometimes*: 30–60 percent of the time; *rarely*: less than 30 percent of the time; *no/does not*: never.

C. Natural Ecosystems (Beyond): The class has areas of natural ecosystems for exploration outside of the natural play area.*

Item 1: The class has access to natural ecosystems.

1	2	3	4	5	6	7	Supporting Evidence
☐ The class has *no* access to natural ecosystems outside the natural play area.		☐ The class accesses *1* natural ecosystem (e.g., pond, river, wetland, marsh, meadow, field, prairie, lake/beach, vernal pools, woodlands, parks) throughout the year.		☐ The class accesses 2 *two* natural ecosystems (e.g., pond, river, wetland, marsh, meadow, field, prairie, lake/beach, vernal pools, woodlands, parks) throughout the year.		☐ The class accesses *at least 3* natural ecosystems (e.g., pond, river, wetland, marsh, meadow, field, prairie, lake/beach, vernal pools, woodlands, parks) throughout the year.	

Item 2: The natural ecosystems are healthy.

1	2	3	4	5	6	7	Supporting Evidence
☐ The natural ecosystems are *never* healthy, or they are nonexistent.		☐ The natural ecosystems are *sometimes* healthy.		☐ The natural ecosystems are *often* healthy.		☐ The natural ecosystems are *almost always* healthy (e.g., rich biodiversity and minimal exotic and invasive species).	

Item 3: The natural ecosystem includes loose parts and natural features.

1	2	3	4	5	6	7	Supporting Evidence
☐ There are *no* loose parts and natural features to interact with (e.g., trees, flowers, wildlife), or there is *no* ecosystem available to visit.		☐ There are *few* loose parts and natural features to interact with (e.g., trees, flowers, wildlife).		☐ There are *some* loose parts and natural features to interact with (e.g., trees, flowers, wildlife).		☐ There are *many* loose parts and natural features to interact with (e.g., trees, flowers, wildlife).	

*Examples of natural ecosystems include ponds, rivers, wetlands, marshes, meadows, fields, prairies, lakes, beaches, vernal pools, woodlands, parks, and so on.

SCORING NOTE:
Almost always: every day, or nearly every day, children are present; *often:* more than 60 percent of the time; *sometimes:* 30–60 percent of the time; *rarely:* less than 30 percent of the time; *no/does not:* never.

Section IV: Community Partnerships and Resources

The program uses local, nature-based organizations and/or resources.

A. Nature Educator: An experienced nature educator visits the classroom regularly and has an ongoing relationship with the teacher and students.

Item 1: The nature educator visits frequently.

1	2	3	4	5	6	7	Supporting Evidence
☐ Nature educator visits *once per year or less*.		☐ Nature educator visits *seasonally*.		☐ Nature educator visits at least *once a month*.		☐ Nature educator visits at least *once a week*.	

Item 2: The program has a strong, supportive relationship with the same nature educator.

1	2	3	4	5	6	7	Supporting Evidence
☐ The program *does not* have a relationship with a nature educator.		☐ Nature educator is *sometimes* the same individual.		☐ Nature educator is *often* the same individual.		☐ Nature educator is *almost always* the same individual.	

B. Artifacts/Resources—On-Site: The class has access to artifacts and resources that support a nature-based curriculum.

Item 1: The program has access to artifacts and resources.

1	2	3	4	5	6	7	Supporting Evidence
☐ The class *does not* have access to a variety of artifacts and resources on the school grounds.		☐ The class *sometimes* has access to a variety of artifacts and resources on the school grounds.		☐ The class *often* has access to a variety of artifacts and resources on the school grounds.		☐ The class *almost always* has access to a variety of artifacts and resources on the school grounds (e.g., diverse habitats, greenhouses, apiary, raptors, sugarhouse, gardens).	

Item 2: Wild and/or domestic animals are available to support nature-based learning.

1	2	3	4	5	6	7	Supporting Evidence
☐ Wild and/or domestic animals are *not* available to support programs.		☐ Wild and/or domestic animals are *sometimes* available to support programs.		☐ Wild and/or domestic animals are *often* available to support programs.		☐ Wild and/or domestic animals are *almost always* available to support programs (e.g., wildlife rehab education animal, class pet).	

SCORING NOTE:
Almost always: every day, or nearly every day, children are present; *often*: more than 60 percent of the time; *sometimes*: 30–60 percent of the time; *rarely*: less than 30 percent of the time; *no/does not*: never.

NAture-Based Education Rating Scale (NABERS) for Pre-K Education: Comprehensive Assessment Rubric

C. Special Programs—Field Trips*: The program has access to special nature-based programs and resources that occur at another location.

Item 1: The program attends nature-based field trips that are integrated into the curriculum.

1	2	3	4	5	6	7	Supporting Evidence
☐ Children take *no* nature-based field trips during the school year.		☐ Children attend special nature-based programs (e.g., nature center, zoo, arboretum, apple orchard, dairy farm) away from the school (field trips) at least 1 time a year, *but* experiences *are not* integrated into the classroom curriculum.		☐ Children attend special nature-based programs (e.g., nature center, zoo, arboretum, apple orchard, dairy farm) away from the school (field trips) at least 1 time a year, *and* these experiences *are* integrated into the classroom curriculum.		☐ Children attend special nature-based programs (e.g., nature center, zoo, arboretum, apple orchard, dairy farm) away from the school (field trips) at least 2 *times* a year, *and* these experiences *are* integrated into the classroom curriculum.	

*If your school is located at a nature center, zoo, arboretum, apple orchard, dairy farm, or similar, but you must schedule a time to visit, it's considered a field trip.

SCORING NOTE:
Almost always: every day, or nearly every day, children are present; *often:* more than 60 percent of the time; *sometimes:* 30–60 percent of the time; *rarely:* less than 30 percent of the time; *no/does not:* never.

Section V: Family Engagement

The program supports families to engage with the nature-based approach.

A. Family Communication & Education: The program provides clear communication with and education for families on the benefits and outcomes of nature-based experiences for young children.

Item 1: The program shares nature-related content to families through formal communication.

1	2	3	4	5	6	7	Supporting Evidence
☐ *No* nature-related content is included in family communication.		☐ Nature-related content (e.g., benefits of nature, activities to do at home, appropriate clothing) is embedded in *some* of these communication methods: family handbook*, family orientation, family newsletter, reports of classroom activities to families, and family-teacher conferences.		☐ Nature-related content (e.g., benefits of nature, activities to do at home, appropriate clothing) is embedded in *most* of these communication methods: family handbook*, family orientation, family newsletter, reports of classroom activities to families, and family-teacher conferences.		☐ Nature-related content (e.g., benefits of nature, activities to do at home, appropriate clothing) is embedded in *all* of these communication methods: family handbook*, family orientation, family newsletter, reports of classroom activities to families, and family-teacher conferences.	

Item 2: The program documents its nature-based activities and shares documentation with families.

1	2	3	4	5	6	7	Supporting Evidence
☐ *No* documentation of nature-based activities and/or projects is posted.		☐ *Minimal* documentation of nature-based activities and/or projects is posted.		☐ *Moderate* documentation of nature-based activities and/or projects is posted.		☐ *Extensive* documentation of nature-based activities and/or projects is posted.	

B. Family Nature Experiences: Programs and resources are provided to facilitate families' experiences in nature.

Item 1: The program offers nature-based family programs.

1	2	3	4	5	6	7	Supporting Evidence
☐ *No* nature-based family programs are offered either inside or outside of the school.		☐ At least *1* seasonal, nature-based family program is offered annually.		☐ At least *2* seasonal, nature-based family programs are offered annually.		☐ At least *3* seasonal, nature-based family programs (e.g., owl hikes, camping, catching frogs or insects) are offered annually.	

Item 2: The program shares community resources and events about nature with families.

1	2	3	4	5	6	7	Supporting Evidence
☐ *No* community resources are shared with families.		☐ Community resources for family experiences in nature are *sometimes* included in family newsletters and/or weekly reports.		☐ Community resources for family experiences in nature are *often* included in family newsletters and/or weekly reports.		☐ Community resources for family experiences in nature are *almost always* included in family newsletters and/or weekly reports.	

*The family handbook includes a mission statement and program philosophy related to nature and a list of appropriate clothing to wear for the weather. (This can be part of the entire school handbook or a separate letter to families.)

SCORING NOTE:
Almost always: every day, or nearly every day, children are present; *often*: more than 60 percent of the time, *sometimes*; 30–60 percent of the time, *rarely*; less than 30 percent of the time; *no*/*does not*: never.

C. Family Involvement: The program encourages families to be involved in nature-based classroom activities.

Item 1: Families are encouraged to share their expertise and experiences in nature-based activities with the class.

1	2	3	4	5	6	7	Supporting Evidence
☐ Families are *not* encouraged to share their expertise and experiences in nature-based activities with the class.		☐ Families are *sometimes* encouraged to share their expertise and experiences in nature-based activities with the class.		☐ Families are *often* encouraged to share their expertise and experiences in nature-based activities with the class.		☐ Families are *almost always* encouraged to share their expertise and experiences in nature-based activities with the class.	

Item 2: The program encourages family volunteers to participate in nature-based classroom activities.

1	2	3	4	5	6	7	Supporting Evidence
☐ Families are *not* encouraged to volunteer to participate in nature-based classroom activities.		☐ Families are *sometimes* encouraged to volunteer to participate in nature-based classroom activities.		☐ Families are *often* encouraged to volunteer to participate in nature-based classroom activities.		☐ Families are *almost always* encouraged to volunteer to participate in nature-based classroom activities.	

SCORING NOTE:
Almost always: every day, or nearly every day, children are present; *often*: more than 60 percent of the time; *sometimes*: 30–60 percent of the time; *rarely*: less than 30 percent of the time; *no/does not*: never.

NAture-Based Education Rating Scale (NABERS) for Pre-K Education: Summary Sheet

School Name: _____

School Address: _____

Date of Observation: _____

Observer Name: _____ Observer Email &/or Phone Number: _____

Time Observation Began: _____ Time Observation Ended: _____

Teacher(s) Name(s): _____

- **Teacher 1:** # Years teaching in a nature-based setting _____
  Other relevant teaching experiences (e.g., outdoor education, informal education) _____
- **Teacher 2 (if applicable):** # Years teaching in a nature-based setting _____
  Other relevant teaching experiences (e.g., outdoor education, informal education) _____
- **Teacher 3 (if applicable):** # Years teaching in a nature-based setting _____
  Other relevant teaching experiences (e.g., outdoor education, informal education) _____

# of additional staff present at time of observation (e.g., paraprofessionals) _____

Age range of children _____ # of children _____

Class Structure (e.g., number of days/week; hours class is in session) _____

Enter the numerical rating (1–7) for each item.

SECTION I: Program Goals & Curriculum Practices
_____ **A.** Program Goals
_____ **B.** Program Practices
_____ **C.** Curriculum
    _____ **Total section score**
    _____ **Average section score** (Total score ÷ 3)

SECTION II: Staffing
_____ **A.** Administrator's Role
_____ **B.** Teacher's Role
_____ **C.** Teacher Qualifications
_____ **D.** Professional Development
    _____ **Total section score**
    _____ **Average section score** (Total score ÷ 4)

SECTION III: Environment
_____ **A.** Indoor Classroom (Inside)
_____ **B.** Natural Play Area (Outside)
_____ **C.** Natural Ecosystems (Beyond)
    _____ **Total section score**
    _____ **Average section score** (Total score ÷ 3)

SECTION IV: Community Partnerships & Resources
_____ **A.** Nature Educator
_____ **B.** Artifacts/Resources—On-Site
_____ **C.** Special Programs—Field Trips
    _____ **Total section score**
    _____ **Average section score** (Total score ÷ 3)

SECTION V: Family Engagement
_____ **A.** Family Communication & Education
_____ **B.** Family Nature Experiences
_____ **C.** Family Involvement
    _____ **Total section score**
    _____ **Average section score** (Total score ÷ 3)

_____ **Total of all section averages**
_____ **Average classroom score** (Each average section score ÷ 5)

Observer signature _____

©2023 Patti Bailie, Rachel Larimore, and Arianna Pikus Published by Gryphon House, Inc. All rights reserved.

NAture-Based Education Rating Scale (NABERS) for K–3 Education: Comprehensive Assessment Rubric

The NABERS for K-3 Education is organized into five sections. Within each section are multiple categories. In the K-3 tool there are additional subcategories within the category of Curriculum. Each category has multiple items, with descriptors, Level 1 through Level 7, for each item. There are anywhere from 1 to 6 items for each category, and these differences in the number of items are accounted for in the scoring process.

SECTION I: Program Goals and Curriculum Practices
A. Program Goals
B. Program Practices
C. Curriculum:
   a. Environmental Literacy and Connection
   b. Literacy
   c. Math
   d. Science
   e. Social Studies
   f. Arts

SECTION II: Staffing
A. Administrator's Role
B. Teacher's Role
C. Teacher Qualifications
D. Professional Development

SECTION III: Environment
A. Indoor Classroom (Inside)
B. Natural Play Area (Outside)
C. Natural Ecosystems (Beyond)

SECTION IV: Community Partnerships
A. Nature Educator
B. Artifacts/Resources–On-Site
C. Special Programs–Field Trips

SECTION V: Family Engagement
A. Family Communication and Education
B. Family Nature Experiences
C. Family Involvement

Guidance for Observations and Scoring

Step 1: Observe the classroom and/or conduct teacher interviews as appropriate to document supporting evidence.

- NABERS is designed to rate individual classrooms. Some items will apply to all classrooms in a building or program, but the majority will be specific to a particular classroom setting.

- Observations should last at least three hours on a typical day. With this in mind, try to avoid using the tool within the first or last four weeks of the school year. "Typical" days should avoid special events, guest teachers, and extreme weather events.

- Observers should minimize their impact on the classroom as much as possible. This means not inferring with or participating in classroom activities–including talking with teachers or children during the class session.

- The NABERS for K-3 rating should include observation of at least three different curricular areas (e.g., environmental literacy and connection, literacy, science, math, social studies, art) taught by the primary classroom teacher.

- Supporting evidence includes observation, teacher reports to the assessor, children's work products, and documents such as lesson plans and strategic plans. Supporting evidence may be relevant in multiple sections or subsections of the tool.

If there is a question about whether a particular practice is present, the assessor should ask the teacher about this after the observation.

* If there are multiple teachers in the classroom as coteachers, the scores should reflect the practices of all teachers.

Step 2: Read each item and check one box per item row.

* Once you have observed and collected supporting evidence, score each item by placing a check mark in one of the boxes in the columns labeled 1, 3, 5, and 7. If a category does not apply, make a note to that effect. This will be relevant in Step 3.

* When scoring, keep in mind these clarifications of the terms *daily/almost always*, *often, sometimes, rarely*, and *no/does not*. *Daily* is every day children are present at school. Generally speaking, *often* would be more than 60 percent of the time, *sometimes* would be 30-60 percent of the time, *rarely* would be less than 30 percent of the time, and *no/does not* indicates the program does not practice this.

Step 3: Determine the score for each category.

Circle the corresponding level (1, 2, 3, 4, 5, 6, or 7) at the top of the category. The score for each category is determined using the following criteria:

For categories with **three or more items**:

Level 1: Half or more of the Level 1 boxes are checked (regardless of the Level 3, 5, or 7 boxes that may be checked).

Level 2: Fewer than half of the Level 1 boxes are checked, some of the Level 3 boxes are checked, and no Level 5 or 7 boxes are checked.

Level 3: All Level 3 boxes are checked or one Level 1 box is checked, and the remaining boxes are checked at Levels 5 or 7.

Level 4: No Level 1 boxes are checked, half or fewer of the Level 3 boxes are checked, and the remaining boxes are checked at Levels 5 or 7.

Level 5: All Level 5 boxes are checked or one Level 3 box is checked, and the remaining boxes are checked at Level 7.

Level 6: No Level 1 or 3 boxes are checked, half or fewer of the Level 5 boxes are checked, and the remaining boxes are checked at Level 7.

Level 7: All Level 7 boxes are checked.

For categories with **two items**:

Level 1: Both Level 1 boxes are checked.

Level 2: One Level 1 box and one Level 3 box are checked.

Level 3: Both Level 3 boxes are checked or one Level 1 box is checked, and the remaining box is checked at Levels 5 or 7.

Level 4: One Level 1 or 3 box is checked and one Level 5 box is checked.

Level 5: Both Level 5 boxes are checked or one Level 3 box is checked, and the remaining box is checked at Level 7.

Level 6: One Level 5 box is checked, and the remaining box is checked at Level 7.

Level 7: Both Level 7 boxes are checked.

If a category does not apply or cannot be observed, compute the quality level based on the number of subcategories completed for that category.

Section I: Program Goals and Curriculum Practices

This section addresses dual goals of developmentally appropriate early childhood and environmental education in which nature is the central organizing concept. The program goals, daily structure, and curriculum reflect the intentional implementation of nature-based education.

A. Program Goals: The program demonstrates dual goals of both child development and environmental stewardship based on high-quality practices of early childhood education (ECE) and environmental education (EE).

Item 1: The program has a mission or purpose statement that indicates dual goals of both child development and environmental stewardship.

1	2	3	4	5	6	7	Supporting Evidence
☐ Program has no mission or purpose statement.		☐ Program has a mission or purpose statement that indicates a goal of child development with no mention of nature.		☐ Program has a mission or purpose statement that indicates a goal of child development with mention of nature as a tool to accomplish that goal.		☐ Program has a mission or purpose statement that indicates dual goals of both child development *and* environmental stewardship.	

Item 2: The program models that all children, no matter their background or ability, deserve and can participate in positive outdoor experiences.

1	2	3	4	5	6	7	Supporting Evidence
☐ Program *does not* model that all children, no matter their background or ability, deserve and can participate in positive outdoor experiences.		☐ Program *sometimes* models that all children, no matter their background or ability, deserve and can participate in positive outdoor experiences.		☐ Program *often* models that all children, no matter their background or ability, deserve and can participate in positive outdoor experiences.		☐ Program *almost always* models that all children, no matter their background or ability, deserve and can participate in positive outdoor experiences.	

Item 3: Emphasis is placed on learning with nature.

1	2	3	4	5	6	7	Supporting Evidence
☐ No integration of nature in learning.		☐ Learning primarily emphasizes learning in nature.		☐ Learning primarily emphasizes learning *about* nature.		☐ Emphasis is placed on learning *with* nature versus learning in or about nature (i.e., integration of nature in learning).	

Item 4: Learning topics and scope are developmentally appropriate.

1	2	3	4	5	6	7	Supporting Evidence
☐ Learning topics and scope are above children's understanding (e.g., abstract aspects of climate change, faraway places).		☐ Learning topics and scope are *sometimes* developmentally appropriate (e.g., concrete, locally focused).		☐ Learning topics and scope are *often* developmentally appropriate (e.g., concrete, locally focused).		☐ Learning topics and scope are *almost always* developmentally appropriate (e.g., concrete, locally focused).	

Item 5: Sustainable practices are evident.

1	2	3	4	5	6	7	Supporting Evidence
☐ *No* sustainable practices are evident in the program.		☐ At least *1* sustainable practice* is evident in the program.		☐ At least 2 sustainable practices* are evident in the program.		☐ At least 3 sustainable practices* are evident in the program.	

Item 6: Program implements Leave No Trace® principles in natural ecosystems.

1	2	3	4	5	6	7	Supporting Evidence
☐ The program *does not* practice Leave No Trace principles in natural ecosystems.		☐ The program *sometimes* practices Leave No Trace principles in natural ecosystems.		☐ The program *often* practices Leave No Trace principles in natural ecosystems.		☐ The program *almost always* practices Leave No Trace principles in natural ecosystems.	

SCORING NOTE:
Almost always: every day, or nearly every day, children are present; *often:* more than 60 percent of the time, *sometimes:* 30–60 percent of the time, *rarely:* less than 30 percent of the time; *no/does not:* never.

*Examples of sustainable practices include using real plates, utensils, cloth napkins, recycling, composting, rain barrels, and so on.

Evaluating Natureness: Measuring the Quality of Nature-Based Classrooms in Pre-K through 3rd Grade

B. Program Practices: The class demonstrates a value for ongoing experiences in nature through daily class structure.

Item 1: The class day starts outdoors.

1	2	3	4	5	6	7	
☐ The class *does not* start the day outdoors.		☐ The class *sometimes* starts the day outdoors.		☐ The class *often* starts the day outdoors.		☐ The class *almost always** starts the day outdoors.	Supporting Evidence

Item 2: A majority of the class time is spent outdoors.

1	2	3	4	5	6	7	
☐ The class has *no* outdoor learning time (i.e., no time separate from recess).		☐ The class spends *less than 30 percent* of total weekly class time outdoors (in the natural play area and/or beyond).		☐ The class spends *30–50 percent* of total weekly class time outdoors (in the natural play area and/or beyond).		☐ The class spends *at least 50 percent* of total weekly class time outdoors (in a natural play area and/or beyond).	Supporting Evidence

Item 3: The class regularly visits natural ecosystems.

1	2	3	4	5	6	7	
☐ The class *does not* spend class time in natural ecosystems (wild areas).		☐ The class spends *less than 30 percent* of outdoor class time in natural ecosystems.		☐ The class spends *30–50 percent* of outdoor class time in natural ecosystems.		☐ The class spends *at least 50 percent* of outdoor class time in natural ecosystems.	Supporting Evidence

Item 4: Extensive daily class time is unstructured nature play.

1	2	3	4	5	6	7	
☐ *No* outdoor class time is spent in unstructured nature play.		☐ The class *sometimes* provides unstructured nature play as part of daily outdoor time.		☐ The class *often* provides unstructured nature play as part of daily outdoor time.		☐ The class *almost always* includes unstructured nature play as part of daily outdoor time.	Supporting Evidence

Item 5: Safety-related policies and procedures based on ongoing site and benefit-risk assessments are in place.

1	2	3	4	5	6	7	
☐ *No* safety-related policies and procedures based on ongoing site and benefit-risk assessments are in place for activities.		☐ Safety-related policies and procedures based on ongoing site and benefit-risk assessments are in place for *some* activities.		☐ Safety-related policies and procedures based on ongoing site and benefit-risk assessments are written for *most* activities.		☐ Safety-related policies and procedures based on ongoing site and benefit-risk assessments are written for *almost all* activities.	Supporting Evidence

Item 6: Safety-related policies and procedures are followed.

1	2	3	4	5	6	7	
☐ Safety-related policies and procedures are *not* followed.		☐ Safety-related policies and procedures are *sometimes* followed.		☐ Safety-related policies and procedures are *often* followed.		☐ Safety-related policies and procedures are *almost always* followed.	Supporting Evidence

*A rare exception to this would be days when the weather is dangerous and, as a result, the teachers adjust their schedule for that day. For example, on an extremely cold morning, teachers might shift the schedule so outdoor time occurs an hour later than normal to allow the sun and temperatures to rise.

SCORING NOTE:
Almost always: every day, or nearly every day, children are present; *often:* more than 60 percent of the time, *sometimes*; 30–60 percent of the time, *rarely*; less than 30 percent of the time; *no/does not:* never.

C. Curriculum*: This category evaluates the extent to which nature is the central organizing concept of the program's curriculum and to what extent learning builds on children's interests and experiences in their local natural environment. Note: Subcategory a. and at least two of the five domain-specific categories must be scored.

a. Environmental Literacy and Connection: This category measures the extent to which teachers support children's development of a relationship with the outdoors.

Item 1: Teachers intentionally develop children's outdoor skills.**

1	2	3	4	5	6	7	Supporting Evidence
☐ Teacher-led activities *rarely* develop children's outdoor skills.		☐ Teacher-led activities *sometimes* develop children's outdoor skills.		☐ Teacher-led activities *often* develop children's outdoor skills.		☐ Teacher-led activities *almost always* develop children's outdoor skills.	

C. Curriculum: a. Environmental Literacy and Connection

Item 2: Children reflect on their nature experiences.

1	2	3	4	5	6	7	Supporting Evidence
☐ Children *rarely* reflect on their nature experiences through conversation and documentation.		☐ Children *sometimes* reflect on their nature experiences through conversation and documentation.		☐ Children *often* reflect on their nature experiences through conversation and documentation.		☐ Children reflect *almost always* on their nature experiences through conversation and documentation.	

C. Curriculum: a. Environmental Literacy and Connection

Item 3: Teacher-led activities build on prior nature knowledge and experiences.

1	2	3	4	5	6	7	Supporting Evidence
☐ Teacher-led activities *do not or rarely* build on nature knowledge and experiences over time.		☐ Teacher-led activities *sometimes* build on nature knowledge and experiences over time.		☐ Teacher-led activities *often* build on nature knowledge and experiences over time.		☐ Teacher-led activities *almost always* build on nature knowledge and experiences over time.	

C. Curriculum: b. Literacy: This category measures the extent to which reading and writing activities and materials connect to children's nature-based experiences and learning.

Item 1: Reading and writing activities connect to children's ongoing nature-based experiences.

1	2	3	4	5	6	7	Supporting Evidence
☐ Reading and writing activities are *rarely* connected to children's ongoing nature-based experiences.		☐ Reading and writing activities are *sometimes* connected to children's ongoing nature-based experiences.		☐ Reading and writing activities are *often* connected to children's ongoing nature-based experiences.		☐ Reading and writing activities are *almost always* connected to children's ongoing nature-based experiences.	

C. Curriculum: b. Literacy

Item 2: Reading and writing activities emerge from children's interest in nature.

1	2	3	4	5	6	7	Supporting Evidence

*Score C. Curriculum only if taught by the classroom teacher.

**There are a variety of terms for outdoor skills, including *woodcraft*, *bushcraft*, and even *survival skills*. Whatever term is used, the activities themselves should align with the other quality measures in the NABERS tool, such as *developmentally appropriate* and *environmental impact*.

SCORING NOTE:
Almost always: every day, or nearly every day, children are present; *often*: more than 60 percent of the time, *sometimes*; 30–60 percent of the time, *rarely*; less than 30 percent of the time; *no/does not*: never.

Evaluating Natureness: Measuring the Quality of Nature-Based Classrooms in Pre-K through 3rd Grade

☐ Reading and writing activities *do not* or *rarely* emerge from children's interests in nature.	☐ Reading and writing activities *sometimes* emerge from children's interests in nature.		☐ Reading and writing activities *often* emerge from children's interests in nature.		☐ Reading and writing activities *almost always* emerge from children's interests in nature.	
1	2	3	4	5	6	7

C. Curriculum: b. Literacy

Item 3: Fictional texts represent authentic, local nature and align with seasonal happenings.

☐ Fictional texts provided *do not* or *rarely* represent authentic, local nature and align with current seasonal happenings.	☐ Fictional texts provided *sometimes* represent authentic, local nature and align with current seasonal happenings.		☐ Fictional texts provided *often* represent authentic, local nature and align with current seasonal happenings.		☐ Fictional texts provided *almost always* represent authentic, local nature and align with current seasonal happenings.	Supporting Evidence
1	2	3	4	5	6	7

C. Curriculum: b. Literacy

Item 4: Informational texts represent authentic, local nature and align with seasonal happenings.

☐ Informational texts provided *do not* or *rarely* represent authentic, local nature and align with current seasonal happenings.	☐ Informational texts provided *sometimes* represent authentic, local nature and align with current seasonal happenings.		☐ Informational texts provided *often* represent authentic, local nature and align with current seasonal happenings.		☐ Informational texts provided *almost always* represent authentic, local nature and align with current seasonal happenings.	Supporting Evidence
1	2	3	4	5	6	7

C. Curriculum: b. Literacy

Item 5: Texts represent diverse audiences having positive outdoor experiences.

☐ Texts provided *do not* or *rarely* represent a diversity of people having positive outdoor experiences.	☐ Texts provided *sometimes* represent a diversity of people having positive outdoor experiences.		☐ Texts provided *often* represent a diversity of people having positive outdoor experiences.		☐ Texts provided *almost always* represent a diversity of people having positive outdoor experiences.	Supporting Evidence
1	2	3	4	5	6	7

C. Curriculum: c. Math: This category measures the extent to which math activities and materials connect to children's nature-based experiences and learning.

Item 1: Math activities are connected to children's ongoing nature-based experiences.

☐ Math activities *do not* or are *rarely* connected to children's ongoing nature-based experiences.	☐ Math activities are *sometimes* connected to children's ongoing nature-based experiences.		☐ Math activities are *often* connected to children's ongoing nature-based experiences.		☐ Math activities are *almost always* connected to children's ongoing nature-based experiences.	Supporting Evidence
1	2	3	4	5	6	7

C. Curriculum: c. Math

Item 2: Math activities are connected to children's interests in nature.

						Supporting Evidence
1	2	3	4	5	6	7

*Score C. Curriculum only if taught by the classroom teacher.

SCORING NOTE:

Almost always: every day, or nearly every day, children are present; *often*: more than 60 percent of the time, *sometimes*; 30–60 percent of the time, *rarely*; less than 30 percent of the time; *no/does not*: never.

1	2	3	4	5	6	7	
☐ Math activities *do not* or are *rarely* connected to children's interests in nature.		☐ Math activities are *sometimes* connected to children's interests in nature.		☐ Math activities are *often* connected to children's interests in nature.		☐ Math activities are *almost always* connected to children's interests in nature.	Supporting Evidence

C. Curriculum: c. Math

Item 3: Math materials represent authentic, local nature aligned with seasonal happenings and consist of objects found in nature.

1	2	3	4	5	6	7	
☐ Math materials *do not* or *rarely* represent authentic, local nature aligned with seasonal happenings *or* consist of objects found in nature.		☐ Math materials *sometimes* represent authentic, local nature aligned with seasonal happenings *or* consist of objects found in nature.		☐ Math materials *often* represent authentic, local nature aligned with seasonal happenings *and* consist of objects found in nature.		☐ Math materials *almost always* represent authentic, local nature aligned with seasonal happenings *and* consist of objects found in nature.	Supporting Evidence

C. Curriculum: d. Science

This category measures the extent to which science activities and materials connect to children's nature-based experiences and learning.

Item 1: Science activities are connected to children's ongoing nature-based experiences.

1	2	3	4	5	6	7	
☐ Science activities *do not* or are *rarely* connected to children's ongoing nature-based experiences.		☐ Science activities are *sometimes* connected to children's ongoing nature-based experiences.		☐ Science activities are *often* connected to children's ongoing nature-based experiences.		☐ Science activities are *almost always* connected to children's ongoing nature-based experiences.	Supporting Evidence

C. Curriculum: d. Science

Item 2: Science activities emerge from children's interests in and questions about nature.

1	2	3	4	5	6	7	
☐ Science activities *do not* or *rarely* emerge from children's interests in and questions about nature.		☐ Science activities *sometimes* emerge from children's interests in and questions about nature.		☐ Science activities *often* emerge from children's interests in and questions about nature.		☐ Science activities *almost always* emerge from children's interests in and questions about nature.	Supporting Evidence

C. Curriculum: d. Science

Item 3: Authentic, local, and seasonal natural materials are used to explore seasonally aligned science phenomena.

1	2	3	4	5	6	7	
☐ Authentic, local, and seasonal natural materials *are not* or are *rarely* used to explore seasonally aligned science phenomena.		☐ Authentic, local, and seasonal natural materials are *sometimes* used to explore seasonally aligned science phenomena.		☐ Authentic, local, and seasonal natural materials are *often* used to explore seasonally aligned science phenomena.		☐ Authentic, local, and seasonal natural materials are *almost always* used to explore seasonally aligned science phenomena.	Supporting Evidence

C. Curriculum: e. Social Studies

This category measures the extent to which social studies activities connect to or build on children's authentic, place-based experiences with the natural world.

Item 1: Social studies activities are connected to children's ongoing nature-based experiences.

1	2	3	4	5	6	7	
							Supporting Evidence

*Score C. Curriculum only if taught by the classroom teacher.

SCORING NOTE:

Almost always: every day, or nearly every day, children are present; *often:* more than 60 percent of the time; *sometimes:* 30–60 percent of the time; *rarely:* less than 30 percent of the time; *no/does not:* never.

Evaluating Natureness: Measuring the Quality of Nature-Based Classrooms in Pre-K through 3rd Grade

1	2	3	4	5	6	7	
☐ Social studies activities *do not or are rarely* connected to children's ongoing nature-based experiences.		☐ Social studies activities are *sometimes* connected to children's ongoing nature-based experiences.		☐ Social studies activities are *often* connected to children's ongoing nature-based experiences.		☐ Social studies activities are *almost always* connected to children's ongoing nature-based experiences.	Supporting Evidence

C. Curriculum: e. Social Studies

Item 2: Social studies activities are connected to children's interests in nature.

1	2	3	4	5	6	7	
☐ Social studies activities *do not or are rarely* connected to children's interests in nature.		☐ Social studies activities are *sometimes* connected to children's interests in nature.		☐ Social studies activities are *often* connected to children's interests in nature.		☐ Social studies activities are *almost always* connected to children's interests in nature.	Supporting Evidence

C. Curriculum: e. Social Studies

Item 3: Social studies activities are connected to local history, culture, and natural resources.

1	2	3	4	5	6	7	
☐ Social studies activities *do not or are rarely* connected to local history, culture, and natural resources.		☐ Social studies activities are *sometimes* connected to local history, culture, and natural resources.		☐ Social studies activities are *often* connected to local history, culture, and natural resources.		☐ Social studies activities are *almost always* connected to local history, culture, and natural resources.	Supporting Evidence

C. Curriculum: f. Arts**

This category measures the extent to which arts activities intentionally connect to children's ongoing nature-based experiences, allow children's interests related to nature to guide the expression, and include natural materials in the work.

Item 1: Arts activities are connected to children's ongoing nature-based experiences.

1	2	3	4	5	6	7	
☐ Arts activities *do not or are rarely* connected to children's ongoing nature-based experiences.		☐ Arts activities are *sometimes* connected to children's ongoing nature-based experiences.		☐ Arts activities are *often* connected to children's ongoing nature-based experiences.		☐ Arts activities (e.g., performing and/or visual arts) are *almost always* connected to children's ongoing nature-based experiences.	Supporting Evidence

C. Curriculum: f. Arts*

Item 2: Arts activities are connected to children's interests in nature.

1	2	3	4	5	6	7	
☐ Arts activities *do not or are rarely* connected to children's interests in nature.		☐ Arts activities are *sometimes* connected to children's interests in nature.		☐ Arts activities are *often* connected to children's interests in nature.		☐ Arts activities are *almost always* connected to children's interests in nature.	Supporting Evidence

C. Curriculum: f. Arts*

Item 3: Art materials consist of objects found in nature.

1	2	3	4	5	6	7	
☐ Art materials *do not or rarely* consist of objects found in nature.		☐ Art materials *sometimes* consist of objects found in nature.		☐ Art materials *often* consist of objects found in nature.		☐ Art materials *almost always* consist of objects found in nature.	Supporting Evidence

*Score C. Curriculum only if taught by the classroom teacher.

SCORING NOTE:
Almost always: every day, or nearly every day, children are present; *often*: more than 60 percent of the time, *sometimes*: 30–60 percent of the time, *rarely*: less than 30 percent of the time; *no/does not*: never.

NAture-Based Education Rating Scale (NABERS) for K-3 Education: Comprehensive Assessment Rubric

Section II: Staffing

The teachers' roles are as facilitators, and they are trained in both early childhood education and environmental education. Administration supports professional development, and teachers cultivate their own interest in nature.

A. Administrators' Role: The administrators support teaching staff in implementing a nature-based approach. (Note: Administrators can include a director, owner, or board members.)

Item 1: Administrators allocate time, money, and material resources to implement nature-based education.

1	2	3	4	5	6	7	Supporting Evidence
☐ Administrators *do not* help facilitate a nature-based education.		☐ Administrators *sometimes* allocate time, money, or material resources to implement nature-based education programs.		☐ Administrators *often* allocate time, money, or material resources to implement nature-based education.		☐ Administrators *almost always* allocate time, money, and material resources to implement nature-based education (e.g., in-classroom materials, planning time, professional development).	

Item 2: Organizational planning focuses on the intentional integration of nature-based education.

1	2	3	4	5	6	7	Supporting Evidence
☐ Short- or long-term organizational planning *does not* include nature-based education.		☐ Short- or long-term organizational planning *sometimes* includes nature-based education.		☐ Short- or long-term organizational planning *often* includes nature-based education.		☐ Short- and long-term organizational planning *almost always* focuses on the intentional integration of nature-based education.	

Item 3: Administrators are public advocates for nature-based education.

1	2	3	4	5	6	7	Supporting Evidence
☐ Administrators are *not* public advocates for nature-based education.		☐ Administrators are *sometimes* public advocates for nature-based education.		☐ Administrators are *often* public advocates for nature-based education.		☐ Administrators are *almost always* public advocates for nature-based education.	

B. Teacher's Role: Teachers play a critical role in setting the tone and appropriate behavior to allow for and encourage open-ended nature exploration and play.

Item 1: Teacher(s) facilitate open-ended nature exploration and play.

1	2	3	4	5	6	7	Supporting Evidence
☐ Teacher(s) *do not* facilitate open-ended nature exploration and play during outdoor time.		☐ Teacher(s) *sometimes* facilitate open-ended nature exploration and play during outdoor time.		☐ Teacher(s) *often* facilitate open-ended nature exploration and play during outdoor time.		☐ Teacher(s) *almost always* facilitate open-ended nature exploration and play during outdoor time.	

Item 2: Teachers express and communicate enthusiasm for outdoor time.

1	2	3	4	5	6	7	Supporting Evidence
☐ Teachers *do not* express enthusiasm about scheduled outdoor time.		☐ Teachers *sometimes* express enthusiasm about scheduled outdoor time.		☐ Teachers *often* express enthusiasm about scheduled outdoor time.		☐ Teachers *almost always* express enthusiasm about scheduled outdoor time and communicate this enthusiasm to the children.	

Item 3: Teachers interact with natural environments.

1	2	3	4	5	6	7	Supporting Evidence
☐ Teachers *do not* engage with the natural environment.		☐ Teachers are seen to interact with natural environments in 1 way.*		☐ Teachers are seen to interact with natural environments in 2 ways.*		☐ Teachers are seen to interact with natural environments in at least 3 ways.*	

*For example, by lying on the ground, raking leaves, catching insects, picking up worms, catching tadpoles and frogs, turning over logs, planting and/or harvesting gardens, or tapping maple trees.

SCORING NOTE:
Almost always: every day, or nearly every day, children are present; *often*: more than 60 percent of the time, *sometimes*; 30–60 percent of the time, *rarely*; less than 30 percent of the time; *no/does not*: never.

Item 4: Teachers are comfortable with nature immersion.

1	2	3	4	5	6	7	Supporting Evidence
☐ Teachers *do not* show comfort with nature immersion by dressing appropriately for and communicating positively about the weather (e.g., wearing appropriate footwear for the terrain and weather).		☐ Teachers *sometimes* show comfort with nature immersion by dressing appropriately for and communicating positively about the weather (e.g., wearing appropriate footwear for the terrain and weather).		☐ Teachers *often* are comfortable with nature immersion and show this by dressing appropriately for and communicating positively about the weather (e.g., wearing appropriate footwear for the terrain and weather).		☐ Teachers *almost always* are comfortable with nature immersion and show this by dressing appropriately for and communicating positively about the weather (e.g., wearing appropriate footwear for the terrain and weather).	

C. Teacher Qualifications: In addition to being qualified to teach based on applicable laws (i.e., certification), the teacher has formal training in nature-related topics.

Item 1: Teacher qualifications include teaching certification and formal training in environmental education.

1	2	3	4	5	6	7	Supporting Evidence
☐ The teacher, in addition to being a certified elementary teacher, has *no additional degree or certificate* related to nature-based education *or* natural science (e.g., environmental education, biology).		☐ The teacher, in addition to being a certified elementary teacher, has an *associate's degree or a nonaccredited certificate* in a field related to nature-based education *or* natural science (e.g., environmental education, biology).		☐ The teacher, in addition to being a certified elementary teacher, has a *bachelor's degree, minor, or university certificate* in a field related to nature-based education *or* natural science (e.g., environmental education, biology).		☐ The teacher, in addition to being a certified elementary teacher, has a *bachelor's or master's degree* related to nature-based education *or* natural science (e.g., environmental education, biology).	

D. Professional Development

Item 1: Teachers participate in ongoing professional development to facilitate their interests, skills, and knowledge of nature and nature-based education pedagogy.

1	2	3	4	5	6	7	Supporting Evidence
☐ Teachers *do not* participate in professional development related to nature topics.		☐ Teachers cultivate their own knowledge by participating *once a year* in professional development (e.g., visiting model programs, attending workshops) related to nature-based education pedagogy *or* natural-history knowledge.		☐ Teachers cultivate their own knowledge of and interest in nature by participating *once a year* in professional development (e.g., visiting model programs, attending workshops) related to nature-based education pedagogy *and* natural-history knowledge.		☐ Teachers cultivate their own knowledge of and interest in nature by participating at least *twice a year* in professional development (e.g., visiting model programs, attending workshops) related to both nature-based education pedagogy *and* natural history knowledge.	

SCORING NOTE:
Almost always: every day, or nearly every day, children are present; *often:* more than 60 percent of the time, *sometimes;* 30–60 percent of the time, *rarely;* less than 30 percent of the time; *no/does not;* never.

Section III: Environment

Three distinct spaces—inside, outside, and beyond—are provided to meaningfully integrate nature among the physical environments.

A. Indoor Classroom (Inside): Nature is infused into all areas of the classroom. The classroom generally has a nature-like feel and appearance (plenty of natural light, wood and natural materials, animals, and plants). For classes that do not have an indoor classroom space or have an indoor space that is used only as an emergency shelter space, score the following item and then skip the first three items of the Indoor Classroom category.

Alternate Item 1-3 (for classes without an indoor space): Need for an Emergency Shelter

1	2	3	4	5	6	7	Supporting Evidence
☐ The class *does not* have an emergency shelter.		☐ The class has an emergency shelter, but it is *not* in close proximity.		☐ The class has an emergency shelter in close proximity *most* of the time.		☐ The class has an emergency shelter in close proximity at *all* times.	

Item 1: The indoor classroom has natural lighting and views of outdoors.

1	2	3	4	5	6	7	Supporting Evidence
☐ The indoor classroom has *no* windows.		☐ The indoor classroom has *some* natural light *without* child-level views to the outdoors.		☐ The indoor classroom has *some* natural light *with* child-level views to *any outdoor space*.		☐ The indoor classroom has *extensive* natural light *with* child-level views to a *natural space* outdoors.	

Item 2: The indoor classroom has natural furnishings and colors.

1	2	3	4	5	6	7	Supporting Evidence
☐ The indoor classroom has *no* natural look and feel (e.g., plastic furnishings, primary colors).		☐ The indoor classroom has a *limited* natural look and feel (e.g., mix of natural and plastic furnishings, diverse textures, primary colors).		☐ The indoor classroom has *some* natural look and feel (e.g., mix of natural and plastic furnishings, diverse textures, earth-based colors).		☐ The indoor classroom has an *extensively* natural look and feel (e.g., natural furnishings, diverse textures, earth-based colors).	

Item 3: The indoor classroom affords children access and movement between indoors and outdoors.

1	2	3	4	5	6	7	Supporting Evidence
☐ The indoor classroom has a difficult transition to the outdoors.		☐ The indoor classroom has an easy, but not direct, transition to the outdoors.		☐ The indoor classroom has immediate access through a door to the outdoor classroom.		☐ The indoor classroom has immediate access to the outdoors, *and* children have free-range movement between the indoor and outdoor classroom through a transition space (e.g., a porch or sunroom).	

Item 4: Natural materials are present and reflect local nature.

1	2	3	4	5	6	7	Supporting Evidence
☐ Natural materials are *not* present.		☐ Natural materials are present in *some* areas of the indoor classroom and reflect a variety of local nature.		☐ Natural materials are present in *most* areas of the indoor classroom and reflect a variety of local nature.		☐ Natural materials (e.g., bird parts, animal bones, bird nests, tree seeds, etc.) are present in *all* areas of the indoor classroom and reflect a variety of local nature.	

SCORING NOTE:
Almost always: every day, or nearly every day, children are present; *often:* more than 60 percent of the time; *sometimes:* 30–60 percent of the time; *rarely:* less than 30 percent of the time; *no/does not:* never.

Item 5: Indoor classroom materials are realistic and representative of local nature.

1	2	3	4	5	6	7	Supporting Evidence
☐ *No* indoor classroom materials represent realistic and local nature.		☐ Indoor classroom materials *sometimes* represent realistic and local nature.		☐ Indoor classroom materials *often* represent realistic and local nature.		☐ Indoor classroom materials (e.g., puppets, books, dramatic play materials) *almost always* represent realistic and local nature.	

Item 6: Indoor classroom materials reflect the human diversity of the local community having positive outdoor experiences.

1	2	3	4	5	6	7	Supporting Evidence
☐ *No* indoor classroom materials reflect the human diversity of the local community having positive outdoor experiences.		☐ Indoor classroom materials *sometimes* reflect the human diversity of the local community having positive outdoor experiences.		☐ Indoor classroom materials *often* reflect the human diversity of the local community having positive outdoor experiences.		☐ Indoor classroom materials *almost always* reflect the human diversity of the local community having positive outdoor experiences.	

Item 7: The indoor classroom has plants and animals.

1	2	3	4	5	6	7	Supporting Evidence
☐ The indoor classroom *does not* have living plants and/or animals.		☐ The indoor classroom has 1 or more living plants and/or animals in the indoor classroom (if allergies allow).		☐ The indoor classroom has 2 or more living plants and/or animals (if allergies allow).		☐ The indoor classroom has 3 or more living plants and/or animals (if allergies allow).	

B. Natural Play Area (Outside): The natural play area (outside) includes numerous human- and nature-made loose parts and a variety of features for nature-based play.

Item 1: The natural play area has a natural look and feel.

1	2	3	4	5	6	7	Supporting Evidence
☐ The natural play area has *no* natural look and feel (e.g., plastic furnishings, primary colors).		☐ The natural play area has *limited* natural look and feel (e.g., mix of natural and plastic furnishings, diverse textures, primary colors).		☐ The natural play area has *some* natural look and feel (e.g., mix of natural and plastic furnishings, diverse textures, earth-based colors).		☐ The natural play area has an *extensive* natural look and feel (e.g., natural materials, diverse textures, earth-based colors).	

Item 2: The natural play area contains a variety of natural features.

1	2	3	4	5	6	7	Supporting Evidence
☐ The outside play area is a traditional playground (e.g., climbing structures, sandbox) with few natural features.		☐ The natural play area includes *at least 3* of the following: loose parts, variety of vegetation, vegetable or herb garden, sand and soil, water feature, opportunities for active motor play, opportunities for less-active play, variety of terrain, mix of sunny and shady areas, variety of gathering spaces, variety of features, and variety of seating and tables.		☐ The natural play area includes *at least 5* of the following: loose parts, variety of vegetation, vegetable or herb garden, sand and soil, water feature, opportunities for active motor play, opportunities for less-active play, variety of terrain, mix of sunny and shady areas, variety of gathering spaces, variety of features, and variety of seating and tables.		☐ The natural play area includes *at least 7* of the following: loose parts, variety of vegetation, vegetable or herb garden, sand and soil, water feature, opportunities for active motor play, opportunities for less-active play, variety of terrain, mix of sunny and shady areas, variety of gathering spaces, variety of features, and variety of seating and tables.	

SCORING NOTE:
Almost always: every day, or nearly every day, children are present; *often*: more than 60 percent of the time, *sometimes*; 30–60 percent of the time, *rarely*; less than 30 percent of the time; *no/does not*: never.

Item 3: The natural play area includes natural materials that reflect a variety of local nature.

1	2	3	4	5	6	7	
☐ Natural materials *are not* present.		☐ Natural materials (e.g., bird parts, animal bones, bird's nests, tree seeds, etc.) are present in *some* areas of the natural play area and reflect a variety of local nature.		☐ Natural materials (e.g., bird parts, animal bones, bird's nests, tree seeds, etc.) are present in *most* areas of the natural play area and reflect a variety of local nature.		☐ Natural materials (e.g., bird parts, animal bones, bird's nests, tree seeds, etc.) are present in *all* areas of the natural play area and reflect a variety of local nature.	Supporting Evidence

Item 4: Natural play area materials represent realistic and local nature.

1	2	3	4	5	6	7	
☐ *No* materials represent realistic and local nature.		☐ Natural play area materials (e.g., puppets, books, dramatic play materials) *sometimes* represent realistic and local nature.		☐ Natural play area materials (e.g., puppets, books, dramatic play materials) *often* represent realistic and local nature.		☐ Natural play area materials (e.g., puppets, books, dramatic play materials) *almost always* represent realistic and local nature.	Supporting Evidence

C. Natural Ecosystems (Beyond): The class has areas of natural ecosystems for exploration outside of the natural play area.*

Item 1: The class has access to natural ecosystems.

1	2	3	4	5	6	7	
☐ The class has *no* access to natural ecosystems outside the natural play area.		☐ The class accesses *1* natural ecosystem (e.g., pond, river, wetland, marsh, meadow, field, prairie, lake/beach, vernal pools, woodlands, parks, etc.) throughout the year.		☐ The class accesses *2* natural ecosystems (e.g., pond, river, wetland, marsh, meadow, field, prairie, lake/beach, vernal pools, woodlands, parks, etc.) throughout the year.		☐ The class accesses *at least 3* natural ecosystems (e.g., pond, river, wetland, marsh, meadow, field, prairie, lake/beach, vernal pools, woodlands, parks, etc.) throughout the year.	Supporting Evidence

Item 2: The natural ecosystems are healthy.

1	2	3	4	5	6	7	
☐ The natural ecosystems are *never* healthy, or they are nonexistent.		☐ The natural ecosystems are *sometimes* healthy.		☐ The natural ecosystems are *often* healthy.		☐ The natural ecosystems are *almost always* healthy (e.g., rich biodiversity and minimal exotic and invasive species).	Supporting Evidence

Item 3: The natural ecosystem includes loose parts and natural features.

1	2	3	4	5	6	7	
☐ There are *no* loose parts and natural features to interact with (e.g., trees, flowers, wildlife), or there is no ecosystem available to visit.		☐ There are *few* loose parts and natural features to interact with (e.g., trees, flowers, wildlife).		☐ There are *some* loose parts and natural features to interact with (e.g., trees, flowers, wildlife).		☐ There are *many* loose parts and natural features to interact with (e.g., trees, flowers, wildlife).	Supporting Evidence

*Examples of natural ecosystems include ponds, rivers, wetlands, marshes, meadows, fields, prairies, lakes, beaches, vernal pools, woodlands, parks, and so on.

SCORING NOTE:
Almost always: every day, or nearly every day, children are present; *often:* more than 60 percent of the time; *sometimes:* 30–60 percent of the time; *rarely:* less than 30 percent of the time; *no/does not:* never.

Section IV: Community Partnerships and Resources

The program uses local, nature-based organizations and/or resources.

A. Nature Educator: An experienced nature educator visits the classroom regularly and has an ongoing relationship with the teacher and students.

Item 1: The nature educator visits frequently.

1	2	3	4	5	6	7	Supporting Evidence
☐ Nature educator visits *once per year or less*.		☐ Nature educator visits *seasonally*.		☐ Nature educator visits at least *once a month*.		☐ Nature educator visits at least *once a week*.	

Item 2: The program has a strong, supportive relationship with the same nature educator.

1	2	3	4	5	6	7	Supporting Evidence
☐ The program *does not* have a relationship with a nature educator.		☐ Nature educator is *sometimes* the same individual.		☐ Nature educator is *often* the same individual.		☐ Nature educator is *almost always* the same individual.	

B. Artifacts/Resources—On-Site: The class has access to artifacts and resources that support a nature-based curriculum.

Item 1: The program has access to artifacts and resources.

1	2	3	4	5	6	7	Supporting Evidence
☐ The class *does not* have access to a variety of artifacts and resources on the school grounds.		☐ The class *sometimes* has access to a variety of artifacts and resources on the school grounds.		☐ The class *often* has access to a variety of artifacts and resources on the school grounds.		☐ The class *daily/almost always* has access to a variety of artifacts and resources on the school grounds (e.g., diverse habitats, greenhouses, apiary, raptors, sugarhouse, gardens, etc.).	

Item 2: Wild and/or domestic animals are available to support nature-based learning.

1	2	3	4	5	6	7	Supporting Evidence
☐ Wild and/or domestic animals are *not* available to support programs.		☐ Wild and/or domestic animals are *sometimes* available to support programs.		☐ Wild and/or domestic animals are *often* available to support programs.		☐ Wild and/or domestic animals are *almost always* available to support programs (e.g., wildlife rehab education animal, class pet).	

C. Special Programs—Field Trips*: The class has access to special nature-based programs and resources that occur at another location.

Item 1: The program attends nature-based field trips that are integrated into the curriculum.

1	2	3	4	5	6	7	Supporting Evidence
☐ Children take *no* nature-based field trips during the school year.		☐ Children attend special nature-based programs (e.g., nature center, zoo, arboretum, apple orchard, dairy farm) away from the school (field trips) at least 1 time per year *but* experiences *are not* integrated into the classroom curriculum.		☐ Children attend special nature-based programs (e.g., nature center, zoo, arboretum, apple orchard, dairy farm) away from the school (field trips) at least 1 time per year *and* these experiences *are* integrated into the classroom curriculum.		☐ Children attend special nature-based programs (e.g., nature center, zoo, arboretum, apple orchard, dairy farm) away from the school (field trips) at least 2 times per year, and these experiences *are* integrated into the classroom curriculum.	

*If your school is located at a nature center, zoo, arboretum, apple orchard, dairy farm, or similar, but you must schedule a time to visit, it's considered a field trip.

SCORING NOTE:
Almost always: every day, or nearly every day, children are present; **often:** more than 60 percent of the time, **sometimes:** 30–60 percent of the time, **rarely:** less than 30 percent of the time; **no/does not:** never.

Section V: Family Engagement

The program supports families to engage with the nature-based approach.

A. Family Communication and Education: The program provides clear communication with and education for families on the benefits and outcomes of nature-based experiences for young children.

Item 1: The program shares nature-related content to families through formal communication.

1	2	3	4	5	6	7	Supporting Evidence
☐ *No* nature-related content in family communication.		☐ Nature-related content (e.g., benefits of nature, activities to do at home, appropriate clothing) is embedded in *some* of these communication methods: family handbook*, family orientation, family newsletter, reports of classroom activities to families, and family-teacher conferences.		☐ Nature-related content (e.g., benefits of nature, activities to do at home, appropriate clothing) is embedded in *most* of these communication methods: family handbook*, family orientation, family newsletter, reports of classroom activities to families, and family-teacher conferences.		☐ Nature-related content (e.g., benefits of nature, activities to do at home, appropriate clothing) is embedded in *all* of these communication methods: family handbook*, family orientation, family newsletter, reports of classroom activities to families, and family-teacher conferences.	

Item 2: The program documents its nature-based activities and shares documentation with families.

1	2	3	4	5	6	7	Supporting Evidence
☐ *No* documentation of nature-based activities and/or projects is posted.		☐ *Minimal* documentation of nature-based activities and/or projects is posted.		☐ *Moderate* documentation of nature-based activities and/or projects is posted.		☐ *Extensive* documentation of nature-based activities and/or projects is posted.	

B. Family Nature Experiences: Programs and resources are provided to facilitate families' experiences in nature.

Item 1: The program offers nature-based family programs.

1	2	3	4	5	6	7	Supporting Evidence
☐ *No* nature-based family programs are offered either inside or outside of the school.		☐ At least 1 seasonal, nature-based family program is offered annually.		☐ At least 2 seasonal, nature-based family programs are offered annually.		☐ At least 3 seasonal, nature-based family programs (e.g., owl hikes, camping, catching frogs or insects) are offered annually.	

Item 2: The program shares community resources and events about nature with families.

1	2	3	4	5	6	7	Supporting Evidence
☐ *No* community resources are shared with families.		☐ Community resources for family experiences in nature are *sometimes* included in family newsletters and/or weekly reports.		☐ Community resources for family experiences in nature are *often* included in family newsletters and/or weekly reports.		☐ Community resources for family experiences in nature are *almost always* included in family newsletters and/or weekly reports.	

*Family handbook includes mission statement and program philosophy related to nature and appropriate clothing to wear for the weather. (This can be part of the entire school handbook or a separate letter to families.)

SCORING NOTE:
Almost always: every day, or nearly every day, children are present; *often:* more than 60 percent of the time; *sometimes:* 30-60 percent of the time; *rarely:* less than 30 percent of the time; *no/does not:* never.

C. Family Involvement: The program encourages families to be involved in nature-based classroom activities.

Item 1: Families are encouraged to share their expertise and experiences in nature-based activities with the class.

1	2	3	4	5	6	7	Supporting Evidence
☐ Families are *not* encouraged to share their expertise and experiences in nature-based activities with the class.		☐ Families are *sometimes* encouraged to share their expertise and experiences in nature-based activities with the class.		☐ Families are *often* encouraged to share their expertise and experiences in nature-based activities with the class.		☐ Families are *almost always* encouraged to share their expertise and experiences in nature-based activities with the class.	

Item 2: The program encourages family volunteers to participate in nature-based classroom activities.

1	2	3	4	5	6	7	Supporting Evidence
☐ Families are *not* encouraged to volunteer to participate in nature-based classroom activities.		☐ Families are *sometimes* encouraged to volunteer to participate in nature-based classroom activities.		☐ Families are *often* encouraged to volunteer to participate in nature-based classroom activities.		☐ Families are *almost always* encouraged to volunteer to participate in nature-based classroom activities.	

SCORING NOTE:
Almost always: every day, or nearly every day, children are present; *often:* more than 60 percent of the time, *sometimes:* 30–60 percent of the time, *rarely:* less than 30 percent of the time; *no/does not:* never.

NAture-Based Education Rating Scale (NABERS) for K–3 Education: Summary Sheet

School Name: _____

School Address: _____

Date of Observation: _____

Observer Name: _____ Observer Email &/or Phone Number: _____

Time Observation Began: _____ Time Observation Ended: _____

Teacher(s) Name(s): _____

- **Teacher 1:** # Years teaching in a nature-based setting _____
  Other relevant teaching experiences (e.g., outdoor education, informal education) _____

- **Teacher 2 (if applicable):** # Years teaching in a nature-based setting _____
  Other relevant teaching experiences (e.g., outdoor education, informal education) _____

- **Teacher 3 (if applicable):** # Years teaching in a nature-based setting _____
  Other relevant teaching experiences (e.g., outdoor education, informal education) _____

# of additional staff present at time of observation (e.g., paraprofessionals) _____

Grade _____ # of children _____

Class Structure (e.g., number of days/week; hours class is in session) _____

Enter the numerical rating (1–7) for each item.

SECTION I: Program Goals & Curriculum Practices
_____ **A.** Program Goals
_____ **B.** Program Practices
_____ **C.** Curriculum
　　　_____ **a.** Environmental Literacy and Connection
　　　_____ **b.** Literacy
　　　_____ **c.** Math
　　　_____ **d.** Science
　　　_____ **e.** Social Studies
　　　_____ **f.** Arts
_____ **Number of subcategories scored** (subcategory a. Environmental Literacy and Connection and at least 2 others must be scored)
_____ **Total of subcategory scores** (7 minus number of Curriculum subcategories not rated)
_____ **Average of subcategory scores** (divide total of subcategory scores by number of categories scored)
_____ **Number of categories scored**
_____ **Total section score**
_____ **Average section score** (Total score ÷ Number of categories scored)

SECTION II: Staffing
_____ **A.** Administrator's Role
_____ **B.** Teacher's Role
_____ **C.** Teacher Qualifications
_____ **D.** Professional Development
_____ **Total section score**
_____ **Average section score** (Total score ÷ 4)

SECTION III: Environment
_____ **A.** Indoor Classroom (Inside)
_____ **B.** Natural Play area (Outside)
_____ **C.** Natural Ecosystems (Beyond)
_____ **Total section score**
_____ **Average section score** (Total score ÷ 3)

SECTION IV: Community Partnerships & Resources
_____ **A.** Nature Educator
_____ **B.** Artifacts/Resources—On-Site
_____ **C.** Special Programs—Field Trips
_____ **Total section score**
_____ **Average section score** (Total score ÷ 3)

SECTION V: Family Engagement
_____ **A.** Family Communication & Education
_____ **B.** Family Nature Experiences
_____ **C.** Family Involvement
_____ **Total section score**
_____ **Average section score** (Total score ÷ 3)

_____ **Total of all section averages**
_____ **Average classroom score** (Total of each average section score ÷ 5)

Observer signature _____

©2023 Patti Bailie, Rachel Larimore, and Arianna Pikus Published by Gryphon House, Inc. All rights reserved.

Appendix A: Annotated Bibliography Featuring Stories with Diverse Children in Outdoor Spaces

Curated by Michelle H. Martin, PhD, and J. Elizabeth Mills, PhD

Animals/Insects

Flett, Julie. 2021. *We All Play: Kimâetawâanaw.* Vancouver, BC: Greystone.
  English and Cree picture book about the similarities between what animals and humans do. Lively pastel and pencil illustrations.

Weston, Robert Paul. 2020. *Natsumi's Song of Summer.* Toronto, ON: Tundra.
  A little Japanese girl, Natsumi, eagerly awaits the arrival of her Black American cousin, Jill. When she comes, they delight in spending time outdoors together. Although Natsumi isn't sure she will, Jill even loves Natsumi's favorite insect.

Oceans/Beaches

Bryon, Nathan, and Dapo Adeola. 2020. *Rocket Says Clean Up!* New York: Random House Books for Young Readers.
  A young Black boy spreads the word about the importance of environmental mindfulness through cleaning up the beaches.

De la Peña, Matt. 2018. *Carmela Full of Wishes.* New York: G. P. Putnam's Sons.
  Carmela, a Latina girl, accompanies her grumpy big brother to the laundromat for the first time. After she tumbles off her scooter, he teaches her the best way to make wishes beside the ocean.

DiPucchio, Kelly, and Raissa Figueroa. 2021. *Oona.* New York: Katherine Tegen Books.
  Story of an adventurous, dark-skinned mermaid.

King, Heidi Tyline, and Ekua Holmes. 2021. *Saving American Beach: The Biography of African American Environmentalist MaVynee Betsch.* New York: G. P. Putnam's Sons.
  An immaculately illustrated story of MaVynee Betsch, whose grandfather bought American Beach for Black folks to enjoy when other beaches were segregated. Years later, when the beach was in disrepair, Betsch worked tirelessly to protect it for posterity.

Gardens and Farms

Brown-Wood, JaNay, and Samara Hardy. 2021. *Amara's Farm.* Atlanta, GA: Peachtree Publishers.
  A Black girl with her hair in puffballs searches the yard for her pumpkins while readers learn about lots of other veggies growing on her farm.

Casey, Dawn, and Jessica Courtney-Tickle. 2020. *My Nana's Garden.* Somerville, MA: Templar Books.
  Three generations of a BIPOC family—a grandmother, mother, and granddaughter—tend to Nana's garden while she is with them. Even after she's gone, they keep passing down the tradition of gardening.

Charles, Tami, and Sara Palacios. 2021. *My Day with the Panye.* Somerville, MA: Candlewick Press.
  A little Haitian girl gets her first try at carrying her family's weekly vegetables on her head in a basket, with a cloth *panye* used to balance the basket. Excellent introduction to this custom; text and illustrations feature lots of informative details about Haiti.

Harris, Shawn. 2021. *Have You Ever Seen a Flower?* San Francisco: Chronicle Books.
: The story of a girl's intensely close-up look at a flower; illustrations in pink, green, and blue neon-colored pencils grow more intense with the closer proximity.

Grimes, Nikki. 2020. *Southwest Sunrise.* New York: Bloomsbury.
: An African American boy moves to the desert with his family and thinks there's nothing in the desert . . . until he pays closer attention.

Hibbs, Gillian. 2018. *Errol's Garden.* Swindon, Wiltshire, UK: Child's Play.
: Errol is great at growing things, and when he starts running out of space, he enlists everyone's help to build a community garden on the rooftop of his apartment building.

Hillery, Tony, and Jessie Hartland. 2020. *Harlem Grown: How One Big Idea Transformed a Neighborhood.* New York: Simon and Schuster Books for Young Readers.
: Faced with a food desert, Tony Hillery works with students to turn an abandoned lot into a thriving farm, creating beauty and access to nutrition through collaboration.

Kloepper, Madeline. 2019. *The Not-So-Great Outdoors.* New York: Tundra.
: A biracial girl can't figure out why her parents are dragging her into the "great outdoors" until they see a bear family, which makes her realize some of the benefits of being out of her own urban jungle.

Larsen, Andrew, and Anne Villeneuve. 2019. *Me, Toma, and the Concrete Garden.* Toronto, ON: Kids Can Press.
: The story of a cross-racial friendship and an accidental summer garden that changes both the friendship and the urban neighborhood where it started.

Latham, Irene, and Johanna Wright. 2020. *This Poem Is a Nest.* New York: Wordsong.
: Short nestling poems arranged by season.

Mangal, Mélina, and Ken Daley. 2021. *Jayden's Impossible Garden.* Minneapolis, MN: Free Spirit.
: Jayden, an African American boy, and Mr. Curtis, who uses a wheelchair, together create a magical secret fort garden that counters Jayden's mama's insistence that "there's no nature here in the middle of the city."

Martin, Jacqueline Briggs. 2016. *Farmer Will Allen and the Growing Table.* Bellevue, WA: Readers to Eaters.
: African American former basketball star Will Allen turns an urban food desert into a thriving garden and deliberately creates community along the way.

Martinez-Neal, Juana, and Arlynder Sett Gaspar Paulino. 2021. *Zonia's Rain Forest.* Somerville, MA: Candlewick Press.
: Zonia, an (Indigenous) Ashianinka girl who lives in the Amazon, immerses herself in her lushly illustrated rain-forest home every day. But when she encounters a clear-cut section, she runs home to Mama, alarmed. The ending issues a call to action.

Miller, Sharee. 2021. *Michelle's Garden: How the First Lady Planted Seeds of Change.* New York: Little, Brown Books for Young Readers.
: The story of Michelle Obama's creation of the White House Kitchen Garden with the help of local school children; cartoonish illustrations.

Scanlon, Elizabeth Garton. 2020. *Thank You, Garden.* New York: Beach Lane Books.
: Two children enjoy a community garden from start to finish with lots of others; poetic text.

Zhang, Gracey. 2021. *Lala's Words.* New York: Orchard Books.
: Lala's mom has no idea how powerful Lala's words are . . . until she sees the humongous plants Lala, urban dweller, has talked into growing. Illustrations are in gray, white, yellow, and green.

Peace

Berry, James. 2020. *A Story About Afiya*. London, UK: Lantana Publishing.
   A quiet story of Afiya, a Black girl with very dark skin and Bantu knotted hair, whose white dress always picks up the design of nature she encounters each day and then turns white again overnight. *Afiya*, in Swahili, means "health."

Hooks, Gwendolyn, and Margaux Carpentier. 2021. *Planting Peace: The Story of Wangari Maathai*. Northampton, MA: Crocodile Books.
   Text-heavy biography of Wangari Maathai, Kenyan activist and Nobel Peace Prize recipient, who started a tree-planting movement that helped bring economic stability and food security back to her community.

MacLachlan, Patricia, and Chris Sheban. 2021. *When Grandfather Flew*. New York: Holiday House.
   As Grandpa, a dedicated birder, ages and dies, a bald eagle's appearance gives Milo hope that Grandpa has gotten his heart's desire.

Paul, Baptiste, Miranda Paul, and Estelí Meza. 2021. *Peace*. Zürich, Switzerland: NorthSouth Books.
   A beautifully illustrated poem about peace, featuring children from many different backgrounds and many different types of animals.

Phi, Bao. 2018. *A Different Pond*. Mankato, MN: Capstone Young Readers.
   A Vietnamese boy and his father go fishing together, seeking food for their evening dinner. They also share stories in flashbacks of their family history as recent immigrants from Vietnam. Stunning illustrations done in a graphic-novel style.

Recycling/Reusing/Making New from Old

Messier, Mireille, and Pierre Pratt. 2016. *The Branch*. Toronto, ON: Kids Can Press.
   When an ice storm takes down a girl's favorite branch, she figures out a way to turn it into another favorite thing.

Wang, Andrea, and Jason Chin. 2021. *Watercress*. New York: Holiday House.
   Mom and Dad pause a drive to pick watercress from a ditch along the roadside, mortifying the female protagonist. When Mom tells of her family's suffering through a famine in China, it changes the girl's perspective.

Seasons

Moore, Johnny Ray, and Cbabi Bayoc. 2021. *Seasonal Adventures*. New York: Reycroft Books.
   A little Black boy and his dad experience all four seasons together, reveling in the delights of each.

Otheguy, Emma, and Ana Ramirez. 2021. *A Sled for Gabo*. New York: Atheneum Books for Young Readers.
   A shy Latino boy warms up to a friend on a snowy day.

Pham, LeUyen. 2021. *Outside, Inside*. New York: Roaring Brook Press.
   A beautiful story about growth that continued to happen inside and outside when the world shut down during COVID-19.

Yee, Wong Herbert. 2012. *Summer Days and Nights*. New York: Henry Holt.
   A young Asian-presenting girl explores the natural world around her in an attempt to stay cool, discovering tiny treasures along the way.

Appendix B: Additional Resources for Educators Related to Nature-Based Education

Books for All Nature-Based Early Childhood Educators

Constable, Karen. 2014. *Bringing the Forest School Approach to Your Early Years Practice.* New York: Routledge.

Cree, Jon, and Marina Robb. 2021. *Essential Guide to Forest School and Nature Pedagogy.* New York: Routledge.

Daly, Lisa, and Miriam Belaglovsky. 2015. *Loose Parts: Inspiring Play in Young Children.* St. Paul, MN: Redleaf.

Danks, Fiona, and Jo Scofield. 2005. *Nature's Playground: Activities, Crafts, and Games to Encourage Children to Get Outdoors.* London, UK: Frances Lincoln Ltd.

Danks, Sharon Gamson. 2010. *Asphalt to Ecosystems: Design Ideas for Schoolyard Transformation.* Oakland, CA: New Village Press.

Figueroa, Laura Park. 2019. *Therapy in the Great Outdoors: A Start-Up Guide to Nature-Based Pediatric Practice with 44 Kid-Tested Activities.* Berkeley, CA: Outdoor Kids Occupational Therapy.

Fisher, Cheryl. 2019. *Mindfulness and Nature-Based Therapeutic Techniques for Children: Creative Activities for Emotion Regulation, Resilience, and Connectedness.* Eau Claire, WI: PESI Publishing and Media.

Garrett, Linda, Hannah Thomas, and Hilary Elmer. 2006. *Small Wonders: Nature Education for Young Children.* Quechee, VT: Vermont Institute of Natural Science.

Gull, Suzanne Levenson Goldstein, and Tricia Rosengarten. 2021. *Loose Parts Learning in K-3 Classrooms.* Lewisville, NC: Gryphon House.

Keeler, Rusty. 2008. *Natural Playscapes.* Lincoln, NE: Exchange Press.

Keeler, Rusty. 2020. *Adventures in Risky Play: What Is Your Yes?* Lincoln, NE: Exchange Press.

Knight, Sara. 2011. *Risk and Adventure in Early Years Outdoor Play: Learning from Forest Schools.* Thousand Oaks, CA: SAGE.

Knight, Sara. 2013. *Forest Schools and Outdoor Learning in the Early Years.* 2nd ed. Thousand Oaks, CA: SAGE.

Lingelbach, Jennipher, and Lisa Purcell. 2000. *Hands-On Nature: Information and Activities for Exploring the Environment with Children.* Woodstock, VT: Vermont Institute of Natural Science.

Louv, Richard. 2008. *Last Child in the Woods: Saving Our Children from Nature-Deficit Disorder.* Chapel Hill, NC: Algonquin.

Louv, Richard. 2011. *The Nature Principle: Human Restoration and the End of Nature-Deficit Disorder.* Chapel Hill, NC: Algonquin.

Moore, Robin C., ed. 1992. *Play for All Guidelines: Planning, Design, and Management of Outdoor Play Settings for All Children.* 2nd ed. Berkeley, CA: MIG Communications.

Moore, Robin C. 1993. *Plants for Play: A Plant Selection Guide for Children's Outdoor Environments.* Berkeley, CA: MIG Communications.

Moore, Robin C. 2014. *Nature Play and Learning Places: Creating and Managing Places Where Children Engage with Nature*. Raleigh, NC: Natural Learning Initiative, and Reston, VA: National Wildlife Federation.

Neddo, Nick. 2020. *The Organic Artist for Kids: A DIY Guide to Making Your Own Eco-Friendly Art Supplies from Nature*. Beverly, MA: Quarto Publishing.

Nelson, Eric M. 2012. *Cultivating Outdoor Classrooms: Designing and Implementing Child-Centered Learning Environments*. St. Paul, MN: Redleaf.

Pelo, Ann. 2013. *The Goodness of Rain: Developing an Ecological Identity in Young Children*. Lincoln, NE: Exchange Press.

Powers, Julie, and Sheila Williams Ridge. 2018. *Nature-Based Learning for Young Children: Anytime, Anywhere, on Any Budget*. St. Paul, MN: Redleaf.

Rivkin, Mary. 1995. *The Great Outdoors: Restoring Children's Right to Play Outdoors*. Rev. ed. Washington, DC: NAEYC.

Robertson, Juliet. 2014. *Dirty Teaching: A Beginner's Guide to Learning Outdoors*. Bancyfelin, Carmarthen, UK: Independent Thinking Press.

Robertson, Juliet. 2017. *Messy Maths: A Playful, Outdoor Approach*. Bancyfelin, Carmarthen, UK: Independent Thinking Press.

Schlitz Audubon Nature Center and Brain Insights. *Naturally Developing Young Brains: Supporting Brain Development for 3-5-Year-Olds through Natural Environments*. Card set. Washington, DC: Natural Start Alliance.

Selly, Patty Born. 2014. *Connecting Animals and Children in Early Childhood*. St. Paul, MN: Redleaf.

Shelburne Farms. 2013. *Cultivating Joy and Wonder: Educating for Sustainability in Early Childhood through Nature, Food, and Community*. Shelburne, VT: Shelburne Farms.

Sobel, David. 2008. *Childhood and Nature: Design Principles for Educators*. Portsmouth, NH: Stenhouse.

Solly, Kathryn. 2015. *Risk, Challenge, and Adventure in the Early Years: A Practical Guide to Exploring and Extending Learning Outdoors*. New York: Routledge.

Warden, Claire. 2015. *Learning with Nature: Embedding Outdoor Practice*. London, UK: SAGE.

Wiedel-Lubinski, Monica, and Karen Madigan. 2020. *Nature Play Workshop for Families: A Guide to 40+ Outdoor Learning Experiences in All Seasons*. Beverly, MA: Quarto Publishing.

Wilson, Ruth. 2018. *Nature and Young Children: Encouraging Creative Play and Learning in Natural Environments*. 3rd ed. New York: Routledge.

Worroll, Jane, and Peter Houghton. 2016. *Play the Forest School Way: Woodland Games, Crafts, and Skills for Adventurous Kids*. London, UK: Watkins Publishing.

Young, Jon, Evan McGown, and Ellen Haas. 2010. *Coyote's Guide to Connecting with Nature*. Shelton, WA: Owlink Media.

Books for Preschool Nature-Based Educators

Kenny, Erin K. 2013. *Forest Kindergartens: The Cedarsong Way*. Vashon, WA: Cedarsong Nature School.

Larimore, Rachel A. 2011. *Establishing a Nature-Based Preschool*. Fort Collins, CO: National Association for Interpretation.

Larimore, Rachel A. 2019. *Preschool Beyond Walls: Blending Early Childhood Education and Nature-Based Learning*. Lewisville, NC: Gryphon House.

Merrick, Cindy, ed. 2019. *Nature-Based Preschool Professional Practice Guidebook: Teaching Environments, Safety, Administration*. Washington, DC: NAAEE.

Sobel, David. 2016. *Nature Preschools and Forest Kindergartens: The Handbook for Outdoor Learning*. St. Paul, MN: Redleaf.

Sobel, David. 2020. *The Sky Above and the Mud Below: Lessons from Nature Preschools and Forest Kindergartens*. St. Paul, MN: Redleaf.

Staff of Dodge Nature Preschool. n.d. *Four Seasons at a Nature Based Preschool*. Washington, DC: Natural Start Alliance.

Warden, Claire. 2010. *Nature Kindergartens and Forest Schools: An Exploration of Naturalistic Learning within Nature Kindergartens and Forest Schools*. Auchterarder, Perthshire, Scotland: Mindstretchers.

Books for K–3 Nature-Based Early Childhood Educators

Banning, Wendy, and Ginny Sullivan. 2010. *Lens on Outdoor Learning*. St. Paul, MN: Redleaf.

Dargatz, Peter. 2021. *Teaching Off Trail: My Classroom's Nature Transformation through Play*. St. Paul, MN: Redleaf.

Gans, Caylin. 2019. *Forest Schooled, The Book*. Ottawa, ON: Forest Schooled.

Gull, Suzanne Levenson Goldstein, and Tricia Rosengarten. 2021. *Loose Parts Learning in K-3 Classrooms*. Lewisville, NC: Gryphon House.

Minnucci, Eliza, and Meghan Teachout. 2018. *A Forest Days Handbook: Program Design for School Days Outside*. Brattleboro, VT: Green Writers Press.

Web Resources

Children and Nature Network, www.childrenandnature.org

Learning Through Landscapes, https://www.ltl.org.uk/

National Wildlife Federation, How-To Guides, https://www.nwf.org/ECHO/Resources?fbclid=IwAR3bTkkxhTWUUY4f5u4LJnnpIYdpDVMG-9jzT_ee6GNXmwQxMH2Ws6yQe-w

Natural Start Alliance, www.naturalstart.org

North Carolina State University, NC State Design Natural Learning Initiative, https://naturalearning.org/

Samara Early Learning, www.samarael.com

University of Illinois at Urbana-Champaign Landscape and Human Health Laboratory, http://lhhl.illinois.edu/

University of Minnesota Duluth Flourishing in Nature Research Briefs, https://sites.google.com/d.umn.edu/jernst/home/flourishing-in-nature-research-briefs?authuser=0

Appendix C: Recommended Questions to Ask During Teacher/Administrator Interviews

Program Goals
- What are the goals of the program?
- Where are these goals documented (for example, in a mission statement, family handbook, poster, or other forms of written documentation)?
- How are the goals of the program communicated to families and the community?

Identifying Emphasis on Learning with Nature
How do you identify the activities for upcoming class sessions?

Learning Topics and Scope Are Developmentally Appropriate
- How do you decide what curriculum to teach in your classroom?
- How do you decide what nature-based content to focus on?

Sustainable Practices
- What do you do in your classroom to promote environmental sustainability?
- How do you model sustainable practices to children in your class?
- Was your building designed using sustainable practices?
- In what ways are sustainable practices used to maintain the building?

Program Implements the Leave No Trace Seven Principles
- How do you reduce the impact your class has on the natural environment?
- How are these procedures communicated to staff? through a policies and procedures manual? through activity protocols?
- Do other groups use this same space?

The Class Day Starts Outdoors
- If the class starts outdoors during the observation, clarify the frequency by asking, "Are there times you start the day indoors?"
- If the class starts the day indoors during the observation, consider questions such as, "When in the day do you usually go outdoors?"
- In either case, ask questions such as, "Are there times in the year you shift the schedule? If so, when? Why?"

Time Outdoors
On the rare occasion that severe weather limits a program's ability to have children outdoors during the observation, ask the teacher to describe the daily schedule if a printed version is not available.

Visiting Natural Ecosystems

Today we went to the ____. Are there other places you sometimes visit during the class day? If so, how often do you visit those places?

Safety-Related Policies and Procedures

- Tell me about your policies and procedures. How are these developed? How often do you review them?
- Do you have written procedures/protocols for any of the activities you do with children? If so, which activities? How were those procedures developed?

Reflecting on Nature Experiences

Tell me about how you reflect on and document outdoor experiences with the children.

Administrator's Support to Implement Nature-Based Education

- When do teachers or teaching teams plan lessons that incorporate nature? Are they paid for this time?
- How much of the budget is allocated to nature-based materials?
- How much of the budget is allocated to teacher professional development (particularly for nature-based education)? What kinds of professional development have the teachers attended in the past year?
- What types of materials are available to support nature-based education? Are they easily accessible, and are there enough materials for all students to participate?
- How often do paid experts visit to support teachers in planning and implementing nature-based activities?

Intentionality of Organization Planning to Integrate Nature-Based Education

- Is there a strategic plan that intentionally includes nature-based education?
- Are curricula chosen that include nature-based activities? If none is available, are teachers able to include nature-based activities within the plan?

Administrators Are Public Advocates of Nature-Based Education

- How do you talk about nature-based education publicly? In what settings do you usually talk about nature-based education?
- How do you talk about nature-based education in front of teachers, colleagues, and the broader community?
- Have you written articles or op-eds on this topic?
- Are you involved in a nature-based education administrators' PLC?

Teacher's Role in Setting the Tone for Open-Ended Nature Play

Tell me about how you see your role as a teacher when you're outdoors with the children.

Teachers Are Comfortable with Nature Immersion
- Do you go outside with the children on cold and/or rainy days? If so, how do you dress for that type of weather?
- What do you say to children about going outdoors in all weather, including on rainy and cold days?

Pre-K and K–3 Teacher Qualifications
- What is the preschool director's educational background related to early childhood education and/or environmental education? Do they have formal degrees or training in either or both?
- What are the teachers' educational backgrounds in early childhood education and/or environmental education? Do they have formal degrees or training in either or both?

Pre-K and K–3 Professional Development
- Do the teachers attend conferences, workshops, or trainings that relate to nature-based education pedagogy (including safety skills)? Which ones have they completed and how often?
- Do the teachers attend conferences, workshops, or trainings that relate to natural-history knowledge? Which ones have they completed and how often?

Indoor Classroom Natural Light and Views of the Outdoors
- Are there windows in the classroom? If so, how big are they? Do they allow natural light to come in?
- Are there skylights that provide natural light?
- What is the view out of the windows? natural views or human-made?

Transition between Indoors and Outdoors
- Is there a door in the classroom that opens directly to the outdoors? If not, is there easy access to the outdoors nearby?
- Is there a transitional space such as a porch outside the classroom?
- Do the children have a choice of being indoors or outdoors during class time or free-choice time?

Natural Materials Found in the Indoor Classroom
- What types of natural materials are used in the classroom?
- Do the animal artifacts and natural materials reflect local nature?

Indoor Classroom Materials and Books Are Realistic and Representative of Local Nature
- What types of puppets are found in the classroom?
- Is there a mix of fiction and nonfiction children's nature picture books in the classroom?

Natural Play Area Features

- Are there other materials you bring outdoors, in addition to what is here today?
- Tell me about how this play area changes from season to season. For example, are there different materials or features at other times of the year?
- Do children have access to natural materials? If so, what kinds?

Natural Ecosystems

- Where do you go to access natural ecosystems outside the fenced play area?
- How often does the class visit these natural ecosystems?

Loose Parts and Natural Features Available in Different Ecosystems

- Describe the natural ecosystems you visit with the children. What types of features are there? What types of loose parts are available for the children to use there?
- Talk a bit about children's engagement in the different places you visit beyond the fence. Do they get bored and find it difficult to interact with the space, or do they get deeply lost in play?

Nature Educator Visits Frequently

- Do you have a relationship with a nature educator or environmental education expert? If so, do they visit your classroom? How often?
- What is the role of a nature educator in your classroom?

Ongoing Relationship with the Same Nature Educator

- Do you have a nature educator who visits regularly?
- How often is the nature educator the same person? How often is it a different person?

Access to Artifacts and Resources

- Where are resources and artifacts stored?
- What types of collections do you use with your teaching?
- Do you need to make a special request for these resources or artifacts?
- Do you share resources and artifacts with other programs and/or community organizations?

Wild and/or Domestic Animals

- Tell me about your classroom pets or other animals children interact with during the day.
- How often, if ever, do you have visitors bring animals into the classroom?

Nature-Based Field Trips

- Have you gone on any field trips this year? Where have you gone?
- Do you have any field trips planned? Where will you go?
- How do you prepare for field trips?
- What, if any, follow-up activities do you plan related to the field trip?

Nature-Related Communication

- In what ways do you communicate with the families that attend your program? Can I see some examples?
- Does your program offer a family orientation? What does that consist of?
- Do you hold family-teacher conferences? If so, to what extent is nature-related content discussed during conferences?

Documentation of Nature-Based Activities

- How do you share with families the nature-based activities that occur as part of the class?
- Do you use a document-sharing system for communicating with families? If so, what do you typically share with them?

Nature-Based Family Programs

Do you offer any family or adult-only events that are nature based?

Community Resources and Events

Do you share community events with families? If so, how do you share these events with families?

Family Expertise and Experiences

- Do you have families share their nature-based expertise with the class?
- If so, how often? What do these events look like?

Family Volunteers

- How often, if ever, do families volunteer in your classroom?
- When volunteers are here, what do they typically do?

References and Recommended Readings

Andrachuk, Heather, et al. 2014. *Forest and Nature School in Canada: A Head, Heart, Hands Approach to Outdoor Learning.* Ottawa, ON: Forest School Canada.

Armitage, Kevin C. 2009. *The Nature Study Movement: The Forgotten Popularizer of America's Conservation Ethic.* Lawrence, KS: University of Kansas Press.

Ball, David, Tim Gill, and Bernard Spiegal. 2013. *Managing Risk in Play Provision: Implementation Guide.* 2nd ed. London, UK: National Children's Bureau.

Bailie, Patti Ensel. 2010. "From the One-Hour Field Trip to a Nature Preschool: Partnering with Environmental Organizations." *Young Children* 65(4): 76-82.

Bailie, Patti Ensel. 2012. "Connecting Children to Nature: A Multiple Case Study of Nature Center Preschools." Doctoral diss. Lincoln, NE: University of Nebraska-Lincoln. http://search.proquest.com/docview/1266824736?accountid=12598

Bailie, Patti Ensel. 2016. "Best Practices in Nature-Based Early Childhood Education." In *Nature Preschools and Forest Kindergartens: The Handbook for Outdoor Learning.* St. Paul, MN: Redleaf Press.

Bhagwanji, Yash. 2011. *Early Childhood Environmental Education Rating Scale.* Washington, DC: North American Association for Environment Education.

Bishop-Josef, Sandra J., and Edward F. Zigler. 2011. "Play and Head Start." In *Play in Clinical Practice: Evidence-Based Approaches.* New York: Guilford Press.

Chawla, Louise. 2015. "Benefits of Nature Contact for Children." *Journal of Planning Literature* 30(4): 433-452.

Copple, Carol, and Sue Bredekamp, eds. 2009. *Developmentally Appropriate Practice in Early Childhood Programs Serving Children from Birth through Age 8.* 3rd ed. Washington, DC: NAEYC.

Curtis, Deb, and Margie Carter. 2015. *Designs for Living and Learning: Transforming Early Childhood Environments.* 2nd ed. St. Paul, MN: Redleaf Press.

Dopko, Raelyne L., Colin A. Capaldi, and John M. Zelenski. 2019. "The Psychological and Social Benefits of a Nature Experience for Children: A Preliminary Investigation." *Journal of Environmental Psychology* 63(2019): 134-138.

Eagles, Paul F. J., and Robert Demare. 1999. "Factors Influencing Children's Environmental Attitudes." *The Journal of Environmental Education* 30(4): 33-37.

Edwards, Carolyn P., Lella Gandini, and George Forman, eds. 1998. *The Hundred Languages of Children: The Reggio Emilia Approach–Advanced Reflections.* 2nd ed. Greenwich, CT: Ablex Publishing.

El Nokali, Nermeen E., Heather J. Bachman, and Elizabeth Votruba Drzal. 2010. "Parent Involvement and Children's Academic and Social Development in Elementary School." *Child Development* 81(3): 988-1005.

Epstein, Joyce L. 2010. "School/Family/Community Partnerships: Caring for the Children We Share." *Phi Delta Kappan* 92(3): 81-96.

Ernst, Julie, Hannah Juckett, and David Sobel. 2021. "Comparing the Impact of Nature, Blended, and Traditional Preschools on Children's Resilience: Some Nature May Be Better Than None." *Frontiers in Psychology* 12: 724340. DOI: 10.3389/fpsyg.2021.724340

Faber Taylor, Andrea, and Frances E. Kuo. 2009. "Children with Attention Deficits Concentrate Better after Walk in the Park." *Journal of Attention Disorders* 12(5): 402-409.

Faber Taylor, Andrea, Frances E. Kuo, and William C. Sullivan. 2001. "Views of Nature and Self-Discipline: Evidence from Inner City Children." *Journal of Environmental Psychology* 21(1-2): 49-63.

Finch, Ken, and Patti Ensel Bailie. 2015. "Nature Preschools: Putting Nature at the Heart of Early Childhood Education." Bank Street Occasional Paper Series 2015(33): 9. https://core.ac.uk/download/pdf/230082328.pdf

Fjørtoft, Ingunn. 2001. "The Natural Environment as a Playground for Children: The Impact of Outdoor Play Activities in Pre-Primary School Children." *Early Childhood Education Journal* 29(2): 111-117.

Galindo, Claudia, and Steven B. Sheldon. 2012. "School and Home Connections and Children's Kindergarten Achievement Gains: The Mediating Role of Family Involvement." *Early Childhood Research Quarterly* 27(1): 90-103.

Gray, Peter. 2013. *Free to Learn: Why Unleashing the Instinct to Play Will Make Our Children Happier, More Self-Reliant, and Better Students for Life.* New York: Basic Books.

Greenman, Jim, and Mike Lindstrom, eds. 2017. *Caring Spaces, Learning Places: Children's Environments That Work!* 2nd ed. Lincoln, NE: Exchange Press.

Heras, Raquel, Rosa M. Medir, and Olga Salazar. 2020. "Children's Perceptions on the Benefits of School Nature Field Trips." *Education 3-13* 48(4): 379-391.

Hughes, Karen, Jan Packer, and Roy Ballantyne. 2011. "Using Post Visit Action Resources to Support Family Conservation Learning Following a Wildlife Tourism Experience." *Environmental Education Research* 17(3): 307-328.

Jordan, Cathy, and Louise Chawla. 2019. "A Coordinated Research Agenda for Nature-Based Learning." *Frontiers in Psychology* 10: 766. doi: 10.3389/fpsyg.2019.00766

Keeler, Rusty. 2008. *Natural Playscapes: Creating Outdoor Play Environments for the Soul.* Redmond, WA: Exchange Press.

Kenny, Erin K. 2013. *Forest Kindergartens: The Cedarsong Way.* Vashon, WA: Cedarsong Nature School.

Larimore, Rachel A. 2011a. *Establishing a Nature-Based Preschool.* Fort Collins, CO: National Association for Interpretation.

Larimore, Rachel A. 2011b. "Nature-Based Preschools: A Powerful Partnership between Early Childhood and Environmental Education." *Legacy Magazine* 22(3): 8-11.

Larimore, Rachel A. 2016. "Defining Nature-Based Preschools." *International Journal of Early Childhood Environmental Education* 4(1): 33-37.

Larimore, Rachel A. 2018. "Using Principles of Nature-Based Preschools to Transform Your Classroom." *Young Children* 73(5): 34-41.

Larimore, Rachel A. 2019. *Preschool Beyond Walls: Blending Early Childhood Education and Nature-Based Learning.* Lewisville, NC: Gryphon House.

Larimore, Rachel A. 2020. "Preschool Science Education: A Vision for the Future." *Early Childhood Education Journal* 48: 703-714.

Larimore, Rachel A. 2021. "Investigating Teacher-Child Interactions in a Nature-Based and Non-Nature Preschool." Doctoral diss. East Lansing, MI: Michigan State University.

Leave No Trace. 1999. "The Seven Principles." Leave No Trace. https://lnt.org/why/7-principles/

Lee, Hannah, Marc J. Stern, and Robert B. Powell. 2020. "Do Pre-Visit Preparation and Post-Visit Activities Improve Student Outcomes on Field Trips?" *Environmental Education Research* 26(7): 989-1007.

Lerstrup, Inger, and Cecil Konijnendijk van den Bosch. 2017. "Affordances of Outdoor Settings for Children in Preschool: Revisiting Heft's Functional Taxonomy." *Landscape Research* 42(1): 47-62.

Martin, Michelle H. 2019. "Black Kids Camp, Too . . . Don't They? Embracing 'Wildness' in Picture Books." The Horn Book. https://www.hbook.com/story/black-kids-camp-too

Martin, Michelle H., and J. Elizabeth Mills. 2022. "Welcoming Black Children into Literary Wildscapes: Wildness in African American Children's Picture Books." *Children's Literature* 50.

Merrick, Cindy, ed. 2019. *Nature-Based Preschool Professional Practice Guidebook: Teaching Environments, Safety, Administration.* Washington DC: NAAEE.

Montessori, Maria. 1912. *The Montessori Method.* Translated by Anne E. George. New York: Frederick A. Stokes.

Moore, Robin C. 2014. *Nature Play and Learning Places: Creating and Managing Places Where Children Engage with Nature.* Raleigh, NC: Natural Learning Initiative, and Reston, VA: National Wildlife Federation.

Moore, Robin, and Nilda Cosco. n.d. *Natural Learning Initiative Outdoor Learning Environment Toolkit: Best Practices Indicators.* Raleigh, NC: Natural Learning Initiative, North Carolina State University.

Moore, Robin, and Nilda Cosco. 2014. "Growing Up Green and Healthy: Naturalization as a Health Promotion Strategy in Early Childhood Outdoor Learning Environments." *Children, Youth and Environments* 24(2): 168-191.

Morrison, George S. 2001. *Early Childhood Education Today.* 8th ed. Upper Saddle River, NJ: Prentice-Hall.

National Association for Interpretation. 2019. *Interpretation Standards: A Pathway Towards Excellence.* Fort Collins, CO: NAI.

National Association for the Education of Young Children (NAEYC). 2022. *Developmentally Appropriate Practice in Early Childhood Programs Serving Children from Birth through Age 8.* 4th ed. Washington, DC: NAEYC.

National Research Council. 2011. *Sustainability and the U.S. EPA.* Washington, DC: National Academies Press.

National Research Council. 2012. *A Framework for K-12 Science Education: Practices, Cross-Cutting Concepts, and Core Ideas.* Washington, DC: National Academies Press.

National Council for the Social Studies. 2013. *College, Career, and Civic Life (C3) Framework for Social Studies State Standards.* Silver Spring, MD: National Council for the Social Studies.

Natural Start Alliance and North American Association for Environmental Education. 2020. *Nature-Based Preschools in the US: 2020 Snapshot.* Washington, DC: NAAEE.

North American Association for Environmental Education. n.d. *Guidelines for Excellence: Early Childhood Environmental Education Programs.* Washington, DC: NAAEE.

Pelo, Ann. 2013. *The Goodness of Rain: Developing an Ecological Identity in Young Children*. Lincoln, NE: Exchange Press.

Pikus, Arianna E., Lori E. Skibbe, Rachel Larimore, and David Sobel. 2020. "Academic Outcomes from Nature-Based Kindergarten and First Grade Classrooms." Poster presentation. July 29-31. Nature-Based Early Learning Conference (virtual).

Schein, Deborah. 2018. *Inspiring Wonder, Awe, and Empathy: Spiritual Development in Young Children*. St. Paul, MN: Redleaf Press.

Schwartz, Eugene. 2009. "Anthroposophy and Waldorf Education: The Kindergarten Years." *Millennial Child*. https://millennialchild.wordpress.com/article/anthroposophy-and-waldorf-education-the-110mw7eus832b-9/

Sims Bishop, Rudine. 1990. "Mirrors, Windows, and Sliding Glass Doors." *Perspectives: Choosing and Using Books for the Classroom* 6(3): ix-xi.

Skibbe, Lori E., Arianna E. Pikus, Rachel A. Larimore, and David Sobel. 2019. "Nature-Based Educational Programming in Relation to Literacy and Mathematics Development in Kindergarten and First Grade." Poster presentation. July 17-21. Toronto, ON: Society for the Scientific Study of Reading.

Sobel, David. 2013. *Beyond Ecophobia: Reclaiming the Heart in Nature Education*. 2nd ed. Great Barrington, MA: Orion Society.

Sobel, David. 2014a. "Learning to Walk between the Raindrops: The Value of Nature Preschools and Forest Kindergartens." *Children, Youth and Environments* 24(2): 228-238.

Sobel, David. 2014b. "Look, Don't Touch: The Problem with Environmental Education." In *Children and Nature: Making Connections*. Great Barrington, MA: The Myrin Institute.

Sobel, David. 2015. *Nature Preschools and Forest Kindergartens: The Handbook for Outdoor Learning*. St. Paul, MN: Redleaf Press.

Sobel, David, and Rachel Larimore. 2020. "Nature Cements the New Learning: Expanding Nature-Based Learning into the K-5 Curriculum." In *Research Handbook on Childhoodnature: Assemblages of Childhood and Nature Research*. New York: Springer.

Sobel, David, et al. 2017. *Executive Summary for Researching Impacts of Nature-Based Early Childhood Education*.

Tilden, Freeman. 1957. *Interpreting Our Heritage*. Chapel Hill, NC: The University of North Carolina Press.

Warden, Claire. 2012. *Nature Kindergartens and Forest Schools*. 2nd ed. Perthshire, Scotland: Mindstretchers Ltd.

Warden, Claire. 2015. *Learning with Nature: Embedding Outdoor Practice*. London, UK: SAGE.

Warden, Claire. 2019a. "Nature Kindergartens." ScooNews. https://www.scoonews.com/news/nature-kindergartens-5579

Warden, Claire. 2019b. "Nature Pedagogy: The Art of Being with Nature Inside, Outside and Beyond." *Pedagogy+ Magazine* 6: 34.

Warden, Claire. 2019c. "Nature Pedagogy: Education for Sustainability." *Childhood Education* 95(6): 6-13.

Index

A

Access and movement between indoors and outdoors, 141-142

Activities emerge from children's interests, 64, 89, 98-99, 103-104, 107, 110

Administrator's role, 8, 114-120

Advocacy, 119-120

Allocating resources, 114-117

Animals
- in the classroom, 147-151
- wild or domestic, 177-178

Artifacts/resources on-site, 8, 175-178

Arts activities, 8, 109-112

Assessment, 3

Attention-deficit hyperactivity disorder (ADHD), 2

Authentic experiences, 1, 60

Authentic materials, 104-105

Authentic nature, 13, 59-60, 79, 90-91, 99-101

B

Benefit-risk assessments, 44-46, 57

Best practices, 4

Beyond. See Natural ecosystems

C

Child development, 20

Child-centered curriculum, 4

Child-led activities, 13, 24

Children of color, 20-23, 77-79

Children with disabilities, 20-23

Class day starts outdoors
- K-3, 49-51
- pre-K, 36-37

Class spends extensive time outdoors
- K-3, 52-53

Class visits from families, 190-193

Classroom materials, 145-147

Common Core, 80, 86, 96

Community partnerships and resources, 8, 171-180, 207-208, 225

Conversation and documentation, 65-67

D

Developmentally appropriate topics and scope, 26-28

Diversity. See Inclusivity

Documenting nature-based activities, 183-185

E

Early childhood education (ECE), 128-129

Emergency shelter, 136

Environment, 135-170, 203-206, 222-224

Environmental education (EE), 13, 128-129

Environmental literacy and connection, 2, 8, 13, 81-86

Environmental stewardship, 1-2, 18-20

F

Family engagement, 181-193
- communication and education, 8, 181-186
- involvement, 8, 190-193
- NABERS, 209-210, 226-227
- nature experiences, 8, 186-189

Fictional texts, 72-73, 76-79, 90-91

Field guides, 75, 93

Field trips, 8, 178-180

H

Healthy ecosystems, 13, 167-168

I

Inclusivity, 20-23, 76-79, 94-85, 146-147

Indoor classroom, 8, 13, 136-151

Informational texts, 74-79, 91-92, 146

K

K-3
- arts, 109-112
- curriculum, 79-112
- environmental literacy and connection, 81-86
- literacy, 86-95
- math, 96-101
- NABERS, 8, 212-228
- program practices, 8, 48-58
- science, 101-105
- social studies, 105-108
- staff qualifications, 130-131
- teachers have certification and formal training, 130-131

L

Learning *about, in,* and *with* nature, 14, 24-26
Leave No Trace Center for Outdoor Ethics, 14, 31-34
Literacy, 8, 86-95
Local history and culture, 108
Local nature, 14, 59, 79, 142-146, 160-163
Loose parts, 168-170

M

Managed outdoor spaces, 14, 135
Maps, 76, 94
Math activities, 2, 8, 96-101
Mission/program statement, 18-20
Most class time is spent outdoors, 37-40

N

National Association for Interpretation (NAI), 3-4
National Association for the Education of Young Children (NAEYC), 3
National Council for the Social Studies, 104
National Project for Excellence in Environmental Education, 4
National Research Council, 28, 101
Natural ecosystems (beyond), 8, 13-14, 40-42, 53-54, 164-169

Natural materials, 14, 68-77, 142-144
- in science activities, 101, 104-105
- in social studies activities, 108, 111-112

Natural play area, 8, 14, 151-163
Natural Start Alliance, viii, 3, 134, 234
Nature educator, 8, 14, 171-174
Nature-based early childhood education (NbECE), 1-4, 14
NAture-Based Education Rating Scales (NABERS), 2-5, 194-228
- explanation of terms, 13-15
- for K-3 education, 8, 212-228
- for pre-K education, 7-8, 211
- guidance for observations and scoring, 9-12, 194-195

Nature-based family programs, 187-188
Nature-based pedagogy, 2-3, 14, 131-134
Next Generation Science Standards, 80, 101
North Carolina State University, NC State Design Natural Learning Initiative, 134, 234

O

Observations, 7, 9-12, 194-195
Ongoing site and benefit-risk assessments, 44-46, 56-59
Organizational planning, 117-119
Outdoor skills, 61-62, 81-86

P

Plants and animals, 147-151
Play, 4, 15, 42-44, 55-56
Pre-K
- curriculum, 59-79
- example time scoring, 39
- program practices, 8, 35-48
- staff qualifications, 8, 128-130

Professional development, 8, 131-134
Program goals, 8, 17-33
- example time scoring, 39
- K-3 arts, 109-112
- K-3 curriculum, 79-81

K-3 environmental literacy and connections, 81-86
K-3 literacy, 86-95
K-3 math, 96-101
K-3 program practices, 48-59
K-3 science, 101-108
Leave No Trace© Seven Principles, 32
NABERS, 200-202, 220-221
pre-K curriculum, 59-79
pre-K program practices, 35-48
risk-related terms, 46
sustainable practices, 29-30

Program practices
K-3, 8, 48-59
pre-K, 8, 35-48

Q

Questions to ask during teacher/administrator interviews, 235-239

R

Reading/writing activities, 88-89
Reflecting on nature experiences, 83-86

S

Safety-related policies and procedures, 44-48, 56-59
Science activities, 2, 8, 101-105
Scoring, 9-11, 194-195
Seasonal experiences, 15, 59, 64-65, 79, 90-92, 99-101
Sharing nature-related content with families, 182-183
Sharing resources and events with families, 188
Site assessments, 44-46, 56
Social studies activities, 8, 105-108
Spirituality, 81
Staff qualifications, 3, 128-131
Staffing, 113-114
administrator's role, 114-120
K-3, 8, 130-131
NABERS, 200-202, 220-221
pre-K, 8, 128-130
professional development, 131-134
Sustainable practices, 28-31

T

Teacher qualifications, 3, 8, 130-131
Teacher's role, 8, 121-128
Teacher-led activities, 15, 67-68, 85-86
Terminology, 13-15, 46
Tips for growing, 12, 71, 73, 75-76, 78-79, 93-94, 101, 112, 134, 151, 160, 167, 177, 189, 193
Tips for the observer, 12, 20, 23, 26, 28, 31, 34, 37, 40, 42, 44, 48, 51, 53-54, 56, 59, 62, 67, 70, 83, 85, 116-117, 119-120, 123, 126, 128, 130, 133, 138, 140, 142, 150, 159, 166, 170, 173-174, 176, 178, 180, 183, 185, 188-189, 191-192